Financial Innovation

As the global financial system continues to evolve it has attracted considerable interest. The contributors to *Financial Innovation* provide an authoritative analysis of recent developments in the arena of international finance.

The book opens with a general analysis of the role and functions of financial systems, looking at the root causes of present day change. Contributions by international experts – academic and practitioner – focus on specific areas of financial innovation to provide a comprehensive analysis of issues such as security trading, the globalization of financial markets, monetary policy, and market regulation. In addition, the book discusses the consequences of innovation for international finance: whether the changes in the American system have eased the volatile climate of the 1980s, and whether the re-orientation of the French system has resulted in greater flexibility in the market mechanism. It also explores the efficacy of measures taken in Brussels to promote innovation within the EEC.

The theoretical and practical knowledge presented by the contributors as they tackle the issues raised by financial innovation makes this book important not only to students of business and finance but to all those involved in analysing financial markets.

Henry Cavanna is Director of the Fondation Internationale des Sciences Humaines and has lectured widely in European and American Universities. He has also organized many international symposiums and seminars in various countries.

Financial Innovation

Edited by Henry Cavanna

ROUTLEDGE

London and New York

First published 1992 by Routledge
11 New Fetter Lane, London EC4P 4EE

Simultaneously published in the USA and Canada
by Routledge
a division of Routledge, Chapman and Hall, Inc.
29 West 35th Street, New York, NY 10001

Typeset by LaserScript Limited, Mitcham, Surrey
Printed and bound in Great Britain by Mackays of Chatham PLC, Chatham, Kent

British Library Cataloguing in Publication Data
Financial Innovation
1. International finance
I. Cavanna, Henry
332.042

ISBN 0–415–05869–4

Library of Congress Cataloging-in-Publication Data
Financial Innovation/Edited by Henry Cavanna
p. cm.
Includes bibliographical references and index
ISBN 0–415–05869–4
1. International finance. I. Cavanna, Henry
HG3881.F436 1992
332′.042–dc20

Contents

Figures

Tables

Notes on contributors

T.R. Gavin Bingham specializes in financial markets, international debt and international liquidity at the Bank for International Settlements, Basle, Switzerland and is also Adjunct Professor at the Helsinki School of Economics. He received his doctorate from Oxford University, and is the author of *Banking and Monetary Policy* (OECD, 1985) as well as numerous articles on financial affairs.

Didier Bruneel, previously Deputy General Manager of the Research Department, is now the Bank of France's Secretary General as well as being Deputy Secretary General of the Conseil National du Crédit. A graduate of the University of Paris II and of the Institut d'Etudes Politiques de Paris, he has taught at the University of Paris I, at the Centre d'Etudes Supérieures and at the Institut des Techniques de Marchés. He is the author of numerous articles and papers on monetary economics.

Henry Cavanna is the Director of the Fondation International des Sciences Humaines, Paris. He received a doctorate in Law from the Universidad Complutense and has done research in the field of Political Science at Dublin and Oxford. In Dublin he edited *The University Gazette* and was later editor of the Parisian monthly *La Table Ronde*. While lecturing widely in European and American universities, he has contributed to various publications and edited several books.

Jean-Claude Chouraqui is head of the Monetary and Fiscal Policy Division of the OECD in Paris. He received his doctorate in Economics from the University of Paris and later studied at the Institute of World Affairs in New York. He is the author of numerous articles and papers, mostly in OECD publications but also in the series Etudes Monétaires.

Paolo Clarotti is Head of the Commission on Banking and Financial Establishments Division of the European Communities – DG XV. He was a graduate of the University of Paris (Pantheon-Sorbonne). He is the author of more than 170 articles and studies in banking and financial magazines.

Richard Harrington is Senior Lecturer in Economics at the University of Manchester. He was educated at the University of Wales and at the London School of Economics. He spent a number of years working in insurance in London before entering academic life. He is the author of *Asset and Liability Management by Banks* (OECD, 1987) as well as a number of other books and articles on financial institutions and financial markets.

David Llewellyn is Professor of Money and Banking at Loughborough University and Chairman of the Loughborough University Banking Centre. He was educated at the London School of Economics. Previous posts include periods at HM Treasury, Nottingham University and the International Monetary Fund in Washington. He has written extensively in the areas of monetary policy, financial regulation, and the financial markets, institutions and systems.

Thomas D. Simpson is Associate Director of Research and Statistics of the Board of Directors of the Federal Reserve System in Washington, DC. He received his doctorate from the University of Chicago, and was Associate Professor at Malcastor College before joining the Board of Governors of the Federal Reserve System. He is the author of *Money, Banking and Economic Analysis* (Prentice-Hall, 1987) and a number of articles on financial innovation.

Acknowledgement

The chapters and structure of this work were presented and discussed at a recent International Seminar organized by the Fondation Internationale des Sciences Humaines in co-operation with the Fundacion Fondo Investigacion Economica y Social. The main editorial task was undertaken by Dr Henry Cavanna, Director of the Fondation Internationale des Sciences Humaines, with the assistance of Richard Harrington.

The financial system in transition

Richard Harrington

INTRODUCTION

For upward of two decades, financial systems and financial markets, both domestic and international, have been undergoing a series of profound changes. It is not the fact of change which is surprising – financial innovation in itself is not new – but the pace and the extent of change. Many new financial instruments and techniques have been developed and existing ones have been modified; new financial markets have been created and existing ones have been adapted to meet new demands and new circumstances. At the same time, there has been growing competition between all types of financial intermediary as traditional demarcations, both functional and geographic, have faded. Out of these changes a new global financial order is emerging.

The main causes of this series of changes are not in dispute although, not surprisingly, different writers assign different weights to individual causes. In this chapter we look at the causes of what has justifiably been called the financial revolution and then consider some of the consequences of this – in particular the consequences for monetary policy and for official control of the financial system. This will serve as an introduction to the chapters that follow which will take up these issues in greater detail.

THE IMPACT OF NEW TECHNOLOGY

One of the prime movers of past change and one which continues to shape the evolution of all parts of the financial industry is technological progress. Rapid advances in microelectronics have brought about both a dramatic increase in computer capabilities and a drastic decrease in computing costs whilst, at the same time, producing nothing less than a revolution in telecommunications. This has meant that banks can now transact a wide range of business in many different countries throughout the world without incurring prohibitive costs and whilst still maintaining an adequate and timely flow of information in order that senior management can exercise due control. Distance is no longer the obstacle that it was in earlier times: technology has, in effect, shrunk the world and made possible a much greater integration of financial markets worldwide.

Money can now be moved round the world easily and cheaply; banks and other financial institutions can communicate easily and cheaply with customers, with their own branches and suboffices and with other financial intermediaries in foreign countries; people can move around the world easily and relatively cheaply. What were once remote places are now accessible and national frontiers are becoming of less and less economic significance. The consequences of these changes can be seen throughout all economic life, but they are of particular importance for finance.

Most financial activity involves the storage, retrieval and regular updating of large amounts of data. In consequence, it was inevitable that the provision of financial services would be profoundly affected by the information technology revolution. Details of assets and liabilities, of transactions and commitments and of rates of interest and security prices are now stored in powerful computer systems; such data can be accessed almost instantaneously and can be updated regularly or, in particular cases such as money-market transactions, continuously. Information can be transmitted where needed and can now be used across the world with greater ease than would have been possible within one country as recently as twenty-five years ago.

The same technological changes have, of course, influenced the clients of financial institutions and have made it possible for large non-financial companies to manage their affairs including their financial affairs on a worldwide basis. The desire of such companies to hold financial assets and to raise loans in a range of different currencies no longer has much to do with official controls on interest rates or on capital movements in particular countries; it is more a reflection of the on-going internationalization of modern economic life.

Modern technology has also reduced the cost of many financial transactions with the result that it is no longer necessary for financial institutions to restrict themselves to a limited number of not-too-complex financial products. When all transactions were processed manually, it was necessary to limit the range of products to what staff at different levels could cope with; but with modern computer hardware and software, once staff have been trained in basic keyboard skills, there are few limits to the number of different financial products that an institution can deal in. The consequence is that many banks, large security houses and other financial institutions have become multi-product firms and are able to create new products by bundling and unbundling existing ones.

One important result of all this is that nowadays both the form and the geographical location of many financial transactions are easily variable. This has obvious implications for the powers of legal and regulatory authorities including central banks. Many types of direct control aimed at financial transactions of a specific type or occurring within a specific geographical area have become ineffective. This is an important reason for the trend towards deregulating the financial sector which has been evident in most developed countries in recent years.

INTERNATIONALIZATION

A rapidly evolving microelectronic technology has made it progressively easier for financial intermediaries to operate in many different countries around the world. But, for banks and other financial institutions to choose to take advantage of this possibility, there has to be sufficient economic incentive. Originally, during the 1960s and 1970s, much of the incentive came from a desire to avoid national restrictions on financial activity such as controls on interest rates, credit controls, exchange controls and controls on the activities that different institutions could undertake. Such restraints existed in most developed (and less developed) countries and most importantly in the United States. The early development of the Eurocurrency markets can be explained in terms of banks and security houses doing that business abroad that they were either prevented from or otherwise restricted in doing at home. Emphasis is usually put on American banks avoiding domestic ceilings on interest rates and the various exchange-control measures introduced during the 1960s but, although this was an important part of the story, it was not the whole story. European and Japanese institutions also had their own reasons for doing business outside the jurisdiction of their own national authorities.

In addition, as pointed out earlier, the world was becoming a smaller place: large non-financial companies were increasingly operating on an international scale and this inevitably led to pressure for financial institutions, especially banks, to follow their clients abroad. And, as certain international markets became established, there was naturally a snowball effect: more institutions were attracted in and the markets grew further.

These new international markets were in bank products – deposits and loans – and in securities. They were truly international in that business was transacted between financial institutions and clients in many different countries, but they tended to be centred in a limited number of geographical locations such as London, Zurich, Luxembourg and Paris. Over time the number of such locations has grown.

It was inevitable that these new markets would be highly competitive. After all, in large part they had arisen because of participants' desire to escape from the obstacles to competition existing in their own domestic markets. In addition, they were composed of a heterogeneous collection of banks and security traders from many different countries, each having their own different financial practices and traditions and hence their own approach to doing business. And the number of participants and potential participants was large, so any attempt at collusion or at concerted action would have been unlikely to succeed.

Competition meant that transaction costs – margins in the case of banking, issuing and dealing costs in the case of securities business – tended to be low relative to those prevailing in national markets. In addition the international markets were highly innovative: the coming together of institutions from many different backgrounds led to much cross-fertilization and the introduction and dissemination of new ideas and new techniques unhindered by official controls. The international markets were not only competitive internally and between themselves, they were in competition with domestic financial markets; this could not fail, in time, to have profound effects on these markets.

A MORE COMPETITIVE ENVIRONMENT

Most national financial markets, during the 1960s and 1970s, exhibited a mixture of competition and concertation: financial intermediaries competed with one another, but there were many agreements, conventions and restrictions – many of them officially inspired – which limited competition. In a number of European countries, rates of interest were officially controlled and there were regular or intermittent credit controls. In North America and in Japan there was a legally imposed separation between commercial banking and security trading, and in virtually all countries stock exchanges were highly controlled institutions with little or no price competition among security traders. In many cases, national markets were partially protected from outside competition by the presence of exchange controls.

But such protection, always less than total, became of less and less relevance. As business became more and more international and as large firms became multinational, corporate treasurers were increasingly able to choose where to invest funds and where to borrow. In those centres where there were large concentrations of foreign banks, this inevitably led to more competition, at least as far as corporate business was concerned. Although the foreign banks may have been attracted to centres such as London or Paris in order to conduct international banking business, once there, they were usually ready to compete for local corporate business and for other wholesale business. In one European country after another, interbank markets akin to the US federal funds market were developed: other short-term markets followed.

In the field of security trading, the many restrictions surrounding national stock exchanges were usually sufficient to prevent outsiders competing directly with established dealers. But the same restrictions also kept national security dealers out of the growing international securities markets and, in addition, for the business of both large borrowers and large investors, each securities market was ultimately in competition with all others. Most national stock markets increasingly faced a choice between, on the one hand, deregulation and competing for a share of the worldwide securities business and, on the other hand, maintaining restrictions, accepting the role of a narrow 'regional' exchange and missing out on much of the business of large multinational borrowers.

In the end, most adopted the path of deregulation and competition: New York had done so in 1976, London did so in 1986 and, since then, other European exchanges have followed. In banking also, the growing international competition made necessary some deregulation, but this involved the monetary authorities directly.

DEREGULATION

By the early 1980s, it had become apparent that many of the official controls and restrictions which, for so long, had been a feature of the financial systems of most countries had outlived their usefulness. There were two main reasons for this. First, the internationalization of finance and consequent wider competition meant that central banks, governments and other authorities were losing *de facto* sovereignty. No longer could they see themselves as controlling individual national financial systems, distinct and separate from other national systems; rather, they were faced with a situation where they were controlling a part of an increasingly interdependent world financial system. Not only could they not stand aside from trends abroad, but it was evident that the long-term prosperity of the national financial community was increasingly dependent on its ability to compete internationally. Those rules and regulations that hindered this ability were inevitably called into question.

At the same time, there was renewed questioning about the effects of many restrictions on economic efficiency. Credit controls were seen to be an inefficient way of allocating credit and high reserve ratios imposed on banks were argued by many to be an unnecessary tax on financial intermediation by banks. Limits on price competition appeared to encourage financial institutions to be profligate in their use of resources, e.g. by opening too many branch offices. Exchange controls gave rise to many elaborate schemes of avoidance and also limited the growth of much legitimate trade in financial and other services. Such arguments gained credence and so, for reasons both of domestic efficiency and international competitiveness, national authorities began to ease or to abolish many of the controls and restrictions that they had hitherto imposed.

As far as banks and other deposit-taking institutions were concerned, the main changes were that reserve requirements were eased, credit controls were eased or abandoned altogether and direct controls on rates of interest were lifted. Where official actions still differentiated between different types of deposit-taking institution, there was a tendency to cease such differentiation, to treat all alike and actively to encourage competition between institutions. As far as the issuing and trading of securities were concerned, governments generally promoted or supported the deregulation of stock exchanges and the admission of new member firms including those of foreign ownership. In a number of countries foreign-owned companies were allowed to become active dealers in government securities. Further, in a number of countries the authorities have promoted, or at least not hindered, the development of markets in short-term and medium-term paper which bring into direct competition both banks and security dealers.

Finally, affecting all financial institutions and reinforcing all other liberalizing measures, there has been a progressive and widespread relaxation of exchange control, in many cases leading to total abolition.

All these changes reflect a recognition by national authorities that they cannot, in the modern world, continue to compartmentalize and protect their financial markets – not that is, if they wish these to be efficient and internationally competitive. These changes themselves, however, by removing artificial obstacles, provided a further push to competition, enabling financial firms to move more easily into new activities and new markets.

INNOVATION AND DESPECIALIZATION

There is no space here to describe in detail the range of new financial innovations that have occurred, nor is there need as the reader will find much about them in the pages which follow this chapter, but it is appropriate to note the main developments.

In banking, a whole new range of short-term markets have been created giving banks new scope actively to manage assets and liabilities. Banks have taken advantage of this and have developed new types of interest-bearing accounts and new types of loan facilities for non-bank clients. There has been a notable blurring of traditional divisions between banking and security dealing with the securitization of bank assets, the appearance of new types of security and the growth of markets in short-term and medium-term paper. In addition, there has been a rapid growth in new techniques of risk management in the form of financial futures, tradeable options and swaps.

These dramatic changes have been accompanied by a process of despecialization, i.e. a decline in the traditional demarcations between different types of financial institution and a growth in the number of intermediaries offering a wide range of financial services. The distinctions between commercial banks, savings banks and co-operative banks were already fading: this process has continued and, in most developed countries, most banks now compete for the whole range of traditional banking business.

Beyond this, many of the large banks have become actively involved in security dealing, both as issuers and as traders. In a limited number of cases – chiefly banks in Germany and neighbouring countries – this was always the case, but for other banks it is a new development. In international markets there is now direct competition between banks and security houses and, in many domestic markets, banks now regularly deal in securities either in their own name or through wholly owned subsidiary companies. Moreover, the line between what is banking business and what is securities business has become blurred both by the growth of markets in commercial paper and other short-term and medium-term negotiable assets and by the increased willingness to 'securitize' bank assets. Finally, it should be noted that there are growing links between banking and insurance: a number of banks have taken stakes in insurance companies and, in a smaller number of instances, the reverse has happened.

MONETARY POLICY

These changes have had important consequences for a number of government policies and especially monetary policy. It is an important feature of monetary policy that it is not aimed at the financial system as such, but it uses the financial system as a means of achieving other government objectives such as influencing the pressure of demand in the economy or obtaining finance for public expenditure on favourable terms. Monetary policy has usually been operated in two ways: (a) market transactions designed to influence market prices (e.g. open-market operations, foreign-exchange operations) and (b) regulations designed to control quantities or to fix prices at other than market-clearing level (e.g. credit controls, ceilings on interest rates). In many cases, the regulations were institution specific, i.e. they applied only to certain categories of institution.

These regulations were affected by financial innovation and were in many cases made completely untenable and, as we have already seen, most have now been modified or dropped altogether. The ability of modern financial institutions to change the form and/or the location of financial transactions made many specific controls avoidable and hence unworkable. The various national authorities were faced with a choice between multiplying controls and making them ever more detailed or adopting policies of deregulation, i.e. drastically reducing the controls imposed on banks and other intermediaries. The first option appeared to have serious consequences for efficiency and international competitiveness and so, invariably among developed countries, the authorities adopted policies of deregulation. This has meant that the exercise of monetary policy has had to rely largely on market transactions, in particular open-market operations.

In most countries, at least those large enough to have active short-term money markets, this still leaves the authorities considerable scope to influence the level of domestic interest rates. But there still remains a problem concerning the intermediate target of monetary policy. During the 1970s, many countries had adopted control of the money supply (as defined) as the target of policy. Statistical evidence had appeared to show that certain measures of money were correlated with important macroeconomic variables, such as nominal national income; the implication was that controlling the money supply would be an efficient way of controlling aggregate demand in the economy. However, in a number of countries, financial innovation and the changing characteristics of financial assets, both those regarded as money and those regarded as substitutes for money, have played havoc with previously established statistical relationships. Often it has proved difficult to control particular monetary aggregates and it has become less clear what would be the economic effects of so doing. This has affected different countries differently but there has been a trend towards downgrading quantitative targets such as particular measures of the money supply and focusing instead on key prices such as the level of interest rates and/or the level of the exchange rate.

SUPERVISION

As well as having far-reaching effects on monetary policy, financial innovation has brought about profound changes in the way that the authorities supervise the financial system. As finance has become more complex and more international and as financial institutions have become more interdependent, so official supervision has had to adapt.

Most progress has been made in the regulation of banking. National authorities have sought two broad goals: (a) a more systematic and more comprehensive surveillance and control of bank operations and (b) sufficient harmonization of national controls to ensure that international trade in banking services is equitable and undistorted. The Group of Ten countries have pursued these aims through a committee of bank supervisors meeting regularly in Basel, Switzerland, and have reached a number of important agreements which have formed the basis for a wider international consensus on the control of banking. The agreements cover essentially who would exercise control and how. As far as the 'who' is concerned, it has been agreed that the competent authorities of the country wherein lies the bank's head office should have primary responsibility for supervising the worldwide activities of that bank including such subsidiary companies as it owns or controls. As far as the 'how' is concerned, it has been agreed that all banks should maintain adequate amounts of capital (as defined). Adequacy is determined in relation to the weighted total of bank assets, the weights reflecting the degree of risk inherent in the different types of assets.

Regulating securities markets has proved more difficult owing to the diverse nature of such markets and of the assets traded therein. In individual countries, both legal controls and stock exchange regulations have long sought to suppress fraud and to promote high ethical standards of behaviour, and many countries have recently sought to tighten requirements both in standards of disclosure by companies and in standards of market behaviour, e.g. the prevention of insider trading. Within Europe, the European Economic Community (EEC) has taken a number of steps towards the harmonization of regulations and the creation of a genuine community-wide capital market, but much remains to be done. Even more so is this true in the wider international context.

FINANCIAL INTEGRATION IN EUROPE

Against the background of a financial system that is changing in all respects and in which the national and the international are rapidly merging, the authorities of the EEC have been seeking to remove remaining obstacles to free trade in financial services within the Community and to move towards an integrated European financial system. Many of the changes have actually been helpful to these efforts in that they have reflected or promoted the internationalization of finance and have contributed to the decline of a number of controls imposed nationally. But, of course, there remain many differences of detail between EEC member countries in the way finance is organized and in the regulations which apply, and also a number of surprisingly large differences in certain areas – notably housing finance. The EEC has sought to reduce those differences seen as obstacles to the free trade in financial services.

In the field of banking, much has already been achieved to enable banks to operate throughout the twelve countries of the Community on the basis of common prudential requirements for capital and common standards of managerial competence and probity, all enforced by the home-country supervisory authority. Needless to say, the European Commission has sought to ensure that these common requirements do not conflict with those agreed by the Committee of Bank Supervisors meeting in Basel. There have been measures to promote common requirements on accounting information and other measures taken or planned to harmonize national approaches to such issues as limits on large risks, the collection of financial statistics and measures against the laundering of moneys of criminal origin.

In the fields of security trading and investment management, a number of steps have been taken on such things as the freedom to buy and sell securities across the Community and on harmonizing requirements for issuing and listing securities. There is now free movement of capital throughout the EEC apart from a few exceptions due to be phased out. The big issue of a sufficiently uniform control regime for all security traders (including compulsory minimum capital requirements) along with home-country supervision has been tackled in a proposed directive issued by the Commission in April 1990. But it will be some time before this directive or an amended version thereof is adopted.

These issues are discussed in more detail in the chapters which follow. Each one considers a different aspect of financial change and its consequences and together they provide wide coverage of this topic. The authors have different national backgrounds, different work experience and hence different viewpoints on the questions under discussion. It was not seen as desirable to try to harmonize in any way the views put forward; rather, it was seen as preferable that readers should benefit from the different experience and different perspectives of the several authors. But since the same economic forces have been operating throughout the world, the essays are complementary and offer the reader a set of different approaches to the same general phenomenon of financial innovation.

Llewellyn's paper provides an appropriate start by giving a general analysis of the financial system, its purposes and functions, before looking at the nature of financial innovation: how one may categorize the innovations that have taken place and how one can explain why they took place. After detailed consideration of swaps as a prime example of a new financial technique, Llewellyn considers the effects and benefits of financial innovation.

Harrington also looks at the causes of financial innovation and specifically at the role of the international markets as originators or diffusers of change. Although he finds that this role has been considerable, he inclines to the view that the fundamental cause of financial change has been the advent of new telecommunications and information technology and that the other influences are best seen as proximate causes.

Chouraqui considers briefly the main types of innovation under the headings of (a) new techniques, (b) institutional despecialization and (c) internationalization and then takes us on to the consequences of financial change. He discusses some advantages and disadvantages for users of the financial system and then considers the main consequences for government policy. These include a more pragmatic approach to monetary policy (with a reduced role for monetary targets) and a much greater effort to achieve a satisfactory and equitable (across institutions and across countries) system of prudential control.

Bingham considers a number of important changes that have taken place in securities markets and their consequences. He notes that activity in both primary and secondary markets grew rapidly during the 1980s and that this growth was accompanied by an increased variety in assets traded and by increased internationalization. These trends raise important questions about the liquidity of markets and about the probable heightened systemic risk, questions which again lead to the importance of proper official supervision within a framework that is co-ordinated internationally. But the history of different and frequently complex national systems of control makes international co-ordination difficult. Bingham concludes with a consideration of the nature and function of regulation and distinguishes between those types of regulation which are likely to reduce the efficiency of markets and those which are likely to promote it.

The foregoing chapters offer a general perspective on the issues that they address, and are not restricted to the experience of any one country. However, although the issues and the problems they discuss are common to all developed countries, it remains the case that national financial systems still have individual features and traditions of their own and it is important to see how specific systems adapt and how specific governments respond to the challenges presented by financial innovation. The next two chapters provide just such a national perspective.

Simpson looks at the profound changes that have occurred in the American financial system as it struggled to come to terms with a remarkable period of financial volatility during the early 1980s, volatility which encompassed the inflation rate, the level of interest rates and the international value of the dollar. At the same time there was a sharp rise in the deficit of the Federal Government and large increases in banks' bad debts both domestically and internationally. Also a major programme of financial deregulation was in process. As a result of these pressures, both bankers and bank regulators became more aware of risk and especially interest rate risk. There was a growth in the use of hedging instruments such as futures and options and an increase in the proportion of loans and deposits at variable rates of interest.

The authorities increased capital requirements on banks and this led to a growth in off-balance-sheet activity and in the securitization of bank assets. There were increases in the number of adjustable rate mortgages arranged by thrift institutions and increased capital requirements imposed on such institutions, although not in sufficient time to prevent a large number of them becoming insolvent by the end of the 1980s, thereby imposing enormous costs on the federal agency responsible for insuring deposits of savings and loan associations and ultimately on the Federal Government.

Bruneel considers the no less profound changes in the French financial system and also places these against a background of volatile interest rates and exchange rates. The changes reflect a major shift from what Bruneel calls a debt economy to a market economy: from an economy in which the predominant form of finance was bank finance at administratively fixed rates of interest and often within a rigid framework of official credit controls to an economy in which most finance is provided via active financial markets in which rates of interest vary according to the pressure of supply and demand. There has been a rapid growth in both equity and bond markets, in short-term financial markets and, after its creation in 1986, in the market for financial futures. This had led to some disintermediation as companies, including many of the large prime-quality borrowers, have been able to raise funds in their own name without relying so much on bank lending. French banks have responded by policies of diversification, both in terms of type of activity undertaken and geographically. As in other countries, as the authorities dismantled direct controls over the banks, they significantly increased prudential regulation.

In the final chapter, Clarotti discusses the measures that the EEC has taken or is taking to promote a single European financial market. Initially, the measures were relatively few and were aimed at securing freedom of establishment throughout the Community for suppliers of financial services and at making a start at removing the many barriers to fair competition. But following the proposal and subsequent adoption in 1987 of the Single European Act, the pace of activity has increased. Instead of laboriously trying to harmonize financial conditions throughout the Community, the

Commission has adopted the approach of recognition by all member states of each others' regulations along with the notion of home-country control of financial institutions. The objective is a situation where any financial institution duly authorized and controlled in one EEC country is free to operate in all the other member states. Progress to date has been uneven. Measures to create a single market in banking have been agreed and will come into force on 1 January 1993; measures to create a single market in security dealing have been proposed, but not yet adopted.

Of course, some efforts at harmonization remain necessary and Clarotti discusses a number of such measures that have been agreed or proposed. These tend to fall under one of three headings: (a) measures to protect the users of financial services; (b) measures to promote the efficiency of financial markets; and (c) measures to promote the integration of the hitherto separate national markets. In many respects, the EEC has been helped by the changes that are the subject of this book. In seeking to break down the obstacles to free trade in financial services, the Brussels authorities have had a powerful ally in financial innovation.

1 Financial innovation: a basic analysis

David Llewellyn

Notwithstanding recent interest in the topic, financial innovation is not a new phenomenon. All instruments, markets and financial techniques in any financial system that now exist were at one time created. What is new, however, is the acceleration since 1980 in the pace and range of financial innovation, and the emergence of several secondary markets in which new instruments are traded. During the 1980s new financial instruments, markets, facilities and techniques have emerged on a large scale, most especially in the British and American financial systems and in international financial markets. In most developed financial systems there has been a substantial growth in the range and issue volume of short-term financial instruments, together with a much higher volume of secondary market transactions. This in turn is a reflection of a more general feature of recent years, namely the shift in the structure of financial intermediation towards credit *instruments* rather than financial institutions. Direct financing and financial intermediation via markets has tended to displace the central role of institutions, with two immediate implications: (a) the risk is borne by the ultimate lenders and (b) liquidity is created via secondary markets in the instruments. Many financial innovations have had their origin in international financial markets, and one of the features of the globalization of financial markets is that financial innovation generated in one market is easily transferred to others.

The object of this review chapter is not to offer a survey and detailed analysis of the many examples of financial innovation that have recently emerged, but to consider the theory of financial innovation within a general analytical framework. The central theme is that financial innovation is not an arbitrary or random process but can be analysed systematically in terms of the factors that create supply and demand conditions for new facilities and markets. The first section establishes a general framework by considering the general functions of a financial system and the role that financial innovation can play in increasing the efficiency of these basic functions.

The next section considers the precise nature of financial innovation and offers a broad classification. This is followed by a 'model' of the financial innovation process by reviewing the factors that give rise to it. The analysis is illustrated by considering two particular examples: swaps and securitization. The final section offers an assessment in terms of benefits and problem issues.

THE GENERAL FRAMEWORK

Financial innovation should be viewed as a reflection, and partly a cause, of structural changes evident in many financial systems since the early 1980s. In this period there has been a general trend towards securitization (financial intermediation with a counterpart in a tradeable financial asset) and a growing importance of the off-balance-sheet business of banks. In line with this there has been a proliferation of new markets and a large rise in the volume of new capital market issues and secondary market activity. The emergence of many new instruments, but most especially secondary market trading in these instruments, is a central feature of the financial innovation of the 1980s. Increasingly, the international aspect to finance has become more pervasive, and several innovations reflect this in several dimensions: they may be designed to deal with the special risks encountered in international finance; they frequently give access to international or foreign markets to borrowers who would otherwise be excluded; and they have the general effect of increasing the integration of national financial markets and systems. In the process the formal distinction between banking and capital market financial intermediation has become less powerful in many financial systems. There have also been significant changes in many financial systems in the money transmission mechanisms and, as with many other aspects of structural change and financial innovation, the role of new technology is a significant force.

The starting point to any systematic analysis of financial innovation must be the financial system and its basic functions, for two reasons. First, financial innovation is an integral part of the working of a financial system and is the process whereby the basic functions are performed in different ways. This is basically in response to the portfolio objectives and constraints of the users and suppliers of financial intermediation services, and how these respond to changes in the general economic and financial environment. Second, the functions of a financial system must be the initial focus because the ultimate criterion when judging financial innovation is the extent to which it increases the efficiency of financial intermediation in particular and the functions of the financial system in general. When considering particular examples of financial innovation they can be related to one or more of the general functions of the financial system.

It is possible to draw a parallel between financial innovation and a similar process in other industries. Industries vary in the extent to which product innovation is a significant aspect in competitiveness. A computer company, for instance, seeks to enhance its competitive position in the market place by offering sometimes fundamentally new products, by improving upon the technical characteristics of existing products and by combining into one machine the characteristics of existing different machines. In doing so it seeks to exploit the potential of new technology and also responds to what it believes customers will buy. In the process the basic function of 'computing' becomes more efficient. A theme of this paper is that there is a direct parallel between financial innovation and the process of innovation in industry: they both respond to similar forces.

There are significant differences between the two, however, which distinguish financial innovation from the generality of innovation. First, unlike in many other industries, the research costs in devising new products are comparatively low. Second, there are no protective patents, and financial innovations are very easily copied. All innovations have the potential to be copied but in some industries this may take a long time because of the very nature of the process. The research costs in innovation may be high but the firm, while accepting that its superior product will eventually be copied, nevertheless believes that it gains a significant market advantage in the period before the product can be copied. That advantage must be sufficient to cover the initial research costs. This is not the case in finance as the characteristics of innovation are immediately visible and can be almost instantaneously copied by competitors. Put another way, the lead time in introducing new products is very short, and the 'shelf-life' of a financial product may be measured in only days. This also means that financial innovation developed in one financial system is easily generalized to other markets. In this way financial innovation can have the effect of integrating markets internationally.

A third difference is that financial innovation can be powerfully influenced by regulation in that many new financial instruments and markets have their origin in an attempt to circumvent regulation. A powerful and early example was the creation of the Eurodollar market which owed much of its growth to the desire to avoid the constraints of Regulation Q in the United States (which placed limits on certain US interest rates) and the effect of US capital controls in the 1960s. This process in turn may create a 'regulation dialectic' as regulators seek to bring new instruments into the purview of regulation. In other words, there is a two-way causal link between regulation and innovation. A final difference between financial innovation and industrial innovation is that the former not only is designed to meet the requirements of customers (common to all forms of innovation) but may also reflect constraints met by the suppliers of financial intermediation. A good example is found in the various new techniques of off-balance-sheet business which reflect, in part, capital constraints of banks.

Functions in the financial system

The ultimate criterion when judging the role of financial innovation is the extent to which it enhances the efficiency of the financial system in terms of its basic functions. These basic functions may be summarized as follows:

— to provide mechanisms for saving and borrowing;
— to bridge different portfolio preferences of suppliers and demanders of funds;
— to allocate funds to their most efficient use;
— to price risk and enable risks to be transferred between different parties according to their ability and willingness to absorb them;
— to offer facilities and markets enabling wealth-holders to change the structure of their portfolio of assets and liabilities;
— to offer specialist services, e.g. insurance;
— to manage the payments system.

Financial innovation has the potential to raise the efficiency in each of these areas; only a few examples are selected to illustrate the point.

A basic function is to provide mechanisms for disposing of savings and financing investment. As a general proposition, efficiency in this is enhanced the wider is the range of facilities offered and the more varied are the characteristics of each mechanism, as it is then more likely that individual and particular requirements can be met. This is referred to later as 'spectrum filling'. Thus the level of savings and investment may be determined in part by the available financing options. At the international level an example is the development of syndicated foreign currency roll-over credits (where the rate of interest to the borrower is based upon a fixed margin over a floating base rate) which enabled OPEC to acquire short-term bank deposits while oil-importing developing countries could finance their long-term requirements on terms that did not involve banks in an interest rate risk. The size of international financial imbalances rose during the 1970s, and the banks provided financial intermediation services on terms acceptable at the time to savers, borrowers and themselves.

This also illustrates the contribution that innovation can make to the second function noted. Another more recent example (which is discussed in detail in a later section) is a swap transaction where the different preferences are met by, for instance, swapping interest rate liabilities.

All finance involves some form of risk, and an important function in the financial system is to price risks and to transfer them to parties willing and able to absorb them. In the above example the pricing of risk is in principle reflected in the margin, and in that case the interest rate risk is passed to the borrowers, although this shift proved to be a problem in the 1980s. A more recent innovation illustrating the risk pricing and shifting function is with respect to the securitization of bank assets, where banks in effect convert on-balance-sheet loans into marketable securities. This has two features: (a) it re-prices the risk as indicated by the price of the bond in the secondary market and (b) it enables the risk to be shifted as the bank is able to sell the asset in a secondary market.

Other recent examples include 'equity participation financing' (in which a loan package includes an equity element where the nature of the return is different from a rate of interest on a loan) and 'mandatory convertible debentures' (where a fixed rate bond can be converted into an equity instrument). Futures, forward rate agreements and options also enable risks to be shifted from one party to another. An option, for example, involves the payment of a premium in return for the ability to choose whether to buy or sell an asset at a previously agreed price. Forward transactions enable traders either to take risk deliberately or reduce risk by a hedging operation. Futures contracts, such as those traded on the London International Financial Futures Exchange, also enable interest rate risks to be shifted and priced.

Over the past few years there have been many innovations in the payments system as new institutions have entered (e.g. building societies in the United Kingdom) and new instruments have been introduced (e.g. money-market funds with chequing facilities, sweep accounts). The influence of technology has been particularly powerful in the payments system.

One of the central functions of a financial system is to provide facilities to enable wealth-holders to change the structure of their portfolio of assets and liabilities. This can be done in basically two ways: through sales of assets in secondary markets, or via techniques such as swaps or conversions that change the characteristics of assets or liabilities.

The theme of this introduction has been that analysis of financial innovation should be viewed in terms of the contribution to the basic functions of a financial system and the contribution to the efficiency of the system. A new dimension to this also arises with some types of securitization which have the effect of exploiting the comparative advantage that different institutions have in different aspects of a loan transaction. The example discussed in a later section relates to the recent trend in the United

Kingdom towards securitizing mortgages. A finance vehicle or institution raises funds via the issue of a capital market instrument and the proceeds are used to buy assets (in this case a block of mortgages) from an institution which has previously made loans. It is mentioned briefly at this stage as an example of the contribution of innovation to efficiency. The mechanism is based upon there being three functions in a loan: an initiating procedure where the loan is made in the first place, administration of the loan and the holding of the asset. Traditionally all three functions have been performed by the same lending institution which seeks a borrower and makes the loan, administers the loan contract and holds the loan as an asset on the balance sheet. There is no reason, however, why the functions should not be split if different institutions have different comparative advantages in different functions. A good example is with securitized mortgages in the United Kingdom. A building society or a retail bank may have a comparative advantage in the first two functions in that it has a branch network giving access to customers and may have excess administration capacity (computers etc.). It would therefore be efficient at initiating and administering mortgages. On the other hand, because of funding or capital constraints it may be less efficient than some other institution (such as a wholesale bank with no retail branches) at holding the asset because it cannot fund the asset as cheaply or because its balance sheet is constrained by a shortage of capital (Llewellyn and Drake 1987b). In this case overall efficiency is increased if each institution exploits its comparative advantage: the first institution initiates and administers the loan, while the second buys the mortgage from the initiating institution on terms beneficial to the borrower as it is able to finance the holding of the asset at a lower price than the selling institution. This particular innovation raises efficiency through a process of decomposing the lending process and exploiting the different comparative advantages. This is a common feature in financial innovation as will be seen in the discussion of swaps.

NATURE OF FINANCIAL INNOVATION

Having discussed the role of innovation in the financial system we turn to a more specific analysis of the nature of financial innovation. It has two central aspects:

1 the creation of new financial instruments, techniques and markets;
2 the unbundling of the separate characteristics and risks of individual instruments and their reassembly in different combinations.

Thus the starting point is a review of the characteristics of financial instruments. No instrument is one dimensional in that it has only a single characteristic. All have several characteristics (yield, liquidity etc.) and different instruments combine basic characteristics in different ways. Thus a fifteen-year dollar floating rate note (FRN) issued by the XYZ Company has five immediate characteristics: (a) it has a floating interest rate component; (b) it is denominated in foreign currency; (c) it has a maturity of fifteen years; (d) it is marketable in a secondary market; and (e) it is issued by the XYZ Company. These not only are the characteristics of the instrument but also represent potential risks to the holder. The four basic characteristics (leaving aside the name of the issuer which cannot be changed) are combined in a single instrument. But they can also be unbundled, priced separately and held by different investors. Thus the company, through a swap transaction, can change its floating interest rate into a fixed rate obligation, and through the forward exchange or swap market it can change the currency denomination of the loan and effectively pass the exchange rate risk to someone else. Similarly in the futures market the holder of a floating rate asset can hedge against an adverse movement in interest rates.

A central feature of financial innovation is this unbundling of characteristics and either keeping them separate or combining them in different ways. This enables investors or borrowers to maintain those characteristics of an asset that they particularly want but to give up those features that are not desired.

Through a process of 'spectrum filling' (discussed in the next section) in principle financial innovation could produce a range of instruments which encompassed all possible permutations of characteristics. A simple example is given in Table 1.1 which describes a financial intermediation matrix. Four characteristics of financial intermediation amongst many are identified: form (capital market versus banks); maturity (short term versus long term); pricing (fixed versus floating interest rate); and liquidity (whether there is a secondary market for the asset). The financial intermediation matrix (considering in this case only these four characteristics) describes how the characteristics are combined in particular forms and instruments and how these may change over time. Financial innovation is the process whereby the permutations are extended.

A simple example compares the capital market and bank lending. Traditionally in the United Kingdom capital market instruments (excluding equities) have been long term in maturity and at a fixed interest rate with an active secondary market. Bank lending, on the other hand, has been predominantly short term, at a floating interest rate and with no secondary market. This represents a discontinuity in the spectrum as intermediate cases are not offered. As a result of financial innovation the 'modern matrix' in Table 1.1 allows for both banks and the capital market to offer both fixed and floating rate funds. Thus the capital market offers short-term commercial paper facilities, and through FRNs also floating rate instruments. At the same time banks also offer long-term financing either at fixed or floating interest rates. A recent development (with such techniques as securitization, asset sales without recourse, loan swaps, transferable loan contracts etc.) is for a secondary market to be developed in bank assets.

This simple example illustrates three central features of financial innovation: (a) it increases the range, number and variety of financial instruments; (b) it combines characteristics in a more varied way and widens the combination of characteristics, thereby reducing the number and size of discontinuities; and (c) it has the effect of eroding some of the differences between different forms of intermediation, as in the example cited where an FRN is a capital market instrument similar, except for liquidity, to a floating rate bank loan.

Table 1.1 Financial intermediation matrix

		Capital market	*Banks*
(1)	*Traditional matrix*		
	Maturity	Long term	Short term
	Pricing	Fixed	Floating
	Liquidity	Yes	No
(2)	*Modern matrix*		
	Maturity	Long term and short term	Short term and long term
	Pricing	Fixed and floating	Fixed and floating
	Liquidity	Yes	No/Yes

The financial intermediation matrix in Table 1.1 includes only four characteristics. In practice, there are many more and financial innovation links them in various ways. The more important of the characteristics, in addition to the four already mentioned, are the following:

— price risk, i.e. the extent to which the price of an asset or liability may change;
— earnings risk, e.g. the difference between equities and loan contracts;
— credit risk, i.e. the possibility of a default;
— country risk, i.e. the risk that a shortage of foreign currency in a country may inhibit debt-servicing;
— pricing formula (in addition to the fixed versus floating interest rate

formula already discussed) including, in the case of floating rate facilities, differences in the 'base rate' used, the frequency of changes and whether any upper or lower limits are imposed;
- conversion characteristics, i.e. the extent and circumstances in which the instrument can be converted into something else, e.g. convertible debentures;
- size of the facility;
- exchange rate risk;
- discretion, i.e. the extent to which the instrument allows either the issuer or holder to exercise a discretion, e.g. an options contract;
- hedging facility, i.e. the extent to which an instrument enables risks to be avoided, e.g. forward contracts.

In effect, financial innovation is about linking these different characteristics of financial instruments in various combinations.

Financial innovation is also about the unbundling of risks so that each can be priced separately and redistributed to those who are most able and willing to absorb them. For instance, a particular instrument may be denominated in foreign currency and carry a floating interest rate. To the holder there are two risks in addition to the general credit risk that the issuer might default. As a single instrument the issuer must find one holder prepared to take both risks simultaneously. The demand for the instrument is likely to be less than when the two risks are separated and priced independently so that those who are prepared to take an interest rate risk carry that part of the risk, while others who are able to absorb exchange rate risk take that component. This separation can be organized through swap or forward transactions.

In this context a distinction is made between what might be termed instrument innovation and *ex post* innovation. In the former case a new instrument is created with a particular set of characteristics. In the second case the same effect can be achieved by a technique that enables the characteristics of an asset or liability to be changed after the event; not by changing the inherent characteristics of the instrument but by some form of exchange of liabilities. The obvious example of this (discussed in detail in a later section) is a swap whereby two parties exchange fixed and floating interest rate liabilities. We shall see that, like the securitization process noted earlier, swaps enable different borrowers to exploit their comparative advantages in different markets and to sell that advantage to others.

A classification

A useful two-dimensional classification of financial innovation is given in a recent Bank for International Settlements (BIS) study (BIS 1986) and shown in Table 1.2. The BIS distinguishes between innovations related to on-balance-sheet and to off-balance-sheet business of banks. In terms of function, using a slightly narrower but similar categorization of financial functions to that described earlier, the individual innovations are related to the basic functions of a financial system that they contribute to.

On this basis the BIS classifies financial innovations as follows:

1 risk-transferring innovations
   (a) price risk
   (b) credit risk
2 liquidity-enhancing innovations
3 credit-generating innovations
4 equity-generating innovations

Risk-transferring innovations either reduce the risk inherent in a particular instrument (e.g. floating interest rates reduce the price risk of a loan for a lender) or alternatively enable the holder to protect against a particular risk. For instance, an investor may be holding an asset or claim whose price or value may vary but a parallel forward contract, while it does not reduce the probability of the risk, nevertheless offers protection in the event that the risk materializes. Within this category a distinction is made between price risk (the price of an asset may change) and credit risk (the borrower may default).

Liquidity-enhancing innovations have the effect of increasing the liquidity of instruments and assets. For instance, in Table 1.2 securitized assets enable loans to be sold in a secondary market which offers the lending institution the capacity to change the structure of its portfolio. Credit-generating innovations widen the access to particular credit markets and hence have the capacity to increase the total volume of credit. In Table 1.2 two such instruments are 'junk' bonds (where the registration standards, and hence costs, are low and where no formal rating is required) which give access to the bond market to firms that could not, for various reasons, make issues on the regular bond market with a formal credit-rating. Swaps also give borrowers access to a wider range of domestic and foreign credit and capital markets.

Equity-generating innovations have the effect of giving an equity characteristic (i.e. where the rate of return on the asset is determined by the performance of the issuer) to assets where the nature of the debt-servicing commitment is predetermined. A common example that has emerged recently is the debt–equity swap whereby some Latin American countries are able to transform a floating interest rate loan from a bank into an equity-type liability.

Clearly, some financial innovations perform several functions simultaneously, e.g. note issuance facilities (Table 1.2) which combine two risk-transferring functions and a liquidity-enhancing role.

Table 1.2 A classification of innovations by financial intermediation function

	Function				
Innovation	*Price-risk-transferring*	*Credit-risk-transferring*	*Liquidity-enhancing*	*Credit-generating*	*Equity-generating*
A On-balance-sheet					
Adjustable rate mortgages	•				
Floating rate loans	•				
Back-to-back loans	•				
Asset sales without recourse		•			
Loan swaps		•			
Securitized assets		•	•		
Transferable loan contracts		•	•		
Sweep accounts and other cash management techniques			•		
Negotiable money-market instruments			•		
Money-market mutual funds			•		
Zero-coupon bonds				•	
Junk bonds				•	
Equity participation financing				•	
Mandatory convertible debentures					•
B Off-balance-sheet					
Futures	•				
Options and loan caps	•				
Swaps	•			•	
Forward rate agreements	•				
Letters of credit		•			
Note issuance facilities	•	•	•		
Credit-enhancing guarantees on securities		•	•		

Source: BIS 1986

THE BASIC MODEL

A central theme is that financial innovation is not an arbitrary process but can be analysed in terms of supply and demand. The object of this section is to establish a general framework for the analysis and determination of financial innovation.

Financial innovation is a reflection partly of rising wealth (which creates a demand for an increased variety of financial assets) and changes in the market environment which induce changes in portfolio requirements both of financial institutions and their customers. The emphasis of this approach is to focus upon the requirements of the suppliers and demanders of financial facilities and instruments. The demand for a particular instrument is a derived demand for the characteristics (e.g. pricing formula, maturity etc.) embodied in it. Thus, if, because of changes in the economic environment, there is an increase in the demand for liquidity or lower exchange rate or interest rate risk, this may induce the creation of instruments designed specifically to meet that demand. At the same time the demand can be met only if it can be done in a way consistent with the requirements of the supplier of the instrument. For instance, if a transactor wishes to eliminate a future exchange rate risk, this can be done either by finding a counterparty with the opposite requirement or by creating a mechanism for transferring the risk (at a price) to another party able and willing to absorb it.

Within this general framework, four categories of financial innovation can be identified: (a) defensive (in response to policy and regulatory changes); (b) aggressive (financial institutions create instruments or new products they believe can be successfully marketed); (c) responsive (when an instrument or service is developed in order to meet a change in portfolio requirements of customers); and (d) protective (when institutions adapt techniques because of their own portfolio constraints). Financial innovation is not a random or arbitrary process but can be analysed in terms of portfolio preferences of the suppliers and demanders of products and analysis of the supply of financial intermediation services. Within this framework the impetus to financial innovation can be considered in terms of seven broad determinants.

Wealth effect

Rising wealth increases the demand for financial assets but also for an increased variety of instruments combining standard characteristics in different ways. The process of portfolio growth and diversification would be expected to create a demand for new instruments.

Portfolio behaviour and preferences of users

As the portfolio behaviour and preferences of the ultimate users of financial services change, profit-maximizing financial institutions seek to meet the new preferences on mutually acceptable terms. Part of the process of financial innovation represents market adjustments by the suppliers of financial services to meet the changing requirements of savers and borrowers. Examples are the willingness to engage in maturity transformation, the offer of facilities for offsetting interest rate and exchange rate risks and the provision of long-term finance at short-term rates of interest such as the development in the United Kingdom in the late 1970s of syndicated bank loans to local authorities. Factors in the environment, or the portfolio position of users, that induce a rise in the demand for liquidity or lower risk facilities (either because risk aversion or absolute risks have increased) may induce the creation of new instruments. There may be a demand for access to wider credit facilities and for fund raising with different characteristics (e.g. equity versus fixed or floating interest rate debt) that cannot easily be met through existing instruments.

Portfolio behaviour and preferences of the suppliers of financial services

Financial institutions are not passive but have their own portfolio objectives and constraints which change through time. In this context, financial innovation represents a process whereby the services offered by institutions are designed to tempt customers to use institutions' services in a way consistent with their own portfolio objectives and constraints. Throughout the 1970s, the portfolio behaviour of banks changed towards asset growth objectives, internationalization of portfolios, active and innovative liability management and the desire to increase the range of services. The development of syndicated credits represents a specific example which limits individual banks' commitments in very large credits. More recently, the emergence of capital and portfolio constraints has increased the incentive towards off-balance-sheet activity designed to generate fee income without increasing assets. The development of the interbank market, certificate of deposit and floating interest rate credits (which pass the risk of interest rate movements to the borrower) all fall within this category.

For reasons associated with factors such as capital constraints, changes in risk or risk aversion and the desire for a more liquid balance sheet, institutions may wish to create instruments with characteristics that raise liquidity or reduce or change the nature of risks. Thus it is not only the position of the users of instruments that induces financial innovation; the portfolio preferences and constraints of the suppliers of financial intermediation services are equally relevant. As with all markets, it is the interaction of the two sets of forces that produces financial innovation and the emergence of instruments and facilities with particular characteristics. A recent example is where banks, because of their excessive exposure to developing countries where risks have increased, have sought instruments designed both to remove assets from the balance sheet and to change the characteristics of the assets. Debt–equity swaps and the process of *ex post* securitization are particular examples.

Many recent innovations have been designed to relieve capital constraints faced by banks which implies an advantage to generating business which does not add immediately to bank assets. The whole range of off-balance-sheet business falls within this category. Off-balance-sheet business involves contingent commitments or contracts which generate income to the bank but are not captured as assets or liabilities under conventional accountancy procedures (Lewis 1988). It has two major advantages: it raises the rate of return on assets and equity, and it may avoid regulatory constraints (most especially with respect to capital) imposed on banks' on-balance-sheet business.

Some of the first 'capital-efficient' instrument innovations involving banks were new forms of commitments such as note issuance facilities (NIFs) and revolving underwriting facilities (RUFs). In the early stages they neither generated balance sheet assets nor were regarded as contingent liabilities. But because both instruments create an exposure to risk (as they offer a guarantee that funds will be provided to the borrower if the borrower is unable to borrow from anyone else) regulatory authorities now apply a capital requirement on such commitments (Llewellyn 1988a). Since then, as noted by Coleby (1987), such instruments have lost their appeal.

Changes in the market environment

Financial institutions and their clients also respond to general changes in the economic and financial environment which create a demand for particular characteristics in financial instruments. Many innovations are an immediate reflection of changes in the market environment which influence both users and suppliers of financial services, the demand for particular characteristics and the willingness of institutions and markets to supply them through different instruments. The examples of financial innovation in response to the increased volatility of interest rates, exchange rates and the rate of inflation, and the high level of interest rates, are legion. The most obvious are currency swaps and the development of financial futures and option markets. Interest rate risks of borrowers can also be avoided by writing cap, floor or collar contracts with a bank. A cap is a 'put option' which acts as a hedge to the buyer (the borrower, in this case) against rising interest rates; it sets an upper limit to the interest rate. A floor is the opposite: a series of 'call options' which, in effect, means the lender is protected from falling interest rates. Either party can offset the implied risk by a transaction in a futures market. The two combined (a collar) makes the transaction almost a fixed interest loan.

Changes in the market environment also affect the risk of existing asset structures as when, for instance, the rise in real dollar interest rates in the early 1980s adversely affected the debt-servicing capacity of developing countries. This in turn induced banks to create instruments designed to remove the exposure from the balance sheet or to change the nature of their risk exposure.

in effect

Policy changes

New financial facilities and techniques also emerge through the effect of changes in government policy. Tax incentives generally have had a powerful effect. This is particularly marked in the United Kingdom in the area of life assurance where many innovations have been introduced as tax arrangements change. The abolition of exchange and capital controls is an obvious example of measures which have induced the creation of a new range of options for investing overseas and for banks to develop international business. An additional example in the United Kingdom is the development of leasing finance because the tax system there (before it was changed in 1984) made it more profitable for low-profit companies to lease capital equipment from high-profit financial institutions than purchase it. Leasing instruments were designed to share in the tax-break secured by the leasing company.

Many of the policy changes inducing financial innovation relate to regulation. The defensive motive was identified as a determinant of innovation as regulated institutions seek to circumvent particular regulatory requirements via the creation of new instruments. Regulation (such as the imposition of capital requirements) acts as a tax in that in many cases it increases the costs and therefore supply price of financial intermediation, and changes the competitive position of the regulated sector *vis-à-vis* the non-regulated sector. Thus capital requirements on banks undermine the role of banks relative to the capital market, as has been seen in the United States with the strong growth of the commercial paper market. Koehn and Santomero (1980) observe in this regard that a regulation designed to make the regulated ostensibly less risky can have the effect of increasing vulnerability as the regulation 'tax' enhances the competitiveness of the unregulated (in this case the capital market) to the extent that the best quality customers are able to shift their business. The net result is that the average quality of banks' loan assets is reduced as they are left with those who are unable to switch. This also illustrates how regulation can change the nature of an institution's business: in this case it has induced the banks to create instruments or facilities that enable them to share in the capital market business. Thus US banks are involved with 'back-up' facilities for commercial paper offerings in the United States. Another example from the United States is the inducement given to the creation of money-market mutual funds by the interest rate ceilings imposed on banks' retail deposits.

These five factors are specific and identifiable. The sixth factor is more general and emerges as a product of a competitive financial system.

Spectrum filling

What might be termed 'spectrum filling' reflects the tendency for active financial institutions and markets to innovate by offering facilities to fill gaps or remove discontinuities in the whole range of financial intermediation facilities. It involves the combining of characteristics (such as yield, marketability, maturity) of different financial instruments and facilities so that the advantages of one instrument alleviate the disadvantages of another. This is a natural process in a competitive and adaptive financial system which meets the market requirements of its actual and potential customers. An extreme example would be the case of a blatantly discontinuous system which offered borrowers only short-term floating rate loans or twenty-five-year fixed interest bond issues. A natural process would accommodate intermediate requirements by banks offering term loans and the capital market offering bonds with a variety of maturities. It is the size and frequency of discontinuities in the spectrum of financial instruments and facilities that distinguishes the comparatively few sophisticated financial systems in the world from the rigid and underdeveloped systems which are predominant. In its extreme form, financial innovation would create a smooth continuous spectrum in all dimensions (e.g. maturity, pricing formulae, marketability etc.) where all characteristics of financial instruments could be integrated in any desired combination.

In addition to the discontinuity that exists within the spectrum for any given user, discontinuities also exist between different users. In the latter case the market produces different terms for different market participants. Financial innovation can bridge this gap, as demonstrated by the development of interest rate swaps which are a product of different structures of comparative advantage that exist between different users of fixed and floating rate finance facilities.

Examples of 'spectrum filling' at the international level include FRNs and transferable loan facilities. The same process of 'spectrum filling' can in effect 'manufacture' new securities markets (Lewis 1988). There is an active commercial paper market in the United States but not in Germany. German companies, however, can simulate one by issuing dollar commercial paper, selling the proceeds spot for Deutschmarks and covering in the forward market. For all intents and purposes the company has issued Deutschmark commercial paper. An obvious domestic counterpart in the United States is the development of money-market mutual funds which carry money-market interest rates but also allow holders to write cheques from the account. It breaks the rigid distinction between a current or chequing account (with no market interest paid on outstanding balances) and money-market investments with no money transmission facilities attached.

Technology

The development of technology in finance has had a powerful impact on financial innovation not least because it enables traders in new instruments (options being a good example) to calculate arbitrage opportunities in complex situations immediately. Technology also contributes to the design and pricing of new instruments, and facilitates the identification, measurement and monitoring of risks in portfolios containing complex instruments. It reduces trading costs in international markets, and has the effect of widening the market for new instruments to an international dimension. In the process the supply and demand for instruments in isolated markets can be more readily matched. It also enables international markets to be linked and therefore gives access to foreign markets to borrowers who would not normally have such access. This is true, for instance, with swaps and is discussed in the next section.

The framework established above is analogous to the approach of Silber (1975, 1983) who argues that financial innovation responds to economic forces. His particular perspective is that: 'New financial instruments or practices are innovated to lessen the financial constraints imposed on firms.' In the same approach he argues: 'the stimulus to innovation can be interpreted as an increase in the cost of adhering to existing constraints'. In Silber (1983) the analysis is illustrated by reference to thirty-eight instruments or markets divided into four categories (cash management techniques, investment contracts, market structures and institutional organization). In what might be termed a 'causality matrix' he identifies specific 'causes' of financial innovation (inflation, volatility of interest rates, technology, legislative initiatives, internationalization of finance) and relates each of the identified innovations to one or more of these 'causes'. While this approach is somewhat stylized, it serves to focus the general principle being established in this review that financial innovation is not a random process but can be analysed in terms of the broad economic, technological, financial and regulatory forces producing changes in the supply and demand for new instruments and financial facilities.

ILLUSTRATIVE EXAMPLES

Table 1.2 lists many examples of recent innovations some of which have been discussed in passing. This section is not designed to offer an exhaustive analysis of each, but selects two in particular (swaps and securitized mortgages) to illustrate the basic economic analysis of financial innovation.

Swaps

Since their creation in 1981 there has been a substantial growth in the volume, range and number of transactors in the swaps market. The market has grown from a principal value of around US$3 billion in 1981 to over US$350 billion by the end of 1987. Swaps involve arbitrage between partially segmented markets. They would not exist if all transactors had equal access to all credit and capital markets on the same terms. Swaps enable differences in comparative advantages in different markets to be exploited. They are used by companies, banks and other institutions to reduce borrowing costs, increase asset returns or to hedge interest rate risk (Felgram 1987).

A borrower negotiating a loan has a threefold choice over (a) the currency of the loan, (b) the interest rate formula (fixed or floating) and (c) the interest rate basis (e.g. the London interbank offering rate (LIBOR), US certificate of deposit rate, US prime rate). This structure of choices can be exercised in two ways: (1) by negotiating directly with the supplier of funds or (2) by the use of interest rate and/or currency swaps after the initial loan has been received. There is also the choice over the draw-down period in a loan, and again this can be either negotiated within the initial loan contract or handled via a futures or forward contract.

An interest rate swap involves a contract between two borrowers to exchange interest rate payments. In a currency swap liabilities in different currencies are exchanged, while in interest swaps interest liabilities of different characteristics are exchanged. In effect, through the swap market the borrower secures a different liability than the one contracted with the initial supplier of funds. Figure 1.1 describes the basic mechanics of an

Figure 1.1 Swap transaction

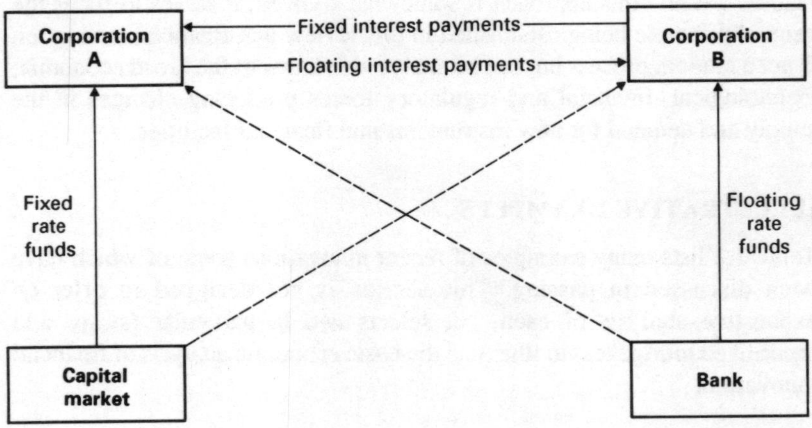

interest rate swap transaction. Corporation A issues a fixed interest bond in the capital market for a maturity of ten years although it would prefer to have a floating interest rate liability. Corporation B prefers a fixed interest liability but borrows for ten years from a bank on a floating interest rate basis. Either directly or through a broker the two corporations, while maintaining their existing obligations to their initial lenders, agree to swap the interest payments. Thus corporation A pays a flow of floating rate payments to corporation B while the latter pays a flow of fixed interest rate payments to corporation A. The broken lines in Figure 1.1 represent the two simulated borrowing transactions that result from the swap. Thus a floating rate borrower can exchange floating rate payments for fixed rate interest

Figure 1.2 Quality spreads over time

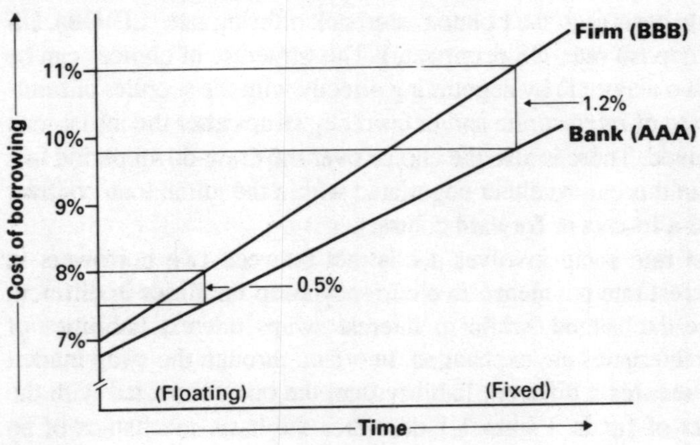

Table 1.3 Interest rate savings

		Firm	Bank
1	Credit rating	BBB	AAA
2	Direct borrowing costs	(LIBOR + 0.75%)	(9.8%)
3	Fixed rate payments swapped	(10.0%)	9.9%
4	Floating rate payments swapped	LIBOR	(LIBOR)
5	All-in costs of borrowing	(10.75%)	(LIBOR -0.1%)
6	Alternative direct borrowing costs	(11.0%)	(LIBOR +0.25%)
7	Savings	25 basis points	35 basis points

Note: Payments are swapped at dealer price: 9.9%/10.0% for six-month LIBOR. Numbers in parentheses are negative interest flows; otherwise positive flows.

payments by becoming a fixed rate payer in a swap transaction. The borrower swaps payments of fixed rate interest for receipt of floating rate interest, which covers the floating rate borrowing cost and creates a fixed rate payment obligation. The price at which the exchange is made is determined in the market and reflects the strength of the comparative advantage of the two parties in the relevant markets.

The key to a swap transaction is the difference in *comparative* advantage that two borrowers have in different markets. A swap can be mutually beneficial even though one of the parties has an absolute advantage in both markets. Figure 1.2 and Table 1.3 are taken from Felgram (1987). We assume the two parties are a triple A rated bank and a triple B rated company. For both parties, as the maturity of a loan lengthens so the cost of funds rises but at different progressions dependent upon their credit standing. Thus investors would require the lower-rated borrower to pay relatively high risk premiums when borrowing long-term fixed interest funds rather than short-term floating rate funds. This implies, as in Figure 1.2, that although the bank can borrow more cheaply in all markets, the lower-rated company faces the lowest relative cost in the short-term floating rate market, while the higher rated bank has its greatest comparative advantage (lowest relative costs) in the long-term fixed rate market.

A swap is designed to exploit these comparative advantages in a situation where the best market for each is not what the borrower actually desires. Each borrows in his best market and exchanges the interest liability with the other. In Figure 1.2 the bank could borrow either at a fixed rate of 9.8 per cent or at a floating rate of LIBOR plus 0.25 per cent; if

LIBOR is 7.25 per cent this gives a total of 7.5 per cent. However, the company would face a fixed interest cost of 11 per cent (i.e. 1.2 per cent higher than the bank) or can opt to pay 0.75 per cent above LIBOR for floating rate finance, i.e. 8 per cent. In Figure 1.2 the widening gap between the two schedules (from 0.5 to 1.2) indicates the worsening position of the company relative to that of the bank as maturity lengthens.

To exploit the comparative advantages, each borrows in the market where they have a comparative advantage and exchanges (swaps) the interest payments. The costs and results of the transactions are summarized in Table 1.3. The bank borrows long-term fixed interest funds (at 9.8 per cent in line 2) even though it prefers short-term floating rate borrowing. The rate at which the swap is made (i.e. the swap price) is determined in the market. In this case the price is such that the company makes fixed rate payments to the bank of 10 per cent (line 3) while the bank makes floating rate payments to the company equal to LIBOR (7.25 per cent). The receipts of floating rate payments (7.25 per cent) from the bank cover the company's direct floating rate borrowing costs (8 per cent) less 0.75 per cent. Thus the company's total cost (line 5) is equal to the payments made to the bank (10 per cent) plus the 0.75 per cent 'cost' of the swap. But this is less than the 11 per cent it would have had to pay to borrow long term at a fixed rate. The bank receives 9.9 per cent from the company (line 3) which exceeds by 0.1 per cent the cost of its fixed rate loan (line 2). Thus the effective cost to the bank (line 5) is what it pays in interest flows to the company (LIBOR at 7.25 per cent) minus the 0.1 per cent advantage in the swap price. This cost of 7.15 per cent compares with the cost it would have incurred (7.5 per cent) had it borrowed directly in the floating rate market.

Thus both parties gain and in this case the bank gains more than the company because it is likely that the price will reflect the fact that the bank has a superior position in both markets. There are several mechanisms through which a swap transaction can be executed. In its simplest form as described above, two principals (one of which might be a bank) exchange interest payments directly with each other having been brought together by a broker. The second possibility is for a bank itself, acting as an intermediary (i.e. taking a position) between two principals, to receive and make the payments from and to the principals. The bank sets the swap price, i.e. how much interest the principals pay to and receive from the bank. In this case the bank may offer a swap facility to a principal without having an immediate counterparty in mind. The bank can subsequently hedge its own position that results from individual swap deals that it offers to principals either by a forward or futures market transaction or by an equal and opposite swap with another principal. Thus a bank may act as a broker, an intermediary or a principal in the swaps market. If it acts as a broker the role is purely informational. As an intermediary it has a balance sheet position and hence potential risk which needs to be covered in its pricing. As a principal it may, for its own balance sheet purposes, exploit its comparative advantage in a particular market.

The interest rate swap developed as a means of both parties exploiting the advantage they have in different markets. In this example the bank has a comparative advantage in the capital market but prefers floating rate finance, while the company has the opposite advantage and preference.

Four basic types of swap can be identified:

1 Interest rate swap.
2 Basis swap: two floating rate payments streams are exchanged but each is calculated on a different basis or formula, e.g. LIBOR and prime rate.
3 Currency swap: two borrowers in different currency markets exchange their interest and principal liabilities.
4 Hybrid swap: two borrowers swap both the currency and the interest rate formula. Corporation A issues a fixed interest rate bond in the Eurodollar bond market and makes the floating interest rate payments payable to corporation B which pays to A a stream of fixed rate Swiss franc funds. This combines a currency and an interest rate swap. Alternatively, given that an exact swap may not be possible, the transaction may involve different counterparties for each component.

In terms of the analysis of the last section, the possibility of swaps arises because, for individual borrowers, there are discontinuities in the spectrum of financial facilities which are effectively smoothed by transactions undertaken after a loan has been received. Swaps reflect either imperfections in the market, segmented markets or different perceptions of risk. They can arise only because different borrowers have different comparative advantages in different markets as otherwise they would borrow directly in the market and on the terms they prefer. If one borrower has a comparative advantage in a fixed interest bond market it implies that his characteristics are more preferred by the subscriber to bonds than those of the counterparty to the subsequent swap. This may arise because, for instance, investors have a preference for multinational companies or household names. It may also reflect regulation that limits the type of investment that can be made. It can reflect portfolio-balance considerations as when banks and institutions already have a concentrated portfolio in a particular direction. Alternatively it may simply reflect differences in risk perception between the suppliers of funds and the counterparties in the swap. It can also reflect differences in information with each borrower raising funds in the market in which it is already known and swapping the liabilities to mutual advantage. Regulation limits the access of some borrowers to particular markets, as in Japan where access to different sectors of the capital market is subject to regulation.

Swap transactions may also reflect changes in the portfolio preferences that occur after original loans have been contracted. Both parties might originally have been content with their own fixed and floating rate obligations but preferences might change within the maturity of the loan.

Swap transactions can reflect market imperfections. An example is with respect to forward transactions where markets are efficient and active for maturities up to one year but not beyond. In this case currency swaps have the properties of hedge instruments where it is difficult to secure long-dated foreign-exchange cover. Thus a fixed-to-fixed currency swap is similar in effect to long-dated forward foreign-exchange transactions. In this way currency swaps allow longer maturity 'forward' transactions than are actually provided in the forward foreign-exchange market. The swap is a technique of simulating a market that does not exist in its pure form or improving upon one that does exist but is inefficient.

The essence of the swap is that each borrower exploits his comparative advantage and trades with a counterparty to mutual advantage. It performs many of the roles of financial innovation: giving effective access to a wider range of markets, creating a smoother spectrum of facilities, breaking or eroding some of the formal distinctions between banking and capital markets and increasing the efficiency of financial intermediation.

The securitized mortgage market

The second case study of financial innovation relates to the mortgage market and securitized mortgages. It emphasizes the role of financial innovation in circumventing regulatory constraints.

The most established secondary market for mortgages is found in the United States and is discussed by Llewellyn and Drake (1987b). The initial catalyst for the emergence of a secondary mortgage market in the United States was a form of market imperfection associated with regulation: the need to even out regional imbalances in the supply of and demand for mortgage finance associated with regulations inhibiting interstate banking. The US secondary mortgage market expanded dramatically following the earnings crisis experienced by the savings and loan associations and mutual savings banks in the early 1980s. This again was a product in part of regulation which limited the extent to which these institutions could raise interest rates in line with market trends. When short-term interest rates rose sharply in the early 1980s the institutions found themselves holding low yielding, fixed rate, long-term mortgage assets.

Although a secondary mortgage market has been well established in the United States (and other countries) for a number of years, such a market is only in its embryonic stage in the United Kingdom. The recent emergence of such a market in the United Kingdom is due primarily to a fundamental structural change in key interest rate relationships, with the mortgage rate rising relative to wholesale money-market interest rates. In addition, as in the United States, a securitized mortgage market may also emerge more substantially in the United Kingdom because of constraints on building societies associated with regulation and, most especially, imposed limits on funding in cheaper wholesale markets.

'Securitization' refers to the conversion of mortgages into securities which are comparable with other investments available on the capital markets. It may also imply removing the assets from the balance sheet of an institution. It is a process of changing the structure and possibly also the size of an institution's portfolio of assets. Securitization occurs when the mortgage assets are removed from the balance sheet of an initiating or original institution (e.g. a building society) through the mechanism of a parallel capital market transaction either by the institution itself (perhaps through a specially created finance vehicle) or a different institution. An obvious example is where a finance vehicle issues FRNs on the capital market and uses the proceeds to purchase a package of mortgages from an initiating institution. This particular market is an example of financial innovation eroding the formal distinction between banking and the capital market.

At a very basic level, financial transfers through a financial system which involve the borrowing and lending of funds may be of three basic kinds: (a) direct (where a direct loan is made by a saver to a borrower), (b) through the capital market where the borrower issues a tradeable security or (c) through the intermediation of a deposit-taking financial institution or other institution acting as a principal. However, this traditional and standard distinction is too restrictive in the context of securitization in two dimensions. First, the very process of securitization represents a mechanism whereby an initial structure of financial intermediation involving a deposit-taking financial institution is subsequently (i.e. after a loan has been made) transferred into a capital market instrument. In other words, a set of financial flows begins as (c) but ultimately becomes part of (b). In this way the form of the initial financial mechanism does not necessarily determine either the nature of the ultimate assets and liabilities created or the balance sheet position of the financial institution providing the initial intermediation service.

The second dimension challenging the traditional distinction made between financial institutions and the capital market is that the various functions in the process of providing loans have become more differentiated. Thus a loan involves an origination process, administration and an asset to be held. An institution (such as a bank or building society) may perform each. But there is no reason why each necessarily has to be undertaken by the same institution. An institution may have a comparative advantage in originating loans perhaps because it has a branch network. On the other hand, it may not be the most efficient institution to hold the asset, perhaps because of a capital constraint or because it cannot fund the asset as cheaply as a different institution which does not have an advantage in originating loans. Because of different comparative advantages (induced in part by a structural change in the pattern of interest rates) the hitherto rigid distinction in the United Kingdom between the role of initiating institutions and the capital market has been eroded as in some cases the various functions in a loan transaction have come to be performed by different agencies. This is central to the issue of securitization in the mortgage market.

A finance vehicle (either specially created or an existing institution) issues a capital market instrument (in the United Kingdom in practice it would be an FRN) and uses the proceeds to purchase a package of mortgage assets from an institution that has made mortgage loans. The original institution may use the funds in two ways. It can substitute other assets for the cash received, thus maintaining the total size of the balance sheet and the initial capital ratio. In effect, the original institution has substituted other assets (e.g. other types of loan) for mortgages, and for this reason this may be termed the 'asset transformation' role of securitization. Alternatively, the institution can choose to use its cash injection to allow deposits to be reduced, and to reduce the total size of the balance sheet. One reason why this option might be chosen is a capital constraint faced by the institution; the effect of the transactions is to raise the capital ratio. This route is termed the 'balance sheet constraint' role of securitization.

The mechanism described has related to the role of securitization in changing an existing balance sheet structure. An alternative mechanism is designed to exploit different comparative advantages and can be advantageous where a holder of mortgages (originating institution) which wishes to create additional mortgages faces a funding constraint (in that it could not raise deposits as cheaply as some other institutions) but faces no capital constraint inhibiting balance sheet growth. In this case the finance vehicle or other institution raises funds in the capital market at a lower cost than could the original institution. With the funds raised it effectively purchases from the originating institution a 'participation right' in its interest receipts from the assets with the rate of interest being some fixed margin over the finance vehicle's cost of funds. The finance vehicle's profit is reflected in the agreed margin over the cost of funds. The source of payment to the finance vehicle by the originating institution is the interest received on the new mortgage loans.

These simple examples illustrate the basic rationale of a securitization procedure involving a secondary market transaction:

1 to enable the institution to change the structure of its assets – asset-transformation motive;
2 to allow the institution to reduce the size of its balance sheet – balance sheet constraint motive;
3 to generate fee income relative to assets and to exploit the comparative advantage that the institution may have in either initiating and/or administering the loan that has been securitized with a secondary transaction – fee income motive.

With respect to the income motive, this necessarily raises the average rate of return on assets retained on the balance sheet. The potential for fee income via securitization arises if the securitizing institution has a comparative advantage *vis-à-vis* competitors in initiating and administering loans relative to holding the asset. This may be because it is profitable for a competitor to hold the asset although it is unable to initiate loans; in this case the competitor is prepared to pay fees to the initiating institution as a cost of obtaining profitable assets. It may also arise because the initiating institution cannot fund the asset at as low a cost as the competitor. In the final analysis it is an issue of comparative advantage in the various functions involved in a loan. It enables some institutions to profit from what they do best – originating and servicing loans – rather than necessarily holding them as assets on the balance sheet.

The emergence of a securitized mortgage market in the United Kingdom reflects financial innovation as a response to portfolio constraints of originating institutions (*protective* innovation) and because of changes in the market environment (the change in the structure of interest rates noted above).

The UK mortgage market has changed substantially in recent years: new mortgage institutions have been established since 1984 which are funded exclusively in the wholesale markets (and usually through capital market issues of one sort or another), and an embryonic secondary market has evolved. The impetus to the entry of capital-market-based mortgage companies has been a major structural change in the pattern of interest rates, with the mortgage rate rising relative to LIBOR (Llewellyn and Drake 1987a). As the mortgage rate has risen relative to wholesale money-market rates mortgage assets are now attractive to a whole range of institutions, such as banks, pension funds, insurance companies and any intermediary funding mortgage assets through wholesale borrowing.

An embryonic secondary mortgage market has developed in the United Kingdom with so-called 'third-tier' mortgage-lending institutions securitizing part of their mortgage portfolio via the issue of mortgage-backed securities (typically FRNs), sometimes through a finance vehicle company so as to remove the mortgage assets from the balance sheet (see Boleat 1987). Institutions such as the National Home Loans Corporation are specializing in the wholesaling, rather than the retailing, of mortgages, obtaining much of their business in the form of referrals from life companies. Furthermore, institutions are emerging which are dedicated to providing a securitization service to other institutions (First Mortgage Securities and the Mortgage Funding Corporation) or to providing an efficient mortgage administration service.

In effect this example of financial innovation represents an unbundling of the components of a loan transaction (origination, administration and the holding of the asset) and enhances overall efficiency by allowing each role to be performed by institutions which are the most efficient at it. Again, financial innovation is about efficiency and an 'unbundling' process.

ASSESSMENT

Financial innovation is not a new phenomenon. In many ways the history of finance, and the evolution of financial systems, is the history of financial innovation. All financial instruments, techniques, facilities and markets that now exist and are taken for granted as natural features of finance came into being at one time, and at that time would have been described as financial innovation. Nevertheless, the pace of innovation in finance has accelerated markedly in the current decade in both national and international markets.

This in itself is a phenomenon to be explained. While it is a complex process, we may identify five major features accounting for this marked acceleration. First is the role of competition: the competitive environment in all financial systems, and internationally, has greatly intensified in the 1980s. A second and major factor has been the parallel development of information and trading technology. If changes in the economic and financial environment have created a demand for new instruments, the development of technology has enabled these demands to be met. A third factor has been the volatile financial environment, most especially with respect to interest rates and exchange rates. Many of the new instruments have been designed to offer some form of protection against this volatility. Fourth, and as part of the more competitive market environment, a 'marketing ethos' has developed in the management of financial institutions. The creation of new instruments and facilities partly represents an attempt by the suppliers of financial services to capture market share and to create demand.

A further characteristic feature of the 1980s has been a steady 'internationalization' in finance (Llewellyn 1988b), which can be counted as a fifth factor in the acceleration of financial innovation. Many of the new instruments and facilities created were developed initially in international markets (partly because of the special risk characteristics of international financial intermediation and the more intensive competitive environment) and as a response to regulation in national markets. They have subsequently been adopted in national financial systems. In various ways financial innovation has been a significant integrating force contributing to a further globalization of finance (BIS 1986).

For example, interest rate and currency swaps have had the effect of increasing the integration of markets and national systems as they facilitate access of both borrowers and lenders to markets which would otherwise be closed to them either through regulation or cost. They frequently increase cross-border links and straddle different sectors of the same currency market. The BIS study cites examples of where less highly rated companies have been able to raise fixed rate finance. Also (via interest rate swaps linked to the issues of 'capped' FRNs), savings and loan associations in the United States have been able to locate non-US counterparties willing to assume some of the risk associated with their interest rate mismatches, some of which are a product of regulation.

Benefits of innovation

The analysis of financial innovation can be summarized by considering in general terms the benefits that accrue through innovation in financial systems. These can be outlined briefly as they are implicit in much of the previous discussion.

1 The costs of financial intermediation can be reduced in two major ways: (a) they give borrowers access to a wider range of markets and facilities and (b) in some cases they allow different institutions to exploit their comparative advantages. This was seen in the case study of securitization of mortgages.
2 New instruments facilitate arbitrage between markets in different countries and instruments and in principle erode pricing anomalies. This may reduce market imperfections.
3 Some instruments and techniques also allow individual borrowers to

exploit their comparative advantage in different markets which again lowers the costs of financing. Swaps are a good example.

4 Several instruments (such as futures, options etc.) widen the range of hedging possibilities and hence enable risks to be protected against.

5 As part of the same process some instruments allow risks to be priced (one of the basic functions of a financial system) and to be shifted to those able and willing to absorb them.

6 To the extent that innovations create secondary markets they facilitate the management and adjustment of portfolios and also serve to price risks.

7 Many instruments allow various risks to be unbundled, separately priced and 'sold'. If the risks are correctly priced this contributes to the financial system's role of allocating resources efficiently.

8 By increasing the range of financial instruments the process of 'spectrum filling' offers a wider range of choice with the presumption that the requirements of users are more readily and efficiently met.

Efficiency of the financial system

In this survey we have considered the issue of financial innovation in the financial system, and a major consideration is the extent to which it has contributed to the basic efficiency of the financial system (see Revell 1983). The concept of efficiency is difficult both to define and measure in finance and a distinction is made between structural efficiency (the range of choice offered in the system and its adaptability to changing circumstances and preferences of users) and allocative efficiency (the ability of the system to price risks accurately and to allocate funds to where the risk-adjusted rates of return are highest). A third concept of resource efficiency (the extent to which financial institutions and markets use efficiently the real resources absorbed in the supply of financial services) raises different issues and is not considered further. However, there is a presumption that competition (both domestic and international) imposes a powerful discipline on the use of resources, as in all industries.

The basic requirements of an efficient financial system are outlined in Table 1.4. In general, and compared with those in most other countries, the British financial system meets these requirements well. This is due in part to four major characteristics: the minimum of regulatory limits on the business of financial institutions; the freedom of entry of foreign institutions; the ability of those using financial facilities to use foreign markets; and the generally competitive conditions in the markets for financial services.

A brief consideration of the contribution of financial innovation to

Table 1.4 Requirements of an efficient financial system

Structural efficiency	
1	Institutions and markets should offer a wide range of instruments and facilities with respect to maturity, risk, rate of return, marketability etc. so that different portfolio preferences can be readily accommodated
2	Particular financial services should be provided in a competitive environment by the most efficient suppliers as reflected in consumers' choice
3	All users of the system should have access to the full range of financial facilities
4	Facilities should exist for changes in the structure of portfolios without disturbing prices
5	Institutions and markets should be innovative, responsive to changing market conditions and able to accommodate changing customer requirements
Allocative efficiency	
6	The system should facilitate the accurate identification, pricing, diversification and transfer of risk
7	All interest rates and prices of financial instruments should be equally flexible so as to minimize financial flows due solely to price rigidities
8	Pricing signals should contribute to an optimum allocation of real resources
9	The system should provide for savings to be channelled to where the rate of return on capital is highest
10	Regulation should be competitively neutral between potentially competing institutions and markets and directed exclusively to issues of consumer protection and systemic risk
11	Allocation effects due to the taxation system should be based only upon market failure and market imperfection considerations, and should be competitively neutral betwen potentially competing institutions and markets

enhancing the efficiency of the financial system is given with reference to the basic functions of the financial system identified at the outset.

Saving and borrowing

There is a presumption that an increased variety of instruments increases the efficiency of saving and borrowing. The costs of financial intermediation can be reduced in two main ways: (a) some instruments such as swaps give borrowers access to a wider range of markets and facilities and (b) in some cases they allow different institutions to exploit their comparative advantages. This was discussed earlier in the case of mortgages. There is a general presumption that the level of saving and investment is likely to be higher the greater is the range of options available for each.

Matching portfolio preferences

By the same argument innovation is presumed to increase efficiency as the wider range of facilities increases the probability that different portfolio preferences are met. On the assumption that users know their requirements and the full implications of the instruments they use, then variety contributes to efficiency. In principle the process of 'spectrum filling' moves the financial system closer to the Arrow–Debreu ideal where all transactors can ensure for themselves delivery of goods and services in all future contingencies. Arrow and Debreu (1954) demonstrate that the existence of risk can be an impediment to the efficient allocation of resources unless there exists a complete set of contingent commodity markets. In principle, therefore, the creation of new instruments moves closer to an approximation of the number of 'states of nature'. However, Tobin (1984) questions this on the grounds that, in practice, there are few instruments catering for longer-term risks and uncertainties.

Allocate funds to most efficient use

There is also a presumption that, to the extent that some innovations enable component risks to be identified, separated and accurately priced, funds are allocated more efficiently. To the extent that risks can be effectively managed through particular instruments, finance is potentially made available to higher-risk investment projects although it is doubtful, in practice, whether instruments contribute significantly in this direction. Welfare is reduced if risks are under-priced because it induces a higher volume of real and financial resources to be devoted to a particular use. However, this argument assumes that particular instruments and innovations do in fact correctly price risks. In addition, new instruments facilitate arbitrage between markets in different countries and instruments and in principle erode pricing anomalies, which may also have the effect of reducing imperfections.

Pricing and distributing risks

If risks are reduced in total (e.g. through futures contracts) there is an unambiguous benefit. Several instruments (such as futures, options) widen the range of hedging possibilities and hence enable risks to be protected against. In itself this is too strict a requirement as efficiency is also increased if a facility enables a risk to be transferred (rather than reduced in total) to an agent more able to absorb it. However, this potential benefit should not be exaggerated as instruments such as options and forward transactions only deal with unanticipated changes given that anticipated movements in, for instance, interest rates and exchange rates are incorporated in the pricing of the instrument.

Changing portfolios

The fifth function noted earlier identifies as a basic function of the financial system the offering of facilities and markets enabling wealth-holders to change the structure of their portfolio of assets and liabilities. All secondary markets perform this function, as do swaps in some cases. This is beneficial to the extent that it enables both asset and liability holders to respond to changing circumstances. In the process it reduces the extent to which transactors need to forecast market conditions and their own circumstances accurately over the maturity of the loan or asset. On the other hand, the proliferation of instruments may actually reduce liquidity by distributing a given total demand across a larger number of instruments and markets, thereby making each market comparatively 'thin'.

Specialist services

Many specialist services (e.g. insurance) are performed in a financial system. If innovation increases the efficiency in the supply of these services then there is an unambiguous benefit. An obvious example is the ever widening range of 'pension-type' facilities currently on offer.

Payments section

A particular function is the management of the payments system. Some recent innovations (CHAPS etc.) have increased efficiency. Similarly innovations such as money-market mutual funds with chequing facilities enable users to integrate savings balances and transactions balances, thereby securing economies of scale and reducing the number of accounts that need to be kept. SWEEP accounts also enable users to economize on non-interest-bearing current accounts.

Overall, there is a presumption that the process of financial innovation does contribute to efficiency.

Problem issues

While there can be undoubted benefits from new instruments created by financial innovation, there can also be associated problems. A full discussion takes us beyond the scope of this review but the major problem issues can be highlighted.

The proliferation of financial instruments with sometimes complex characteristics creates problems for the conduct of monetary policy. The issues are surveyed by Akhtar (1983). A central one is that the definition of the 'money supply' becomes more ambiguous and uncertain when a wider range of instruments have characteristics of a transactions nature. The mechanisms of the money supply process are similarly affected with the unique role of banks becoming less important. At the same time the demand for 'money' has become less stable and less sensitive to movements in interest rates. In addition, to the extent that many instruments straddle different markets, measures of credit control operate with less certainty and precision. 'Goodhart's law' suggests that the meaning of a particular monetary aggregate changes when it becomes the target of monetary policy. In fact many instruments are created precisely in order to circumvent the constraints imposed by monetary policy operations. The growth of acceptance credits in the United Kingdom in the early 1980s is a good example.

The same phenomenon also arises with respect to financial regulation of a prudential nature. In an earlier section we identified the defensive motive as one category of financial innovation. Regulation tends to lag developments in innovation and in the process a 'regulation dialectic' emerges as regulation responding to innovation induces further circumventing moves by financial institutions. In general regulation becomes more difficult as the complexity of financial instruments and facilities is increased. Regulation frequently relates to particular institutions and this approach becomes more problematic to the extent that innovation has the effect of, for instance, eroding the distinction between banking and capital market instruments. New instruments also create new risks which may be difficult to identify, measure and locate. A good example relates to off-balance-sheet facilities designed in part to circumvent capital constraints of banks. To the extent that these create contingent liabilities they need to be brought within the purview of regulation. Regulatory authorities have responded to this by assigning a capital requirement against such contingent liabilities, although the process (involving 'credit-equivalents') is complex (see Llewellyn 1988a). Overall, financial innovation has made regulation a more complex issue as the identification, measurement and location of inherent risks are more difficult to define than with more conventional forms of financial intermediation. Keeping pace with the implications of financial innovation has become a major challenge to the regulatory authorities (BIS 1986).

Institutions must also be aware of the difficult question of the implications for contingent liability involved with new instruments such as NIFs, forward rate agreements etc. These need to be incorporated in portfolio management procedures though, by definition, there is little experience to be guided by. The process of identifying, measuring and locating risks is as difficult for the regulated as it is for the regulator. Put another way, the business of banking becomes more difficult as complex instruments are created and managed by institutions and markets. Mayer and Kneeshaw (1988) note that the incorporation of exposures resulting from new instruments into the overall risk and income strategies of institutions poses formidable management problems with the possibility that it may not be done efficiently.

More generally problems of portfolio management intensify as complex instruments with varying combinations of risk are added to the business of institutions.

The same problem arises for the users of new instruments. Given the complexities involved it might be questioned whether users are totally familiar with the implications of the complex instruments they use. Additionally, the issue of asymmetric information arises in some cases. The full risk implications of some instruments (e.g. options) can sometimes be determined only by involved mathematical procedures and these have to be appreciated as much by the users as by the institutions and regulators. The full risk and other implications of new instruments have not been tested in all circumstances.

Some innovations also have the effect of raising the risk of on-balance-sheet positions. Thus Koehn and Santomero (1980) find that in the US banks business with prime borrowers has been lost to the commercial paper market. As it is only the best credit risks that have effective access to this market, banks are left with less creditworthy business on the balance sheet which raises the average risk of the balance sheet. A similar implication could arise with British building societies in the securitization process to the extent that it is higher-quality mortgages that are included in the mortgage pool to be securitized.

A controversial issue is the extent to which some instruments and techniques add to the volatility of spot prices. A recent example is the contention that the use of, for instance, programmed computer trading and insurance arbitrage techniques were factors in the precipitous decline in equity prices on the New York Stock Exchange in October 1987. Mayer and Kneeshaw (1988) also note that 'delta hedging' in options markets can exaggerate exchange rate and interest rate volatility.

One of the benefits cited earlier was that, if the pricing of risks through new instruments and markets is accurate, efficiency in the allocation of funds is raised. But this begs the question as to whether in practice they are accurately priced. In complex instruments and markets, and in the absence of experience, there can be no guarantee that this is always the case. Mayer and Kneeshaw (1988) argue that there is a tendency to under-price new instruments with the result that retained earnings may be insufficient protection against the risks incurred. Such under-pricing may be because (a) institutions adopt a long-run profit-maximizing strategy with less concern for the short-run implications of their business strategy, (b) they have little, if any, experience of the new instruments, (c) it is genuinely difficult to assess the risks and (d) the evaluation of risks can be made in terms of the current macroeconomic environment which may change and cause several different risks to emerge simultaneously. Related to the last possibility is the added difficulty of integrating and combining each of the separate risks implied in the range of new instruments into the total portfolio position rather than treating each set independently. Mayer and Kneeshaw also postulate a macro problem and use as an example option writing, which is comparable with insurance but with two major differences. First, the parameters involved (e.g. exchange rate movements) are more unstable than those found in most insurance contracts. Second, there is not the portfolio benefit of the law of large numbers; thus if the exchange rate moves substantially all buyers of an option will exercise their rights.

To the extent that instruments have an international dimension by, for instance, further integrating different national markets, it is likely that 'shocks' are similarly transmitted internationally.

Thus, while there are undoubtedly clear benefits from financial innovation, there are also associated problems deriving from the complexities involved. It may also be the case that an excessive volume of resources is devoted to finance and the creation of differentiated products. In general financial innovation is beneficial in three major respects: (a) it lowers the cost of finance or the transactions costs of doing what is already possible; (b) it allows users to do things that could not be done before and provides new sources of finance to some borrowers; and (c) it reduces or reallocates risks. In these ways there is a potential beneficial impact on the real economy. However, the use of some instruments and facilities may be a zero-sum game exclusively within the financial system with no benefit to the real economy, though such 'intra-system transactions' may be beneficial in that they raise the potential of financial institutions to perform their services more efficiently. Thus, interbank transactions may on the face of it appear to confer no benefit on the real economy and yet they undoubtedly do facilitate business with the real economy and, for instance, enable banks to economize on low-yielding liquid assets.

In the final analysis the issues raised are empirical. A certain scepticism is offered by Vinals and Berges (1988) who have investigated the use of instruments and conclude that: 'the available empirical evidence indicates that the potential effects have not been very important in practice'. They suggest two reasons for this. First, the evidence on investment functions suggests that new instruments that mainly reduce the cost (rather than the availability) of finance have only a limited impact on firms' investment. Second, instruments that do relax firms' external financial constraints are neither very significant in terms of market size nor extensively used.

Conclusion

Financial innovation has become a major feature of financial systems and finance in general. In the process it has contributed, in some countries more than others, to major structural change in national financial systems and to a general integration of such systems. The process of financial innovation contributes to four specific functions of a financial system: (a) it increases the variety of financial instruments for both borrowers and lenders by offering various combinations of standard characteristics; (b) it increases the liquidity of the system to the extent that tradeable assets and markets are created; (c) it enables particular risks to be priced and transferred; and (d) it may give borrowers access to particular markets from which they were hitherto excluded. These may be viewed as the basic 'functions' of financial innovation.

Financial innovation in general has had the effect of increasing the integration of markets, including between financial centres as many instruments straddle different types of markets and markets in different countries. As part of this the formal distinction between bank and capital market intermediation has tended to become less powerful. In this sense financial innovation has contributed to a more general structural change evident in some financial systems (most especially the United States, United Kingdom, Canada and Australia) implying a less structured, more integrated system with the specialist nature of different types of financial institutions becoming less pronounced. In fact some innovations have the effect of enabling traditional services to be provided by non-traditional suppliers. A particular example in the United States is the emergence of money-market mutual funds with transactions facilities. So just as some instruments have the effect of integrating and linking markets, so they may also have the effect of eroding specialist functions of financial institutions. Both are a reflection of the 'spectrum filling' role of innovation which is a natural product of a competitive financial system.

The objective of this review has been to demonstrate that financial innovation is not a random process but can be analysed systematically within a general analytical framework. A central theme has been that the ultimate criterion of judgement is the extent to which the instruments and facilities created in the process of financial innovation increase the efficiency of the financial system in the execution of its basic functions.

REFERENCES

Akhtar, M. (1983) 'Financial innovations and their implication for monetary policy: an international perspective', *BIS Economics Papers* no. 9.

Arrow, K. and Debreu, G. (1954) 'Existence of an equilibrium for a competitive economy', *Econometrica* 22: 256–90.

BIS (Bank for International Settlements) (1986) *Recent Innovations in International Banking*, Basel: BIS.

Boleat, M. (1987) 'Secondary mortgage markets', *Building Societies Association Journal*, July.

Coleby, A. (1987) 'The state of banking: a UK perspective', Mimeo, Bank of England.

Felgram, S. (1987) 'Interest rate swaps: risk and prices', *New England Economics Review*, Federal Reserve Bank of Boston, December.

Koehn, J. and Santomero, A. (1980) 'Regulation of bank capital and portfolio risk', *Journal of Finance*, December.

Lewis, M. (1988) 'Off-balance sheet business', in J.S.G. Wilson (ed.) *Bank Assets and Liability Management*, London: Euromoney Publications.

Llewellyn, D.T. (1988a) 'The policy issues: capital adequacy', in J.S.G. Wilson (ed.) *Bank Assets and Liability Management*, London: Euromoney Publications.

—— (1988b) 'Financial intermediation and systems: global integration', in D.E. Fair and C. de Boissieu (eds) *International Monetary and Financial Integration: European Dimension*, The Hague: Martinus Nijhoff.

Llewellyn, D.T. and Drake, L. (1987a) 'Structural change in the UK mortgage market: interest rate implications', Chemical Bank, London.

—— and —— (1987b) 'Secondary mortgage markets and the securitisation of mortgages', Loughborough University Banking Centre.

Mayer, H. and Kneeshaw, J. (1988) 'Financial market structure and regulatory change', in A. Heertje (ed.) *Innovation, Technology and Finance*, Oxford: Basil Blackwell.

Revell, J.R.S. (1983) 'Efficiency in the financial sector', in D. Shepherd and A. Silbertson (eds) *Macroeconomic Efficiency and Macroeconomic Performance*, London: Philip Allan.

Silber, W. (ed.) (1975) *Financial Innovation*, Lexington, MA: Lexington Books.

—— (1983) 'The process of financial innovation', *American Economic Review, Papers and Proceedings*, May.

Tobin, J. (1984) 'On the efficiency of the financial system', *Lloyds Bank Review*, July.

Vinals, J. and Berges, A. (1988) 'Financial innovation and capital formation', in A. Heertje (ed.) *Innovation, Technology and Finance*, Oxford: Basil Blackwell.

2 Financial innovation and international banking

Richard Harrington

Prehistorians used to argue whether innovations were 'diffused' from a single source or appeared spontaneously and independently in different places, but so complex a background has made this seem a waste of time and energy.

J.M. Roberts, *History of the World*

INTRODUCTION

It has, on occasions, been suggested that the recent spate of financial innovations owes much to the previous growth of international banking: that innovations are frequently tried out first in the less-controlled international markets and, if successful, are subsequently introduced into different national markets. Alternatively, when innovations occur in domestic markets, they are rapidly adopted in international banking and from there spread quickly to other domestic markets. On this view, the large international financial markets play a crucial role in the innovation process, both as a source of innovation and/or the means of their diffusion.

It is this view which is examined in this paper. In the next section we look at how economists have traditionally discussed innovation: the subject is not new and industrial innovation has long been a source of discussion and debate. Next we look more specifically at financial innovation and see how far attempts to analyse this are similar to the analysis contained in the older literature on industrial innovation. Having thus prepared the ground, we then consider four major financial innovations – (a) certificates of deposit, (b) financial futures, (c) floating rate notes and (d) currency and interest rate swaps – and examine to what extent we should attribute an important role to the international markets in the initiation and/or diffusion of these innovations. The final section provides a brief conclusion.

THE ANALYSIS OF INDUSTRIAL INNOVATION

Financial innovation is a relatively new topic, but innovation as such, usually associated with manufacturing industry, energy production or the extraction of raw materials, has long been a subject of discussion among economists and other writers. But economists, in modern times, have not really been at ease with this subject. Innovation does not fit easily with other established branches of economic theory, and in the case of the standard (neoclassical) theory of the firm, it is more conflicting than complementary. The latter theory, by now well entrenched in the textbooks, sees firms as being in a largely static world in which they are more reactive than innovative and in which reactions are largely confined to changes in output and prices. But whilst innovation may constitute a reaction to changes in the economic environment, it can also be seen as the firm seeking to change its environment. In practice, firms do not just respond to given demand schedules; they frequently try to create new demands for products they can supply. Nor do firms necessarily accept any given state of market competition; they may innovate precisely in order to upstage existing competitors and to earn a degree of market power for their own products.

Faced with this initial problem, economists have tended to describe and to categorize innovation (e.g. product innovation versus process innovation) and then to examine the relationships between market structure and innovative behaviour and between firm size and innovation behaviour. They have not spent too long in trying to answer the question why firms innovate. It has been accepted that firms' actions are motivated by the search for profit and hence the firms will introduce new products or processes whenever this is expected to increase profits. An elaboration of this approach is implicit in the attempt to dichotomize innovations into those proximately caused by 'science-push' and those proximately caused by 'demand-pull'; i.e. did opportunities to raise profit by innovation stem from changes in supply possibilities or from changes in the demands of customers and potential customers?

This is not the place to attempt a survey of the findings of industrial economists about the relationships between market structure and innovative ability and between firm size and innovative activity. These issues have been comprehensively surveyed elsewhere.[1] On the first issue, it is sufficient to say that there is no consensus: it can be argued that a highly competitive industrial structure is conducive to innovation, but it can also be argued that it is situations of monopoly or otherwise restricted competition that generate large profits and thus permit large expenditures on research and development. Faced with this ambiguity, some writers have argued that it is the intermediate situation of oligopoly – where there is interfirm rivalry but restricted price competition – that best provides both the incentive to innovate and the wherewithal to finance research and development. Empirical studies have failed to settle the issue and have themselves been beset with a number of problems. There are considerable difficulties in trying to define or measure innovation, with the result that many studies have instead looked at firms' expenditure on research and development (i.e. the input into the process rather than the output) or at the number of patents taken out (something known to be a poor guide to the number of commercially useful innovations). Also there is the familiar problem of trying to disentangle causation when evidence shows, at best, association. Thus, if one finds that industries dominated by large oligopolistic firms spend a lot on research and development, does this show, as some have argued, that oligopoly is conducive to innovation, or does it rather reflect the fact that, in certain industries, the technological possibilities are such as to bring both a rapid rate of innovation and a requirement for large firms to carry this out? Oligopoly, or indeed monopoly, may just as well be the consequence of innovation as the cause.

Studies that have looked for an association between firm size and innovative activity have, in general, also failed to produce clear-cut results. Beyond finding that there appears to be some minimum size level necessary for firms to undertake research and development, economists have been unable to show any close association between firm size and research and development expenditure or between firm size and the number of patents taken out.

Work continues on these issues and a number of recent developments offer the prospect of some greater understanding of the innovation process. Before turning to financial innovation itself, I would like to mention briefly two relevant recent papers. First, Pavitt *et al.* (1987), using information compiled on more than 4,000 significant commercial innovations made in the United Kingdom between 1945 and 1983, test for a relationship between innovation and firm size. They find that the distribution of innovative activity was U-shaped: an above-average rate of innovation was found among small firms (less than 1,000 employees) and among large firms (greater than 10,000 employees) whereas a below-average rate of innovation was found for intermediate firms. This evidence relates solely to the United Kingdom and, like all economic evidence, it has to be put in context and interpreted with care. Nevertheless, it is significant in that it does actually deal with innovations themselves and not with doubtful proxies such as research and development expenditure or the number of patents taken out.

Second, there is a recent paper by Metcalfe and Gibbons (1986) which is notable for what it says about the theoretical framework within which we usually analyse innovation. The authors reject (for this purpose) conventional static economic models populated by 'representative' firms and argue strongly for economic theory to catch up with industrial reality which they see as characterized by variety and change. Firms are different, processes of production and hence production costs and profits are different, and it is these differences which lead to an on-going process of change due both to more efficient technologies displacing less efficient ones and to the search for yet more efficient technologies. In general terms, this approach is not new, and the authors recognize antecedents in the work of Schumpeter and other writers, but given the importance of innovation, both general and financial, in the modern economy, it is necessary to improve the framework of analysis and Metcalfe and Gibbons's forceful reminder of this is timely.

THE ANALYSIS OF FINANCIAL INNOVATION

When we come to discussions of financial innovation, we immediately find a very different picture. There are some nods to the existing literature on industrial innovation (e.g. attempts to distinguish product and process innovation) but in general the subject is approached in a different way. First, there is concern to describe and to classify what exactly has been going on: innovations are listed and frequently distinguished from each other according to one criterion or another. This is understandable given that recent financial innovation has not only affected what financial 'products' are offered and the ways in which financial institutions 'produce' them – it has also been associated with important changes in the structure of the financial services industry in a number of countries.

Second, there is much concern with trying to explain why financial innovations occur. Writers have not just accepted that banks etc. are profit-maximizing enterprises and will innovate whenever it seems profitable to do so; they have sought more specific causes, such as the avoidance of official regulations. This also is understandable given the extent and speed of change in financial services in recent years: either one must assume that banks were not primarily motivated by profit earlier, or one must concede that other factors are involved nowadays as well as a competitive search for profit.

Third, there has been relatively little concern with the influence of industry structure on innovation. The issue has not been entirely absent from discussions of financial innovation; a number of writers have referred to increased competition as being one causal factor and, more occasionally, intercountry comparisons have been made, but the subject has not been central to the discussion, as it has been with industrial economists. Rather, concern has been with effects going the other way: how does innovation influence industry structure?

A number of factors have been cited as causing financial innovation. The most important appear to be the following:

1. avoidance of constraints, notably official regulations;
2. reduction of costs;
3. increased competition;
4. new technology;
5. the internationalization of finance;
6. changes in the market environment (e.g. volatile inflation rates, interest rates and exchange rates);
7. legislative action.

A number of other more or less specific causes can be found in the literature, but these can usually be subsumed under one of the above.[2]

Different writers put stress on one or more of the above causes and each can be shown to have been an important factor in inducing innovation at some time or in some place. But it is a mistake to see them as separate or independent: for the most part, they are closely interrelated. We are dealing with a complex pattern of events which in combination have led to the recent wave of financial innovation. This will be readily apparent if we consider first the impact of new technology.

The development of microelectronic technology has had profound implications for banks and other institutions. It is a development which took place largely outside the financial sector but which was found to be of widespread application within it. It provides a good example of innovation due to 'science-push'.

Technology has transformed all aspects of banking. Consider first retail banking. The main costs involved in retail banking derive from three sources: (a) the need to store large amounts of information; (b) the need to access this information regularly and quickly and to update it continually; and (c) the need to carry out large numbers of transactions on a regular basis. It was found that all these functions could be mechanized to some extent once the first generation of large mainframe computers had appeared. At first, the computers were in the back office, keeping records and assisting with the processing of transactions, but as technology improved they were installed in the front office and many more transactions became automated. Office banking and home banking (i.e. the facility to initiate a range of automated transactions from your own office or home) are now offered by many banks. Further developments are expected[3] and many writers now question whether the extensive branch networks of retail banks will be required much longer (see for instance Llewellyn 1985).

Wholesale banking is also crucially dependent on modern technology. The wide range of short-term markets are over-the-telephone markets which only exist because of the availability of (a) efficient telecommunications, (b) computerized information systems which provide up to the minute information on rates of interest, exchange rates etc., (c) computer programs which permit rapid calculation of the value of many different transactions or series of transactions and (d) other hardware and software packages which allow banks to monitor continually their changing asset–liability position. In the absence of such modern technological aids, there would be fewer wholesale markets, transactions costs would be higher and the number of transactions would be much smaller.

All this applies, *a fortiori*, to the international markets, which comprise a network of over-the-telephone markets worldwide. These markets are very much a product of modern technology. They exist, in effect, because technology has shrunk the world and made distance no longer a barrier. Improvements in civil aviation and in telecommunications and the appearance of satellite linkages between computers are each important factors.

These technological developments have dramatically reduced costs and in consequence have made new things economically possible. They have made it possible for banks to undertake transactions at a distance and across national frontiers and to undertake many more types of transaction. Thus much banking business and, more generally, financial business is now easily variable both in form and in geographical location. It is from this simple fact that much else follows.

The reduction in costs and the internationalization of finance have inevitably increased competition within the industry. A number of non-financial firms have found it attractive to enter the industry; many existing financial firms have chosen to increase the number of services they offer with the result that certain traditional demarcations between types of intermediary have ceased to be important; and foreign banks and security dealers have become active competitors in many domestic markets. There has been a great interpenetration of markets which has increased competition, especially for wholesale business: margins have been reduced and innovation has frequently been used as a competitive weapon, especially by newcomers seeking to become established.

The new possibilities open to banks have meant that certain types of official regulation can now more easily be circumvented. This has led to changes in regulations in many countries and this, in turn, has been a permissive factor with regard to yet further innovations. The role of financial innovation as a means of avoiding burdensome regulation has been stressed by a number of writers. Silber (1975, 1983) and Ben-Horim and Silber (1977) see this as the prime cause of financial innovation, and this view is supported by de Boissieu (1986a, b). A good case can be made for it, but it needs to be put in the proper context.

Most of the regulations on banks have not been circumvented, nor are they, for the most part, likely to be so. This is the case with the now not inconsiderable amount of prudential regulation applied to banks. The regulations that were subject to widespread avoidance were those that were applied not because of their relevance to banking but where the banks were just a vehicle for macroeconomic policy or for other government objectives. Such regulations, i.e. interest rate ceilings, credit controls, inevitably appeared arbitrary to banks, and both they *and their clients* frequently had an incentive to avoid them where possible. Technology made this possible and monetary policy has had to be adapted to avoid reliance on arbitrary restrictions.

It is interesting to ask how similar financial innovation is to innovation elsewhere. Clearly, financial firms are motivated by profit as are non-financial firms. Technology has been crucial to many financial innovations just as it has been to many innovations in other industries. Competition appears to have been a spur to innovation, but also innovation in financial services has frequently served to promote competition by whittling away the barriers which previously served to isolate markets and to permit local institutions some degree of market power. Among the differences between finance and other industries, it should be recorded that banks were traditionally subject to more controls of an apparently arbitrary nature (as far as the banks themselves were concerned) and that this was the proximate cause of a number of innovations. Second, whilst all goods and services exhibit a range of characteristics and there is scope for varying these, in finance the scope for varying the characteristics of assets and liabilities is nowadays exceptionally great: the form of financial transactions is easily variable. Thus, for example, if interest-bearing overnight deposits are not allowed, the substance of these can be achieved under the form of repurchase agreements.

Finally, what is the role in this of the international market? It is clear from what has been said that the internationalization of finance has had a wide-ranging impact on banking and has been a factor in a number of innovations. But whether the international markets themselves have played a key role as a source of innovations or as a means of diffusion is not so clear. To throw light on this, it is necessary to look in more detail at some specific innovations.

CASE STUDIES: FOUR SPECIFIC FINANCIAL INNOVATIONS

The four innovations chosen for consideration are (a) certificates of deposit, (b) financial futures, (c) floating rate notes and (d) currency and interest rate swaps. They were chosen for a number of reasons. All were important innovations; all created new financial instruments; all have proved durable or seem likely to be so; and, finally, they are widely dispersed in time. Certificates of deposit were introduced in 1961, whereas currency and interest rate swaps became of importance some twenty years later.

Certificates of deposit

Certificates of deposit (CDs) are short-term negotiable instruments issued by banks with terms to maturity, mostly, of up to one year. They were first issued in 1961 by banks in New York City. Whilst this was not the first time that banks had issued short-term instruments that were formally negotiable,[4] it was the first occasion, in modern times, that banks had issued short-term paper which was negotiable in practice as well as in theory and for which an organized secondary market existed. CDs are a funding instrument, from the standpoint of banks, and so their innovation must have been due to a concern to raise more funds or to raise funds more efficiently.

This was in fact the case. During the 1950s, commercial banks in America had been losing market share to institutions such as savings banks, savings and loan associations and finance houses. Among the New York banks, deposit growth was even lower than that of commercial banks elsewhere in the country, whilst they still faced high loan demands from the many corporate clients with head offices in New York. Owing to both federal and state banking legislation, New York City banks could not open deposit-taking branches beyond the confines of that city;[5] and whilst they could expect that, as well as collecting retail deposits, they would take deposits from their large corporate clients, the latter were showing a liking for treasury bills as high-yielding but highly liquid assets. It should be recalled that, at that time, all US banks were prohibited from paying interest on time deposits of less than thirty days.

The CD was an imaginative response to the constraints on the New York banks. It was a means of competing with US treasury bills in that it too was a liquid negotiable instrument and one which would yield a market rate of interest. It was thus a means of attracting large deposits from the corporate sector within New York City; but, in addition, because CDs were negotiable, they could be sold among investors and there would be no way of limiting holders to any geographical area. CDs, in effect, were a means of getting round restrictions on deposit-taking: they could be sold, via dealers, throughout the country, and by this means New York banks could compete for wholesale money across the entire United States.

Clearly CDs were a specific American innovation designed to deal with circumstances facing one particular sector of the American banking industry. Their appearance owed little to new technology – computer usage was then in its infancy – and a lot to avoiding official controls. The international market was not involved in the innovation, but it was to be involved in its diffusion.

CDs were introduced in New York in 1961 and quickly proved popular. In 1966, dollar CDs were introduced in London; the market grew steadily and the number of banks issuing and dealing in CDs also grew. Many non-American banks obtained first-hand experience of this instrument.

Sterling CDs were first issued in London in 1968 and in the following year CDs were introduced in Australia. Banks in a number of other countries started issuing CDs at times during the 1970s, but it was more recently, in the early 1980s, that there was a sudden growth in the issue of non-dollar CDs. They were introduced in Sweden in 1980, in Italy in 1982, in France in 1985 and in Federal Germany in 1986.

Today, CDs are well established in most developed countries. They provide a good example of an innovation which proved successful in circumstances very different from those which brought it about. Initially, CDs were a means whereby New York banks could circumvent certain specific American restrictions; in the long run, it was the combination that they provided of term money to banks and a liquid asset to investors which ensured that they had a role in so many different financial systems. They were not a product of the international market, but they spread to it five years after being introduced in the United States and it is plausible to attribute to the international market an important role in helping to diffuse this innovation.

Financial futures

Forward currency transactions between banks and their clients and between banks themselves have been common for a long time, but the organization of a market in foreign currency futures (i.e. standardized tradeable forward contracts) dates from 1972. Such contracts were first listed in that year on the Chicago Mercantile Exchange. Three years later, in October 1975, the first interest rate futures contract was introduced on the Chicago Board of Trade. Subsequently, other contracts were introduced, not all of them successful. In 1982, a contract on an equity share index was introduced. Also in 1982 the London International Financial Futures Exchange began trading with a number of interest rate and currency contracts. By 1990, financial futures were being traded at exchanges in Australia, Canada, France, Germany, Hong Kong, Japan, the Netherlands, New Zealand, Singapore, Switzerland, the United Kingdom and the United States.

In terms of volume, the US markets remain dominant. During 1989 the Chicago Board of Trade alone handled over 140 million contracts. In comparison, the London market handled approximately 16 million contracts. The most active contracts are those for government bonds, especially US government bonds, three-month Eurodollars and a number of currencies quoted against the US dollar.

Financial futures have quickly become established as an important part of modern finance and must be seen as a highly successful innovation. The risks are risks of changes in the price of assets such as bills, bonds, term deposits and foreign currencies and of synthetic assets such as a stock exchange index. The success of financial futures is usually attributed to the increase in volatility of the prices of many of these assets since the early 1970s, which has increased the desirability of hedging. It is certainly true that, in an era of floating exchange rates and high inflation, both interest rates and exchange rates have shown much instability.

But this is only part of the story. Most of the risks that can be hedged by means of financial futures can also be hedged by other means, and this has long been the case. Consider a German exporter due to receive US dollars in six months from now and who is worried that the dollar may fall in value. He can use a futures contract, with very little initial outlay, to sell the dollars six months forward. He now knows what he will receive in Deutschmarks in six months' time and he is no longer at risk due to changes in the exchange rate. But the same situation could be achieved perfectly well by other means. The exporter can borrow dollars now, switch these into Deutschmarks in the spot market and invest the proceeds short term in Frankfurt. In six months' time the dollar receipts can be used to pay off the dollar loan and the exporter's Deutschmark position is established in advance. Again there is no exchange rate risk. In the same manner, a German importer due to pay dollars in six months' time can borrow Deutschmarks now, sell these spot for dollars and invest the dollars short term in New York. A synthetic forward transaction is thus created.

The position is similar with regard to hedging interest rate risks. Consider the case of bonds. By buying in the cash market with borrowed money, an investor can achieve a position very similar to that obtained from the purchase of a bond future. By selling short in the cash market and lending the money, an investor can achieve a position very similar to that obtained from the sale of a bond future. It is necessary to add that such synthetic forward contracts can mostly only be arranged over short-term horizons. But, to date, the heaviest turnover in futures markets has been on the near-maturity contracts. Financial futures are being used mainly to secure financial positions which could have been achieved by other means.

So why are they so successful? The answer is that new technology has made possible new ways of achieving old objectives at much lower cost. With the establishment of a central market where all transactions become transactions with the exchange itself, the costs of creating positions and unwinding them have been greatly reduced. Financial futures may be seen as a means of creating liquidity at low cost.[6]

This is another example of an innovation that occurred in the United States. Financial futures were started in Chicago by exchanges that had previous experience of commodity futures. By the late 1970s, usage of the new markets had become international and it was the growing interest of bankers and security dealers worldwide which stimulated the growth of new financial futures markets inside and outside America. This shows again how, with the present internationalization of finance, new initiatives, wherever they start, are likely to be quickly copied.

Floating rate notes

The first floating rate notes (FRNs) were issued in 1970. They were essentially a response to rising interest rates and the growing reluctance of investors to accept the risks of fixed rate bonds. FRNs shift the interest rate risk to the borrower and in this they are the capital market equivalent of variable rate lending by banks. Growth of issues was only modest until after 1974, when banks began to issue large quantities of FRNs. This appears to have been a response to the turbulence in financial markets for a period of several months during that year, following the failure of the Herstatt bank in Germany. At that time, a number of banks experienced difficulty in obtaining wholesale funds and many were only able to do so by paying relatively high rates of interest. FRNs were seen as a means of securing long-term funding without upsetting the interest-matching of assets and liabilities. Also, for some banks, FRNs could be made acceptable to bank supervisors as capital.

Banks have also been important investors in FRNs, and so the market has served as an alternative means of interbank lending. Issues by banks and non-banks grew rapidly in the early 1980s until, in 1985, total issues were nearly US$56 billion. However, in later 1986, there was an abrupt decline. Owing to the growth of alternative sources of funds available to borrowers in the form of both short-term paper and interest rate swaps, margins on FRNs had narrowed. Such margins, traditionally expressed as a percentage over LIBOR, had by 1986 become percentages under LIBOR;

and in the case of two sovereign borrowers, issues had been made with yields below LIBID. Starting with perpetual FRNs and spreading to the market as a whole, there was a reaction with heavy selling of outstanding paper. Dealing became difficult and FRNs became relatively illiquid assets. In 1987, new issues dropped to just over US$12 billion but there was a partial recovery the following year with gross issues in excess of US$22 billion.[7]

The growth in issues of FRNs can be seen as an example of an innovation in response to changed economic circumstances. Their initial development owed much to higher and volatile rates of interest. Their rapid growth after 1974 was due to a change in bank demands for medium- and long-term finance. FRNs are clearly a product of the international market and their success led to the issue of similar instruments in a number of national financial markets.[8]

Currency and interest rate swaps

Currency and interest rate swaps were developed in the 1980s out of an earlier practice of parallel or back-to-back loans used to circumvent exchange-control regulations. The latter were used, for example, by British firms having resources in sterling but prevented by exchange controls from switching these resources into foreign currency at normal exchange rates. If they could find a foreign firm having resources in the appropriate foreign currency and desirous of obtaining sterling, then a parallel loan could be arranged.

Such parallel loans were tailormade for each individual case and were costly to arrange. In the early 1980s, the idea was generalized to encompass a number of exchanges of commitments between companies: exchanges usually of streams of interest payments but also, on occasions, of the principal of loans as well. In this way, banks and non-financial companies could arbitrage different credit ratings in different markets. For example, a firm requiring dollar finance but whose credit rating was best in Switzerland could borrow Swiss francs, change these for dollars in the foreign-exchange market and then swap its future repayment obligations in Swiss francs for a comparable series of dollar payments. It was found that by such means, with each party to the transaction borrowing where it had comparative advantage, borrowing costs could be reduced. Swaps were not just between streams of payment in different currencies; different credit ratings could be arbitraged in different national markets or between different segments of the international market both using the same currency. Swaps between fixed interest payments and a stream of floating interest payments have become common.

Initially, swaps were individually negotiated with a bank dealing with both counterparties and drawing a fee. The need to match two counterparties made negotiations long and expensive. But banks soon realized that it was possible to hedge swap commitments by a suitable set of forward and futures transactions. From then on, a number of large banks began what was described as warehousing swaps which meant, in practice, standing ready to arrange swaps directly between themselves and a single counterparty, hedging their own risks and then, perhaps later on, carrying out an offsetting swap with another counterparty and unwinding their interim hedging arrangements. In 1985, the International Swap Dealers Association and the British Bankers' Association produced a set of standardized dealing terms and documentation for interest rate swaps. Nowadays, swap quotations are continually available and deals are arranged in a short time. Some extensions to the standard product, such as forward swaps or options on swaps, are also offered by a number of banks.

The market continues to grow rapidly. Outstanding interest rate swaps at the end of 1986 were estimated to be approximately US$350 billion and outstanding currency swaps at the same date were estimated at between US$80 billion and US$100 billion (see Bank of England 1987a). But such is the growth of the market that estimates from the International Swap Dealers Association put the value of principal involved in new swaps arranged in 1988 at no less than US$1,000 billion for interest rate swaps and US$317 billion for currency swaps.

The innovation of swaps is very much a product of the international markets. Its origins may lie in the avoidance of particular official regulations but the role and purpose of swaps soon went beyond that. In some cases, swaps are only a more efficient way of doing what can be done by a set of transactions in currency futures. So here, as in the case of financial futures, we should see the present-day active market in swaps as a product of modern technology which allows rates to be calculated immediately and offsetting hedging transactions to be carried out promptly. Swaps are also an example of how the growth of one financial market stimulates others. It was the growth of large liquid markets in bond futures and in currency futures which facilitated this quick hedging of swap transactions.

CONCLUSION

In the preceding section, we have considered only four of the many financial innovations of recent years. Each can be classed as a major innovation of considerable importance but, of course, there have been other new products or new techniques, also very important, that for reasons of space have been neglected. Of the four innovations discussed, two originated in the United States and two in the international markets. Extending the list of innovations considered would not alter this picture greatly: most innovations in recent years have stemmed from one or other of these two sources. Of the two, the United States has probably been the most important.

A number of writers have discussed financial innovation in the United States (see for instance Silber 1975, 1983; Wenninger 1984). If minor changes to financial instruments are included as well as wholly new instruments or new markets, the list of innovations is long. For example, John Wenninger (1984) lists no fewer than sixty-two innovations, most of which originated in America. There would seem to be a number of reasons why the American financial system should be so innovative. First, it is the largest and most developed national financial system. Second, banks in the United States have traditionally been subject to a number of constraints, many of which did not apply elsewhere. We saw, in the analysis of industrial innovation, how modern technology had enabled financial instruments to be easily variable as to both form and location. It was probably inevitable that the new technology in the United States should be used to devise ways of getting round controls such as Regulation Q and the restrictions on interstate banking. Indeed much of the early growth of the international markets can be explained in terms of US banks doing abroad that business which was restricted at home.[9]

Finally, we should perhaps mention the cultural factor. It is well known that, whilst some regulations can stimulate financial innovation, too much kills it. There were a number of specific controls on US banks but there was no overall centralized control by the public authorities such that innovations without official consent would have been unthinkable. US banks operate in an environment where the exploitation of gaps in regulations is not only permissible but is also socially acceptable. This is less true in many European countries.[10]

Given that the dollar has long been the most important currency in international banking, and given that American banks and security houses play a large role in international finance, it is inevitable that innovations in the United States are frequently carried over into the international market. But, of course, there are other influences as well. For instance, the first Eurobond was issued by a British merchant bank but one (Warburgs) which had intimate knowledge of the system of issuing and dealing in bonds traditional among German universal banks. The growth of Eurobond dealing was a step towards universal banking on the German and Swiss model. Also, one can note that, whilst roll-over loans were originated in the international market, the practice of bank lending at variable rates of interest was already common in a number of European countries as well as in Australia and New Zealand.

The international markets themselves have been the source of many financial innovations. Born out of the new technology, potentially mobile as to location and free from the constraints of national monetary policies, these markets have usually been quick to overcome obstacles to their efficient functioning. This is hardly surprising. The international markets, by definition, bring together banks and other financial institutions from many different traditions and backgrounds. With their enhanced technological capacity and the confrontation of many different ideas, the international markets have become something of a melting pot. Sometimes these markets originate new solutions to problems, but invariably they also serve to diffuse new ideas from all quarters. International banking has meant that first banks interpenetrated each other's markets and then there began a progressive tendency towards a world financial market with national markets steadily losing their traditional protective barriers. In these circumstances it is inevitable that new ideas spread quickly and that similar innovations are found in countries that, not so long ago, appeared to have quite different financial systems.

In this situation, one may look for causes of financial innovations, but one will often find only a complex picture in which different factors and different influences have all played a part. Like other writers, I have tried to attribute causes for the innovations discussed above, but these are only proximate causes and one can trace many other influences and contributory factors. The international markets themselves, the most important modern innovation of all, have become a new source of innovation but also the means of rapidly diffusing new ideas and new techniques wherever they originate. In the end, what we are dealing with is a dramatic 'science-push': technology has shrunk the world and made many things possible which were not possible before. It is the microelectronic revolution which, for good or ill, has totally changed all aspects of finance. It has brought about an era of rapid evolution and growing complexity, and at such a time attempts to look for precise individual causes of change are likely to prove vain.

NOTES

1 See for instance the relevant chapters in Devine *et al.* (1985), George and Joll (1983) and Sawyer (1985).

2 For instance Wojnilower (1980) argues strongly the importance of credit crunches in the United States, but these can be seen as one form of official constraint, albeit one applying only intermittently.

3 Electronic funds transfer at point of sale (EFTPOS) has long been predicted and continues to be the subject of experiments in many countries.

4 Banks in a number of European countries had earlier issued financial assets which were formally negotiable. For instance, Luxembourg banks had issued bearer certificates denominated in Luxembourg francs since the early 1950s.
5 The right of New York banks to open branches anywhere in the State was only granted by the 1971 Statewide Branching Law and did not become fully effective until January 1976.
6 This view is argued strongly by Cooper (1986).
7 For further details of events in the FRN market in 1986 and early 1987, see BIS (Bank for International Settlements) (1987) and Bank of England (1987b).
8 Some examples of national financial developments which follow the example of FRNs are given in Chapter 3 of Harrington (1987).
9 This thesis is argued by Johnston (1983) among others.
10 The importance of cultural factors is stressed by de Boissieu (1986b).

REFERENCES

Bank of England (1987a) 'Recent developments in the swap market', *Bank of England Quarterly Bulletin* 27 (1) (February).

—— (1987b) 'Developments in international banking and capital markets in 1986', *Bank of England Quarterly Bulletin* 27 (2) (May).

Ben-Horim, M. and Silber, W. (1977) 'Financial innovation: a linear programming approach', *Journal of Banking and Finance* no. 1.

BIS (Bank of International Settlements) (1987) *Fifty-seventh Annual Report 1986/87*, Basle: BIS.

de Boissieu, C. (1986a) 'Les innovations financières en France', *Revue d'Economie Politique* no. 5.

—— (1986b) 'Quelque réflexions sur l'analyse économique des innovations financières', *Economie Appliquée* no. 3.

Cooper, I. (1986) 'Innovations: new market instruments', *Oxford Review of Economic Policy* 2 (4) (Winter).

Devine, P.J., Jones, R.M., Lee, N. and Tyson, W.J. (1985) *An Introduction to Industrial Economics*, 4th edn, London: Allen & Unwin.

George, K.D. and Joll, C. (1983) *Industrial Organisation: Competition, Growth and Structural Change*, 3rd edn, London: Allen & Unwin.

Harrington, R.L. (1987) *Asset and Liability Management by Banks*, Paris: OECD.

Johnston, R.B. (1983) *The Economics of the Euro-Market*, London: Macmillan.

Llewellyn, D.T. (1985) *The Evolution of the British Financial System*, London: Institute of Bankers.

Metcalfe, J.S. and Gibbons, M. (1986) 'Technological variety and the process of competition', *Economie Appliquée* no. 3.

Pavitt, K., Robson, M. and Townsend, J. (1987) 'The size distribution of innovating firms in the UK: 1945–1983', *Journal of Industrial Economics* 35 (3) (March).

Sawyer, M.C. (1985) *The Economics of Industries and Firms*, 2nd edn, London: Croom Helm.

Silber, W. (1975) 'Towards a theory of financial innovation', in W. Silber (ed.) *Financial Innovation*, Lexington, MA: D.C. Heath.

—— (1983) 'The process of financial innovation', *American Economic Review*, May.

Wenninger, J. (1984) 'Financial innovation in the United States', in *Financial Innovation and Monetary Policy*, Basle: BIS.
Wojnilower, A. (1980) 'The central role of credit crunches in recent financial history', *Brookings Papers on Economic Activity* no. 1.

3 Financial liberalization and monetary policy: an overview

Jean-Claude Chouraqui

Over the past ten years there have been profound changes in the operation of the financial markets of many of the industrialized countries. Essentially these changes have taken three forms: the development of financial innovations through the introduction of new techniques and new financial products; 'institutional despecialization' characterized by the disappearance of the traditional demarcations between the various categories of financial institutions; the increasing internationalization of financial transactions, together with considerable expansion of capital flows. All these changes have had important consequences for the activities of financial intermediaries and for the conduct of monetary policy. A positive feature of financial innovation is that it helps to increase competition within the financial sector and offers customers a broader range of financial services. However, it brings with it some disadvantages, notably the difficulty of monitoring monetary aggregates and the risks of financial instability. To cope with problems of this sort, the monetary authorities have usually reacted by introducing greater pragmatism in the implementation of policies and by strengthening the surveillance of banking activities.

In this chapter we review the main characteristics of the structural changes currently affecting financial markets. We then analyse the advantages and disadvantages of these changes as well as their implications for monetary policy and bank supervision.

THE CHANGES IN FINANCIAL MARKETS

The new financial instruments

A whole range of new products and new risk-hedging techniques have recently been introduced in financial markets. The emergence of these innovations has been helped by several factors, in particular the following:

— the easing or abolition of regulations governing financial transactions (such as ceilings on interest rates);
— the desire of economic agents to minimize transactions costs due to taxation and regulations;
— the desire of financial operators to protect themselves against the risk of unexpected fluctuations in interest rates and exchange rates;
— technological progress which, by facilitating the transfer of funds, has enabled financial institutions to broaden the range of services they can offer to their customers.

Within the limited framework of this chapter, it is not of course possible to draw up a complete list of the numerous financial innovations that have been introduced into national and international financial markets.[1] However, among the most common innovations mention should be made of issues of certificates of deposit, commercial paper and other short- and medium-term bonds negotiable on the money market,[2] issues of long-term debentures with various encashment clauses and underwriting provisions,[3] the development of futures markets,[4] the increasing use of floating rate contracts,[5] interest rate and currency swaps and other risk-hedging devices such as options and future rate agreements[6] etc.

These new instruments have contributed to the rapid growth of securities markets – a development known as 'securitization'. For many borrowers, the issuance of negotiable securities has substituted for bank credit. Prime issuers who have a good credit rating are therefore able to obtain capital at rates lower than those charged on the interbank market. Second-class borrowers also resort to securities markets, but in these cases a guarantee or line of bank credit often proves useful or even indispensable. The granting of back-up facilities – a form of off-balance-sheet transaction – allows the banks to charge a commission for the information they gather for the purpose of establishing the credit rating or creditworthiness of customers.

Thanks to financial innovations, banks have also played a direct part in the expansion of securities markets, by issuing debt instruments such as savings bonds, medium- and long-term bonds and negotiable certificates of deposit. In some cases this was brought about by the easing of existing regulations. Thus, in several countries, the volume of certificates of deposit has increased because the interest paid thereon has been deregulated and the restrictions applied to certificate of deposit issues and trading have been eased. In other cases the banks have resorted to issuing negotiable debt instruments – notably bonds – as a means of adding to their capital, in order either to broaden their lending capacity or to strengthen their financial base.

Changes in the mechanisms of financial intermediation

The emergence of new financial instruments, combined with the rapid growth in issues of securities and other negotiable paper, has been accompanied by changes in the nature of the activities of the various categories of financial institutions. In a number of countries the relative importance of deposit-taking establishments (mainly banks) has diminished in favour of institutional investors (such as pension funds, life assurance companies and mutual funds) who hold a substantial proportion of their assets in the form of securities. This means that institutional investors now share financial risks (at least in part) and play a role in activities which were formerly the province of banks.

Banking activity has also been affected by the rapid increase in issues of commercial paper which strengthen direct financing between non-financial economic agents. As stated above, this new form of financing has enabled firms to have less recourse to short-term bank lending, thus contributing to the decline in banks' gross turnover and the reduction in their interest margins. Banks are not totally excluded from these new financial channels, however, since they are intermediaries in the issuance of commercial paper (domiciliation of the back-up credit line, investment function etc.); moreover, the commissions that the banks levy for carrying out these tasks (see above) allow them to diversify the sources of their earnings. This tendency reflects the present practice of systematic charging for banking services.

The development and utilization of sophisticated products such as options, swaps and other risk-hedging devices is one of the main activities that banks are at present undertaking in order to satisfy their customers' needs. By doing this, the banks are better placed to handle the risks inherent in financial transactions, by reducing disparities across interest rates, exchange rates and maturity dates. However, as with the guarantees or back-up facilities extended by banks in the context of issues of negotiable paper, this shift in banking activity has resulted in a considerable increase in off-balance-sheet transactions. Bank risks have consequently become less transparent, a fact that is viewed with concern by the monetary authorities, as will be seen later.

Alongside these changes in the nature of banking activities, there has been a very marked convergence of the functions of deposit-taking institutions, on the one hand, and institutional investors, on the other. In some countries (United States, Japan and France), this convergence was facilitated by the abolition or easing of restrictions that prevented various institutions from carrying out certain activities. Increased competition resulted from this, in the sphere of both deposit-taking and security transactions (including security issues and trading and asset management).

The convergence of the activities of banks and of institutional investors has been more rapid on the international market than on national markets. These two types of institution now play a major role in foreign currency transactions.

The internationalization of financial transactions

The third type of structural change that has affected financial markets is their internationalization. This movement, which had already begun in the 1960s with the development of the Euromarket, gained momentum subsequently because of the marked growth in international capital flows in the context of floating exchange rates. Initially, the same factors were responsible as those that contributed to the emergence of financial innovations in domestic markets, namely[7] the policy of deregulation (several countries have dismantled exchange controls and encouraged the opening up of their markets to foreign banks), the impact of taxation (the tax levied on interest paid to non-residents until recently in some countries – notably the United States – played a part in the growth of the Eurobond market) and technological progress (speedier processing of transactions in different markets). Other factors also played a role, however, in particular the following:

- the growth of issues of new instruments, such as commercial paper, floating rate bonds and zero-coupon bonds,[8] denominated in currencies other than the US dollar;
- the internationalization of stock markets (a growing number of company shares are now quoted and traded on financial markets);
- recourse to the new risk-hedging transactions (swaps, options etc.) mentioned above;
- the tendency towards diversification of financial asset portfolios due to the growing importance of key currencies (yen, Deutschmark) or a basket of currencies (the European ECU) in international transactions.

Broadly speaking, it is mainly the banking systems of the major industrialized countries that have been affected by this phenomenon of internationalization. In fact, the international exposure of banks has increased appreciably in recent years; this is reflected in the changing structure of their balance sheets, with a higher proportion of foreign assets and liabilities, a growth of assets denominated in foreign currency and increased country risks with respect to capital. In addition, there has been a spectacular advance in international interbank financing, which has had a significant influence on the movement of exchange rates.

THE ADVANTAGES AND DISADVANTAGES OF THE PROCESS OF FINANCIAL INNOVATION

Pecuniary and non-pecuniary advantages

Some financial innovations have brought about changes in the pecuniary and non-pecuniary advantages afforded by monetary assets. On the pecuniary front, in many countries it is now possible to earn interest on transactions balances, formerly not authorized, and to be paid rates in line with market rates, formerly subject to a ceiling. Hence, households and firms have seen higher returns on assets deposited with banks or other financial institutions. This has been the case in particular in the United States[9] following the proliferation of interest-bearing demand accounts.

Another pecuniary advantage is the reduced transactions costs of holding, negotiating or transferring financial assets. In the case of deposits, this is largely due to the fact that (especially in the United States, Canada, the United Kingdom and Japan) the range of instruments that can be used as transactions balances has widened and various instruments not used as transactions balances have become more liquid. In some countries (the United States in particular), there has also been a reduction in transactions costs on securities markets. The reason for this is the freedom allowed to financial institutions to set the amount of their commission according to the type of transaction. This has been mainly beneficial to major operators, who have been able to negotiate reduced commission charges; charges on small-scale transactions, however, have tended to increase.

Financial innovations have also induced non-pecuniary advantages which relate, on the one hand, to the greater ease with which economic agents can now hedge against interest rate and exchange rate risks and, on the other, to the diversification of financing services due to disintermediation. More generally, stronger competition among financial institutions has provided households and firms with a wider range of services better adapted to their needs.

The problems of monetary control and the risks of financial instability

The rapid and often uncontrolled development of financial innovations has considerably complicated the task of the monetary authorities, especially in countries that set quantitative targets on the growth of money supply. Indeed, the broader range of financial assets available and their increased substitutability have made monetary aggregates more difficult to interpret. In the past the demand for money on the part of economic agents was fairly stable. This was especially true in countries such as the United States, Canada and the United Kingdom, where there was a close medium-term relationship between national income and the relevant monetary aggregate. This relationship has been seriously disrupted as a result of financial innovations.[10] Moreover, with the introduction of floating rate devices and forward contracts on financial instruments the way in which monetary policy influences real variables, particularly investment, is no longer very clear.[11] As discussed below, although these disturbances could prove to be temporary, the monetary authorities have usually concluded that it was not appropriate in the present climate to set precise targets for specific aggregates and that a more subjective approach was necessary.

A second problem raised by financial innovations is their potential impact on the stability of the financial system. This type of concern has become considerably more acute since the 1987 stock market crash. Several sources of instability can be identified (see Akhtar 1986).

1 With the surge in off-balance-sheet transactions, the situation of financial institutions is no longer transparent. Given that it is difficult to monitor movements in assets and liabilities, it is becoming harder to assess the financial positions of establishments involved in this sort of activity. Risks become 'watered down' along a long line of opaque transactions.
2 Increased competition has prompted financial institutions to use new products to seek highly profitable, but at the same time highly risky, positions. The quality of the claims held by some of these establishments may well prove to be dubious when borrowers are no longer in a position to make their repayments. Sectoral difficulties, such as those in agriculture and the oil industry in the United States, can make this type of situation even more serious. As a result, commercial banks, many of which are already experiencing severe problems because of the inability of developing countries to service their foreign debt, are finding themselves in an increasingly sensitive situation.
3 Some of the new financing techniques involve high risks, making trading delicate, especially for institutional investors. An example is junk bonds – high-yield bonds issued by institutions whose credit rating is low – which have been very fashionable on the US market in recent years.
4 The interdependence and internationalization of financial activities have encouraged speculative 'raiding' by powerful financial operators with a view to gaining control of industrial and commercial groups. This creates a risk of stock market booms totally out of line with

> underlying economic forces, to the point where reference is sometimes made to the 'casino economy'. These risks have become more acute as interest rates have become more volatile post-deregulation.

Certain analysts also view the process of financial innovation as a growing source of both internal and external indebtedness. In some countries (notably the United States), the result has been a continuous rise in the ratio of (private and public) debt to gross domestic product since the beginning of the 1980s. This tendency is probably more serious than statistics suggest because they do not take account of direct lending between non-financial economic sectors, which – as emphasized above – tends to increase rapidly. Such a situation is especially worrying since a large proportion of the debt is held short term (encouraging the growth of new financial instruments) and is not used to finance productive activities.

The emphasis on short-term returns is often seen as a reflection of the present behaviour of financial markets which tends to assign increasing importance to immediate returns over long-term profits.[12] The reasoning here is that most financial operators seem nowadays to judge firms and financial institutions on their short-term performance, which they then systematically extrapolate. This very short-term view of financial markets may have an adverse influence on the investment behaviour of firms to the extent that firms may be increasingly concerned with achieving a quick return. If this were the case, the allocation of resources would be at variance with considerations of long-term growth. Although this viewpoint is widely held at present, it is not really corroborated by the few empirical studies that have recently been carried out on the subject.[13]

THE CONSEQUENCES FOR MONETARY POLICY

More flexible control of monetary aggregates

To cope with problems of monetary control due to financial innovations, the central banks of the countries most affected have on the whole adopted a pragmatic approach. In the conduct of their policy, they have taken a wider range of economic and financial indicators into account (see Atkinson and Chouraqui 1984; BIS 1984). Some countries thus no longer seek to adhere strictly to stated targets for money supply growth but permit deviations from them for short or longer periods depending on the circumstances. Notable examples are the United States and the United Kingdom, where the targets have often been overrun and adjusted in mid-year or the following year in order to allow for the overshoots. Moreover, in these two countries the monetary authorities have been forced to set multiple targets, to alter the relative importance assigned to each of the money aggregates selected as targets or even (as in Canada in 1982) no longer to announce targets for certain aggregates.

Innovations have also influenced the conduct of monetary policy in other major OECD countries, although the problems have been smaller. Thus, in France and Italy the authorities have been compelled to redefine money aggregates or to monitor broader aggregates that include liquid instruments steeply on the increase. Even in Japan and Germany, where financial innovations have not triggered major distortions in the behaviour of the monetary aggregates, the authorities have sought to exercise greater control over the creation of financial claims both by banks and by other (non-bank) institutions.[14]

Against this background of more flexible pursuit of monetary targets, the exchange rate has assumed growing importance. In the United States, it is one of the indicators that has influenced the decisions of the monetary authorities regarding interest rates, although not subject itself to specific targets. In the United Kingdom and Canada the role of the exchange rate has been even more significant; thus, since the decision no longer to announce targets for monetary growth (sterling M3 and M1 respectively), exchange rate stabilization has implicitly become the main intermediate objective of monetary policy. Similarly, in most other European countries, with the exception of Switzerland, the conduct of monetary policy has been constrained by exchange rate considerations, notably because of the limits set on the margins for currency fluctuation within the European Monetary System.

Strengthening bank supervision

The constant preoccupation of the monetary authorities to preserve the stability of the financial system is becoming prominent in the present phase of rapid changes on the financial markets. Because of these changes, the activity of banks and other financial intermediaries now involves greater risks and uncertainty, so that the possibility of the emergence of tensions that could compromise the stability of the financial system at national or international level cannot be ruled out. This means that the traditional prudential rules imposed on financial institutions need to be reviewed and strengthened in the light of the new conditions.[15]

One of the major problems that the monetary authorities have to face at the moment and which has been discussed above is the very rapid growth of off-balance-sheet transactions. In this connection, the authorities' task consists in ensuring that such transactions show up in the published accounts of the banks concerned and that the relevant prudential regulations are applied to them. It is for this reason that several countries (United States, Japan, Germany, United Kingdom) have extended or intend to extend the standards governing capital to short-term issuing notes and to banks' commitments in the form of guarantees provided for certain transactions. The other major issues concerning bank supervision relate to the disappearance of the demarcation between the activity of banks and that of other financial institutions. In particular, will it be necessary to extend supervision to all types of financial intermediaries? Should comparable supervision standards be applied to institutions carrying on similar activities? In most countries, in the present context, the authorities generally agree that functional criteria are preferable to purely institutional criteria when it comes to defining the concepts of a bank and banking activity. This being so, there is a tendency towards application of uniform provisions to institutions carrying on identical activities. Although this approach makes for increased competition, it is not easy to implement in view of the considerable differences in size of the various financial institutions.

Finally, it should be emphasized that the international aspects of these problems are just as important as the national considerations. There is such a degree of overlap in the financial systems of each country that any difficulties experienced by a large bank, or group of banks, could well have consequences that go beyond national frontiers. Close international co-operation is therefore essential if the management of banks is to be better supervised. Considerable progress has been made in recent years, as a result of the measures taken by the monetary authorities of the major industrialized countries to strengthen banks' capital and to harmonize methods of measuring capital adequacy. However, there are still marked differences in the minimum standards imposed on banks and in the supervision methods used. Prudential supervision of the new off-balance-sheet banking activities is also the subject of growing international co-ordination, although the difficulties encountered in this area are on a smaller scale since this type of supervision is still in its early stages of development in most countries.

NOTES

1 For a detailed analysis, see BIS (1984, 1986).

2 These instruments, usually with a high unit value, are more akin to tradeable securities than to traditional deposits, their maturities ranging from ten days (for commercial paper) to three years (for certificates of deposit).

3 Examples of the best known are part-paid bonds (bonds for which the subscriber pays only in part at the time of issue, the other part being paid subsequently on an agreed date), deferrable bonds (bonds for which payment can be deferred

beyond the maturity date, at a rate and for a period agreed at their date of issue), convertible bonds (fixed rate bonds which can be exchanged for floating rate bonds or vice versa), single-coupon bonds (bonds having only one coupon payable on maturity) and zero-coupon bonds (non-interest bonds, the holder's return being the difference between the maturity value and the issue price).

4 These markets provide insurance against unexpected short-term rate variations. As a general rule, the issuer adopts the same position as on the spot market. For example, a firm that intends to issue commercial paper can immediately sell standard contracts corresponding to 'notional' loans (such as short-term treasury bills or long-term government loans). If rates rise, the additional cost of issuing the commercial paper will be offset by a forward market gain given that the price of the standard contracts sold by the firm will simultaneously have gone down.

5 For example, floating or adjustable rate bonds, which were introduced in order to protect issuers and holders against the risks inherent in fixed rate bonds (an excessive interest burden paid by the issuer in the case of a fall in rates, or a fall in market values for the holder in the case of a rise in rates).

6 Interest rate 'swaps' converting fixed rate debt into floating rate debt (and vice versa), or the exchanging of floating rates whose reference rates are not the same. The principle underlying these risk-hedging operations is that it is only the interest that is transferred, never the capital. Each party must thus be in search of identical volumes of capital but have opposite interest rate objectives. It often happens that interest rate swaps are combined with currency swaps. The option, another risk-hedging device, gives the right to buy or to sell a security at a price fixed at the outset. Depending on the arrangement, if movements in rates justify it, the buyer of the option can exercise this right, either at the expiry date or at any time up to that date. Future rate agreements specify an interest rate to hold over a future period but, unlike the instruments above, they relate only to changes in rates (the transaction is completed by cash payment of the difference between the guaranteed rate and the market rate at the end of the specified period).

7 For a fuller analysis, see BIS (1986) and Fukao and Hanazaki (1986).

8 See notes 2 and 3 above.

9 NOW (notice of withdrawal) and SUPER NOW accounts bearing interest at rates close to money-market rates. These accounts and other liquid investment instruments have expanded rapidly on the US markets with the removal of ceilings on interest on deposits.

10 This point is examined in detail by Atkinson and Chouraqui (1986). See also Akhtar (1983).

11 This is one of the major conclusions of Chouraqui *et al.* (1989).

12 The findings of empirical studies on the subjects, however, are fairly mixed. See Nickell and Wadhwani (1987) and Walker (1985).

13 As stated, very few papers have been written on this subject. Among those that support the idea that investment and research spending is influenced by 'short-termism' in financial markets are Mayer (1987) and Bain (1987).

14 In these two countries the regulations governing permission to issue financial claims have been considerably modified. In June 1985 a market for bankers' acceptances denominated in yen was set up in Japan. In December of the same year the Bundesbank decided to relax its position on issues of negotiable

certificates of deposit denominated in Deutschmarks, but to make them subject to compulsory reserves if their maturity was under two years.

15 This aspect is examined in detail by Marquardt (1987). See also Portes and Swoboda (1987) and Shafer (1987).

REFERENCES

Akhtar, M.A. (1983) 'Financial innovations and their implications for monetary policy', *BIS Economic Papers* 9 (December).

—— (1986) 'Recent changes in the financial system: a perspective on benefits versus costs', in *Shifting Frontiers in Financial Markets*, Dordrecht: Martinus Nijhoff.

Atkinson, P. and Chouraqui, J.C. (1986) 'The formulation of monetary policy: a reassessment in the light of recent experience', Working Paper 32, OECD Department of Economics and Statistics, March.

Bain, A. (1987) 'Economic commentary', *Midland Bank Review*, Summer.

BIS (Bank for International Settlements) (1984) *Financial Innovations and Monetary Policy*, Basle: BIS.

—— (1986) *Recent Innovations in International Banking*, Basle: BIS.

Chouraqui, J.C., Driscoll, M. and Strauss-Kahn, M.O. (1989) 'The effects of monetary policy on the real sector: what do we know?', *Banca Nazionale del Lavoro Quarterly Review*, March.

Fukao, M. and Hanazaki, M. (1986) 'Internationalisation of financial markets: some implications for macroeconomic policy and the allocation of capital', Working Paper 37, OECD Department of Economics and Statistics, November.

Marquardt, J.C. (1987) 'Financial market supervision: some conceptual issues', *BIS Economic Papers* 19 (May).

Mayer, C. (1987) 'New issues in corporate finance', Inaugural Lecture, London City University Business School.

Nickell, S. and Wadhwani, S. (1987) 'Myopia, the "dividend puzzle", and share prices', Discussion Paper 272, Centre for Labour Economics, London School of Economics.

Portes, R. and Swoboda, A. (eds) (1987) *Threats to International Financial Stability*, Cambridge: Cambridge University Press.

Shafer, J. (1987) 'Managing crises in the emerging financial landscape', *OECD Economic Studies* 9 (Autumn).

Walker, D. (1985) 'Capital markets and industry', *Bank of England Quarterly Review*, December.

4 Securities markets and banking: some regulatory issues

T.R. Gavin Bingham

The considerable expansion of securities markets in recent years has been both a bane and a boon to the banking community. There can be little doubt that a large proportion of the flows that have passed through the securities markets would have been placed on deposit at banks and lent on to other users in the absence of such markets. However, at the same time, although to varying degrees in different countries, banks have benefited from the growth of these markets by expanding their underwriting, own issuing, market making, trading and investment in securities.

After first identifying the main changes in securities markets and discussing some of their causes and consequences, in this chapter a few personal reflections are presented on three regulatory issues. First, what are the implications for the regulation of securities markets of increased reliance on the ability to sell or issue marketable claims when meeting liquidity needs? Second, what regulatory issues are raised by the growing international character of securities transactions? Finally, how much and what type of regulation is needed and feasible in securities markets?

DEVELOPMENTS IN SECURITIES MARKETS IN THE 1980s

During the 1980s the securities markets have been characterized by four principal trends. First, in response to continuing public sector deficits and steps by the authorities to foster the emergence and growth of certain financial instruments and markets, the number, volume and variety of new issues have increased. Second, and in part because of the buoyancy of new issuing activity but in part because of an upward trend in equity prices, the value of securities outstanding has expanded sharply. Third, despite some retrenchment following the 1987 stock market break, activity in secondary markets has grown dramatically as costs have fallen and administrative restrictions on portfolio holdings and trading have been relaxed. Finally, securities business has become much more international in character, as

Table 4.1 Estimated net lending in international markets

	Stocks at end 1983	*Changes*[a]					*Stocks at end 1988*
		1984	*1985*	*1986*	*1987*	*1988*	
Total international lending claims of reporting banks[b]	2,558.3	152.2	295.4	658.0	760.1	494.4	550.5
Minus double-counting due to redepositing among the reporting banks	1,318.3	62.2	190.4	463.0	460.1	269.4	3,115.0
A Net international bank lending[c]	1,240.0	90.0	105.0	195.0	300.0	225.0	2,390.0
B Net new Euro-note placements	0.0	5.0	10.0	13.0	23.3	19.5	72.1
Total completed international bond issues		105.6	161.9	219.6	181.2	219.4	
Minus redemptions and repurchases		24.6	38.9	59.3	71.1	81.5	
C Net international bond financing	320.0	81.0	123.0	160.3	110.1	137.9	1,085.4
D=A+B+C Total international financing	1,560.0	176.0	238.0	368.3	433.4	382.4	3,547.5
Minus double-counting[d]	60.0	31.0	58.0	78.3	53.4	67.4	347.5
E Total net international financing	1,500.0	145.0	180.0	290.0	380.0	315.0	3,200.0

Notes:

[a]Non-dollar flow banking data are converted into dollars at constant end-of-quarter exchange rates, and non-dollar bonds at rates ruling on announcement dates. Stock data are converted at current exchange rates.

[b]Banks in the Group of Ten countries plus Luxembourg, Austria, Denmark, Finland, Ireland, Norway, Spain, the Bahamas, Bahrain, the Cayman Islands, Hong Kong, the Netherlands Antilles and Singapore, and the branches of US banks in Panama.

[c]In addition to direct cross-border claims on end-users, these estimates include certain interbank positions: first, claims on banks outside the reporting area, the assumption being that these 'peripheral' banks will not, in most cases, borrow the funds from banks in the financial centres simply for the purpose of redepositing them with other banks in these centres; second, claims on banks within the reporting area to the extent that these banks switch the funds into domestic currency and/or use them for direct foreign currency lending to domestic customers; third, a large portion of the foreign currency claims on banks in the country of issue of the currency in question, e.g. dollar claims of banks in London on banks in the United States, here again the assumption being that the borrowing banks obtain the funds mainly for domestic purposes and not for re-lending abroad; a deduction is made, however, in respect of working balances and similar items.

[d]International bonds taken up by the reporting banks, to the extent that they are included in the banking statistics as claims on non-residents; bonds issued by the reporting banks mainly for the purpose of underpinning their international lending activities.

institutional investors and other major market participants have sought to diversify their portfolios, minimize their costs and find the highest returns commensurate with safety and liquidity.

Primary market activity

Statistics compiled by the Bank for International Settlements (BIS) provide some indication of the expansion of primary issues of international securities and their growing importance relative to bank lending (Table 4.1). At the end of 1983 bonds accounted for only a fifth of total international banking and capital market assets. By the end of 1988 the steady expansion of bond financing and the emergence of the Euro-note market had brought the share of these instruments up to a third.

Activity on national securities markets has also been buoyant. Evidence on new issues of bonds, shares and certain traditional types of short-term paper in the national markets of the Group of Ten countries indicates that activity in primary markets has been greater in the 1980s than in earlier periods (Table 4.2). To be sure there are differences among countries and market segments, and slowdowns do occur as happened in 1988. But on the whole a clear expansion in primary market activity is evident in national markets.

One of the reasons for intercountry differences in the growth of national securities markets may be variation in access to international securities markets. For countries like Germany, Japan, the United Kingdom and the United States, which have dispensed with exchange controls and have relaxed or eliminated their portfolio restrictions, security transactions are not confined to national markets. There is ample evidence that Japanese security issues and purchases in foreign markets have been substantial in recent years. For countries which still impose binding exchange and portfolio restrictions, such as until quite recently France and Italy, an increase in securities market activity will tend to occur in domestic markets, as has been the case. Second, there seems to be a fairly close relationship between the size and persistence of the public sector deficit and new issues of bonds. Countries with large and continuing deficits, such as Belgium and the United States, continue to have high new bond issue ratios. Third, since new debt issues will be needed to replace those that mature, it is natural that, relative to gross national product (GNP), new issues of debt are greater than new issues of equity, which may never be retired.

The burgeoning in the variety of financial instruments during the first part of this decade is an aspect of primary market activity that has generated considerable attention. Competition in meeting the specific needs of customers is one cause. The increase in various types of risk is a second one since this has augmented the need to hedge. It is not pure coincidence that the original rapid expansion of futures exchanges, forward contracts and options occurred in the early 1980s when interest rate volatility was at a peak. Earlier, when they were smaller, these risks could be borne more easily by ultimate agents. The greater ease with which financial contracts can be unbundled and repackaged has contributed to increased issuing activity with, for example, a large proportion of new issues being swap driven.

Value of securities outstanding

The second major trend in securities markets, the increase in the value of securities outstanding, is a result of the interplay of supply and demand and is reflected in two simultaneous developments: the steady and rising flow of new security issues just described and the buoyancy of security prices throughout most of the 1980s. The general downward movement in interest rates up through 1987 led to a rise in the market price of fixed rate securities. More importantly, the upward trend in equity prices during the 1980s boosted the value of the stock of securities outstanding. Without the buoyancy in quotations, 'income gearing ratios' or the ratio of GNP to the stock of equity would have deteriorated sharply, and in the United States the amount of equity outstanding would have actually fallen in the wake of the net retirement of equity associated with corporate buyouts and similar operations.

Higher equity prices can be attributed to a number of factors: the reduction in various restrictions which give rise to large once-and-for-all portfolio reallocations, government measures to encourage equity investment, structural adjustments boosting expectations of the long-term profitability of the corporate sector and, in the period up to 1987, a downward trend in interest rates. It is noteworthy that security prices have risen despite an increase in supply resulting from the tendency to issue securities rather than to borrow from banks and from extensive privatization programmes in a number of countries.

Secondary market activity

The marked expansion of transactions in secondary markets is the third major feature of the 1980s and, arguably, the one with the most wide-reaching implications for measures designed to ensure that there is adequate systemic liquidity. This is also the change that is the most dramatic in terms of size. Owing to differences in types of securities traded and in the

Table 4.2 Security issues in national markets (as a percentage of gross national product)

	1966–72,[a] annual		*1973–9,[b] annual*		*1980–6, annual*			
	Average	*Maximum*	*Average*	*Maximum*	*Average*	*Maximum*	*1987*	*1988*
Shares[c]								
Belgium	1.2	1.7	1.0	1.8	2.5	5.7	n.a.	n.a.
Canada	0.7	1.2	1.2	2.8	2.4	3.2	2.4	0.4
France	1.0	1.0	0.8	1.0	1.4	2.8	3.0	2.8
Germany	0.5	0.6	0.4	0.6	0.5	0.8	0.6	0.4
Italy	1.2	1.6	1.3	2.1	1.8	2.6	1.4	1.0
Japan	1.2	1.6	0.8	1.3	0.8	0.9	1.8	2.3
Netherlands	0.2	0.3	0.1	0.2	0.3	0.6	0.5	0.3
Sweden	–	–	0.9	1.2	1.2	1.5	1.5	1.1
Switzerland	0.7	1.0	0.7	1.1	1.1	2.5	2.0	0.8
United Kingdom	0.6	1.1	0.6	1.2	0.8	2.1	3.6	1.2
United States	0.9	1.4	0.4	0.7	−0.5	0.8	−1.2	−2.3
Bonds[d]								
Belgium	–	–	9.8	13.4	9.9	15.5	7.9	9.4
Canada	4.5	7.1	5.1	6.6	5.6	6.1	5.8	4.2
France	2.0	2.2	2.0	2.6	4.0	5.4	2.9	4.0
Germany	2.8	4.1	3.7	4.8	5.0	5.6	5.6	4.2
Italy	5.3	6.9	7.5	10.2	8.1	12.6	7.3	6.4
Japan	5.2	7.0	7.8	9.6	7.5	8.8	4.4	4.0
Netherlands	1.9	2.3	1.9	2.6	4.9	6.5	5.0	8.2
Sweden	–	–	9.3	11.6	12.4	15.5	8.5	11.2
Switzerland	5.4	6.7	5.4	7.3	8.4	10.5	12.5	12.6
United Kingdom	2.2	6.7	3.6	5.2	3.1	4.5	1.2	−0.7
United States	4.5	6.4	6.2	9.3	9.5	14.1	11.0	9.1

	1966–72, [a] *annual*		*1973–9,* [b] *annual*		*1980–6, annual*			
	Average	*Maximum*	*Average*	*Maximum*	*Average*	*Maximum*	*1987*	*1988*
Short-term paper[e]								
Belgium	–	–	1.6	2.7	4.4	6.6	2.4	1.1
Canada (CP)	0.3	0.6	0.5	1.4	0.1	0.5	0.3	0.7
Canada (TB)	0.4	1.1	1.0	1.5	2.9	4.2	2.4	5.1
Italy	0.4	1.3	3.5	5.3	3.6	7.2	2.6	3.4
Japan	0.5	1.1	0.7	2.7	0.2	0.9	1.2	0.2
United Kingdom	–	–	0.2	1.8	0.0	0.1	0.5	0.6
United States	0.6	1.5	0.5	1.1	0.7	1.4	0.7	1.6
Debt certificates								
Netherlands	5.8	8.2	6.5	7.0	5.2	6.6	4.9	5.2

Notes: Based on national sources which differ conceptually from country to country.

[a]For the United Kingdom and France, 1970–2 (for shares for France, 1972 only); for Italy 1967–72 and for treasury bills for Canada, 1969–72.

[b]For Sweden, 1974–9; for bonds and short-term paper for Belgium, 1975–9.

[c]Net issues (for Belgium, Italy, Sweden and Switzerland, gross).

[d]Net issues. For Belgium, Canada and Sweden, domestic currency issues only; for Switzerland, public issues only; for the United States, includes treasury bills.

[e]For Belgium, paper at less than one year; for Canada (TB), Italy and the United Kingdom, treasury bills; for Canada (CP) and the United States, commercial paper.

organization of securities markets in different countries, cross-country comparisons must be made with care (Table 4.3). But in the largest countries secondary market transactions have expanded more rapidly than primary issuing, though retrenchment occurred in the wake of the 1987 stock market break.

Lower transactions costs resulting from technological change and the relaxation of officially sanctioned restrictions on entry and pricing are a principal reason for burgeoning secondary market activity. Further impetus to lower costs and higher volume has been given by the growth of the institutional investor. Pension funds, insurance companies and other institutions trade in large blocks and benefit from discounts; they also carry out operations on such a scale that it may pay them to seek out opportunities for arbitrage or to implement trading strategies that the small investor would find too costly to follow. Moreover, greater competition in underwriting and other primary market activity has induced banks and securities houses to engage in more active trading in a larger portfolio of securities. Greater short- and medium-term volatility of exchange rates and interest rates has also contributed to the growth of transactions. Purchases and sales of securities are often one element in hedging operations, which in the face of greater perceived risk and lower costs of hedging have expanded considerably.

Growing international links between securities markets

The fourth and final feature of securities market activity during the 1980s has been its increasing international character. There has been much facile talk of the 'globalization' of financial markets but, as far as banking is concerned, expanding international activity is neither novel nor undocumented, having occurred at a fairly rapid rate over a span of decades. It is in the securities area that the changes have been most dramatic.

At the beginning of the decade, international securities business was modest. Euro-bond activity was dwarfed by international banking, and foreign presence in national securities markets was confined to a moderate amount of foreign bond issues and only a notional amount of equity issues in a very limited number of national markets. Participation of foreign securities houses in domestic securities markets as brokers, dealers and market makers was virtually unknown, although major securities houses sometimes had small overseas branches providing support for head office operations, principally the underwriting of foreign issues in domestic markets and the provision of portfolio management services.

In the intervening years, securities houses have obtained seats on stock exchanges in the world's three major financial centres and some of the

Table 4.3 Securities markets in selected countries

	1982	*1983*	*1984*	*1985*	*1986*	*1987*	*1988*
United States (New York)							
Turnover[a]	100	156.8	156.8	198.8	284.6	384.0	277.9
Market value of listed securities[b]	1,259	1,522	1,758	1,883	2,128	2,132	2,360
Ratio of turnover to amounts outstanding	0.39	0.50	0.44	0.52	0.65	0.88	0.57
Japan (Tokyo)							
Turnover[a]	100	210.0	193.9	263.9	644.9	1,179.6	1,515.6
Market value of listed securities[b]	417	546	644	948	1,794	2,726	3,789
Ratio of turnover to amounts outstanding	0.35	0.42	0.44	0.41	0.52	0.63	0.59
United Kingdom (London)							
Turnover[a]	100	130.3	145.5	230.3	342.4	1,293.9	878.8
Market value of listed securities[b]	196	226	236	353	473	680	712
Ratio of turnover to amounts outstanding	0.17	0.19	0.2	0.21	0.23	0.63	0.41

Source: Fédération Internationale des Bourses de Valeurs

Notes: [a] Index 1982=100.

[b] In billions of US dollars.

secondary ones, have initiated underwriting of Euro-equities issued and traded simultaneously in several centres and have even begun underwriting and making markets in domestic government securities, traditionally a preserve of national entities.

A number of reasons can be given for the growing international character of securities business. Controls and regulations have played a role in both a positive and a negative way. First, the relaxation of various restrictions such as those on capital movements, portfolio composition and access to markets has allowed securities houses and banks to undertake a greater amount and a wider range of securities business in a larger number of countries. Second, the maintenance of restrictions on the conduct by banks of securities business in the national markets of the United States and Japan, the two countries with the largest financial surpluses and deficits, has deflected competition to the international arena, where these limitations do not apply. In order to maintain market positions in the face of keener competition from deposit-taking banks, which have sought to augment their fee income from securities and related business as margins on bank lending have been compressed, securities houses have expanded their overseas activities.

Further impetus to the expansion of international securities business has been given by the existence of various rules, conventions and oligopolistic market structures in national financial centres which often make it cheaper to issue securities internationally. Moreover, as there are still strong pressures for further, albeit often gradual, liberalization of national financial markets, banks and securities houses operating from regulated national markets such as Japan's may find it in their interest at present to finance the expansion of their international business with domestic revenue in order to establish and solidify their positions in the global market. Once domestic markets are fully liberalized, strategic cross-subsidization will be impossible.

The increased preference of borrowers and lenders for securities rather than bank claims has been a further important factor behind the growth of both national and international securities business. Institutional investors prefer securities holdings to bank deposits. Rates of return on securities tend to be higher, and the growth of secondary markets has augmented their liquidity. Moreover swaps, options and other ancillary facilities allow the redesign of standard securities contracts so that the specific needs of borrowers and lenders can be met more easily than in the past. Borrowers prefer this form of finance since the cost is often lower than that of bank loans. Indeed, some prime borrowers have at times been able to issue securities at rates below those paid by banks on their own liabilities. Some banks now have to pay a higher risk premium than in the past because of a deterioration in the quality of their assets, notably loans to less developed countries and in some countries loans to particular sectors or regions. Lower inflation and in some countries the persistence of large government and current account deficits are factors of a macroeconomic nature that contribute to the expansion of securities business.

REGULATORY ISSUES

The changes in securities markets raise a host of regulatory issues, some of which have received considerable attention in the recent past: insider trading, the conduct of securities business by banks (Glass–Steagall), the implications for efficiency and stability of growing financial activity unaccompanied by a corresponding expansion in real activity, market entry, position taking, risk monitoring and capital adequacy etc. In this chapter we address only a select number of questions.

1 How do the trends discussed above affect the way liquidity needs are met and what regulatory response is appropriate?
2 What are the regulatory implications of the growing international character of securities business?
3 How much and what type of securities market regulation is needed and feasible?

Liquidity and regulation

The growth of securities markets means that the sale of holdings of existing securities and the issuance of new securities have become increasingly important complements to holdings of both money and a portfolio of assets whose maturities and amortization schedules correspond to the expected pattern of payments. The collapse of securities markets would therefore be more detrimental to the working of the entire financial and economic system than in the past when the principal losers were individual holders and new issuers of securities.

In consequence there has been a subtle but significant shift in the rationale for regulation. It ceases to be confined largely to the protection of individual borrowers and lenders and becomes analogous to the rationale for the regulation of banking and the existence of a lender of last resort: ensuring that the benefits to the economy as a whole – the 'externalities' – of the continued provision of liquidity are not jeopardized. Regulation of the securities market thus comes to have systemic consequences and the need for a 'market maker of last resort' for both government and privately issued papers should be considered.

Structure and functioning of secondary markets

The intimate relationship between the structure and functioning of a market, particularly a financial market, makes it useful to examine the main features of secondary markets and to consider the role of the market maker. One important characteristic of active secondary markets is a certain degree of efficiency reflected in narrow bid–ask spreads, modest fees and relatively low price volatility. Market deepness is promoted by the presence of many actual or potential participants and a certain amount of standardization. If there is great diversity in the type of financial contracts, the market inevitably becomes segmented. For this reason, active secondary markets emerge initially in widely held instruments with similar and usually low credit risk characteristics: foreign exchange, treasury paper, certificates of deposit, commercial paper etc. Standardization of other features of the contract, e.g. denominations, maturities, interest rate calculation methods, amortization schedules, also contributes to the emergence of active secondary markets. Indeed, one of the reasons why the creation of financial instruments customized to meet the needs of individual borrowers has abated in the recent past has been the absence of secondary markets for such products. Another reason has been the growing ability to meet specific needs by assembling a synthetic instrument from standard parts.

A second characteristic of many active secondary markets is the presence of market makers. While it is possible for a secondary market to work on the basis of pure brokerage, where deals are struck only when two parties with matching needs are found, markets tend to be deeper and more active when there are houses ready at all times to quote firm buying and selling prices for a minimum predetermined quantity. The market maker must have, or be able to obtain at very short notice, a stock of the financial instrument in question, which generally means that he/she will tend to have an open position. This position is an important source of income over and above that arising from fees and the margin between bid and offer prices, but it also entails risks, sometimes substantial risks. To bear them the market maker should have adequate capital and the profits from market making should be commensurate with the risk.

A third feature of most financial markets – not secondary markets alone – is a tendency towards concentration, at least in the long run. Large institutions often stand at an advantage in financial markets. They are regarded with greater confidence by market participants, have an influence on the regulations that are laid down and often obtain the endorsement of the authorities in the form of primary dealer or similar status more easily than small houses. Although there may be many minor participants, the bulk of the business is often accounted for by only a handful of houses.

This tendency for an oligopolistic structure to emerge in secondary markets can influence price formation. In a concentrated market, market makers, particularly those with large merchandising networks, will be loath to quote firm prices or to disclose information on the volume and prices of their trades as this will allow competitors to infer their strategies. Trading will often take place at prices different from the ones quoted, and prices which are struck will not be homogeneous, i.e. identical contracts negotiated at the same time will have different prices for different counterparties. Market makers may also have an incentive to engage in 'ramping' and short-selling, i.e. influencing prices by varying the amounts supplied to the secondary market. The oligopolistic market structure which prevails in the Euro-bond market explains why it has been difficult to create a screen-based trading system even though the technology is available and the authorities are favourably disposed.

Regulating secondary markets

What are the implications of the relationships between the structure and functioning of secondary markets for the design of regulations? First, they bring to light a basic regulatory dilemma. On one hand, the spread between bid and ask prices should be as small as possible to encourage efficiency and to promote a large volume of transactions. Consequently the promotion of competition, the relaxation of barriers to entry and the elimination of rigidities in commissions and spreads arising from administrative controls or cartel-like behaviour all seem eminently desirable.

On the other hand, since market making generates substantial benefits for the economy as a whole, well in excess of, say, the tax receipts on income from market making, maintenance of continuity in the markets is essential. If the return from market making is not adequate or the risks are too great, securities houses will cease to quote firm two-way prices at reasonable spreads whenever a minor shock occurs. The cessation of market making in the perpetual floating rate note market at the end of 1986 is one illustration of how the seizing-up of a market not only affects the liquidity of outstanding claims but also has an impact on the ability of issuers to sell paper in the primary market. In addition, it shows that events in one market will often affect another where a similar type of paper is traded.

For these reasons the authorities need to strike a balance between these two opposing currents: competition should be promoted but minimum standards should be met. The tendency in most markets has been to strike this balance by doing away with controls on prices and relaxing but not abolishing restrictions on entry, whilst at the same time insisting on certain minimum standards for all market makers. A *sine qua non* for this approach is the maintenance of controls on entry through a system of designation, recognition or licensing. This indeed is the principle underlying the recent financial services legislation in the United Kingdom, which stipulates that only authorized entities will be entitled to conduct financial services business.

Such an approach accords not only with the responsibilities of the authorities to the community at large but also with the interests of the major established institutions. The continued existence of barriers to entry into market making, especially fairly low ones that do not lead to the creation of alternative markets, allows the established houses to appropriate more of the economic rents associated with market maker status and oligopolistic markets than would otherwise be possible. In addition, when fees and commission are no longer controlled, they can price their services below the threshold that causes parallel markets to emerge. This in turn is beneficial to the authorities since they need not be as watchful of circumvention. The policing function is effectively delegated to the securities houses.

The interrelationship between function and structure has several other implications for the design of regulations. First, seemingly small and insignificant rules or conventions may have far-reaching consequences for the functioning of the market. For example, in some countries limit orders allow other (non-market-making) dealers and the public to compete indirectly with market makers, by placing buy and sell orders conditional on prices moving to certain levels. This reduces the oligopolistic power of the market maker and tends to generate more information. Rules requiring market makers to post their prices electronically on screens have much the same effect.

Second, the existence of market makers means that there is a group of agents whose open positions give them a vested interest in stability. This interest can be utilized when laying down rules that promote stable markets: certain types of disclosure, maximum price change rules present on some exchanges, concentration of orders at particular times etc.

Third, as issuers of some of the main securities held for liquidity purposes, the authorities can make sure that the supply of securities is adequate. Indeed, this is why market-making status and privileged access to new government issues through participation in underwriting syndicates or auctions often go hand in hand. In this respect the authorities can act as market makers of last resort.

International regulatory issues

Earlier, when securities business was essentially confined to transactions between residents of the same country and the systemic consequences of a cessation of market making were less severe, there was little need for international co-operation in the design of regulations applying to securities business. National systems of regulation tended to evolve independently of one another with some countries favouring systems of self-regulation, some stressing disclosure and reliance on market discipline, some exercising control through banks, some preventing banks from conducting important types of securities business, some creating national commissions, some assigning regulatory responsibilities to territorial authorities (provinces, states, Länder, cantons) etc. (Table 4.4). This variation in regulatory structures complicates international co-operation and makes some issues such as extra-territoriality and reciprocity more acute in securities market regulation than in banking. Another factor which makes international co-operation more difficult in the securities area is the breadth of concerns of the authorities. Whereas prudential questions are at the heart of banking regulation, ethical concerns (insider trading, conflicts of interest, churning, trading at non-market prices) and questions related to the functioning of the market (prospectus requirements, accounting standards etc.) are important in securities regulation.

Table 4.4 Securities market regulation: institutional framework

Country	*Central supervisory body*	*Provincial/Länder/ cantonal responsibility*	*Self-regulatory organization*
Canada	–	Yes	
France	Commission des Opérations de Bourse		
Germany	(Ministry of Finance)		Stock exchanges
Japan	Ministry of Finance Securities Bureau		
Netherlands	(Ministry of Finance)		Amsterdam Stock Exchange
Switzerland	–	Yes	
United States	Securities and Ex-change Commission		
United Kingdom	SIB/Bank of England		Yes; many

Extra-territoriality and reciprocity

In principle there are four ways that cross-border coherence in regulation can come about:

1. by the creation of general rules applying with equal force in more than one jurisdiction;
2. by the convergence of national rules;
3. by mutual recognition of divergent national rules;
4. by application by one country of its rules outside its own territorial borders.

In practice the four types are blurred. Outside regional groupings like the European community the first form, which carries with it the implication of a loss of sovereignty, is rare and for the three major international financial centres – London, New York and Tokyo – without practical significance. The second type, convergence of national rules, has occurred in banking, at least for the larger countries, in part because the structure of the regulatory systems was not as divergent as for the securities industry and in part because banks' willingness to move the location of their international operations has provided an incentive for co-operation. In the securities business, mutual recognition and transnational application of national rules have been more common. In part this is a consequence of widely varying regulatory approaches and the crucial importance of a few major centres.

The adoption of the principle that financial services can only be provided within the context of some recognized regulatory framework, in the new British legislation governing financial services, has entailed a certain amount of extra-territoriality because of the importance of London as a centre for international securities business. For example, the Association of International Bond Dealers, an entity legally established in Switzerland, has been recognized as the relevant self-regulatory body by the UK authorities. Exchanges outside the United Kingdom are also subject to recognition.

Largely for the same reason, reciprocity, a principle widely regarded as inimical to free multilateral trade, has increasingly been adopted in financial legislation and reflected in bureaucratic practice. This is partly a reflection of a general resurgence of protectionism, but reciprocity has also been used in a tactical sense by countries with important banking and financial interests to open markets that might otherwise have remained closed. Quite apart from any theoretical objections, its application is often difficult and arbitrary, particularly when banks and securities houses have different powers in different countries.

Competition in laxity

Growing international financial integration, diversity in regulatory approaches and parochial advancement of local interests all carry with them the dangers of 'competition in laxity'. In the area of banking this has largely been avoided through dialogue between the authorities of the main parent countries, the adoption of consolidation in supervising returns and recognition that winning a slightly larger market share for the institutions of one's own country would be a Pyrrhic victory if it were achieved by weakening the soundness of an increasingly interdependent international financial system.

It may well be that economies in scale and scope arising from a large volume of transactions and the related importance of the infrastructure needed for the successful operation of securities markets (quotation and order confirmation systems, clearing arrangements, common standards for contracts, methods for resolving disputes etc.) may make securities houses less likely than banks to shift to an entirely new and unregulated locality. Offshore securities markets have clearly not had the same success as offshore banking centres. On the other hand, securities houses may be able and willing to shift their trading business between the major financial centres with established and efficient infrastructures. For this reason attempts to achieve greater regulatory coherence are salutary.

The roles of regulation

Much of what has been said above suggests that regulation serves a number of different purposes and is shaped by a variety of forces. Viewing it as a service for which there is notional demand and supply may help understand the forces at work. On the demand side there are essentially three different sets of actors. First, and probably most important for the precise content of the regulations, are the security market participants themselves. The security houses, in particular, have a direct interest in the operation of the market that is stronger and more focused than that of those who use the markets as a source of funding or a place to invest money. Second, there is the public at large which may not use the security market often or directly but which would be affected by its collapse. The third category consists of regulatory authorities in other countries who are concerned about the shape of regulation in major national markets because of the consequences of disruption in an interdependent world, because of the possibility of competition in laxity and because of the tendency towards the extra-territorial application of national regulations.

On the supply side there is considerable diversity ranging from systems of almost complete self-regulation to ones of rigorous controls by the authorities of virtually all aspects of the operation of securities markets. The distinction between self-regulation and regulation by government, however, is by no means hard and fast. The authorities can and do induce market participants to lay down and police their own codes, and securities houses have a major influence on the shape of administrative rules by virtue of their expertise and the strength of their lobbying. Moreover, market participants may often prefer regulation by the authorities. In this case some of the costs of establishing and even operating the infrastructure may be borne by the taxpayer. The presence of a neutral arbiter may also allow the achievement of a market structure which is in the interest of each individual market participant and of the economy as a whole, but which would not emerge otherwise because of the fear of tactical manoeuvring. This is the classic case of the prisoner's dilemma where co-operation is likely to be beneficial both for the individual and the community but is unlikely to occur without the ability to make and enforce contracts and rules. An analogy can also be drawn with environmental protection. Each individual factory owner may be willing to bear some additional cost for the sake of clean air, but without a system of consultation, monitoring and sanctions he will be loath to bear those costs on his own initiative for fear that another factory owner may have different preferences.

Viewing regulations in this light helps to avoid a common tendency to see them as an obstacle to free and unhindered transactions. While there are some regulations which hamper the efficient functioning of markets and whose justification lies in, say, protection of the small investor, there are other rules that promote market efficiency. In the past decade much of the deregulation that has occurred has involved the removal of rules that hindered the growth and development of securities markets, e.g. exchange and portfolio controls, dual capacity restrictions, regulation of fees and commissions. Many of the new regulations – minimum capital requirements, limits on positions, licensing or recognition requirements etc. – can be seen as conducive to the continued smooth operation of the market in the face of shocks.

Recognizing that some regulations may foster the emergence of externalities and allow market participants to earn an economic rent on them may also be of help in devising a rational approach to the imposition of burdensome regulations needed for some other purpose. The amount of burdensome regulation that can be imposed is a function of (a) the value to market participants of the infrastructure, (b) the costs of entry into the market and (c) the costs of creating or using an alternative infrastructure.

While the foregoing analysis suggests that regulation, being subject to the forces of supply and demand, is unlikely to wither away, it provides no guidance as to just what regulations will tend to augment welfare and which ones will reduce it. As such, it provides no justification for either the maintenance of existing regulations or the introduction of new ones. What it does do is provide grounds for a long-established regulatory practice: the tendency to move in small steps. Since the impact of a change in regulation cannot be predicted with precision, it pays to make gradual changes and assess their consequences before taking the next step. Acting in this manner is less likely to disrupt the financial system and accords with political realities. Vested interests are more likely to accept small gradual changes than systemic ones.

CONCLUSIONS

In conclusion it might be useful to recapitulate the three main propositions concerning the regulation of securities markets that have been advanced in this chapter. First, the tendency to use securities markets, in particular secondary markets, as a source of liquidity has made it increasingly necessary to see the regulation of these markets as part of efforts to ensure the soundness and stability of the financial system as a whole, and not only as a means to ensure the integrity of private transactions having little or no significance for those who are not party to the contract. Second, the growing international character of securities market transactions has given a certain urgency to efforts to achieve coherence in regulation. Moving the process of consultation beyond bilateral contacts could reduce tendencies to advance narrow sectional interests. Third, seeing regulation as the outcome of the interaction of supply and demand brings to light the considerable range of forces that shape the various rules that are laid down. In addition, recognizing that regulation may both promote market efficiency and give rise to positive externalities, provides a foundation for other regulations which are less acceptable to market participants but are none the less necessary.

NOTE

Comments by J.S. Alworth, G.D. Baer, E.P. Davis, H.W. Mayer and C.J. Thompson are gratefully acknowledged. The opinions expressed in this chapter do not necessarily reflect those of the Bank for International Settlements.

REFERENCES

Allen, J.W. (1986) 'The internationalisation of securities trading markets', *Congressional Research Service*, HG 4551 Gen, Library of Congress, Washington, DC.

Boyd, J.H. and Graham, S.L. (1986) 'Risk regulation and bank holding company expansion into nonbanking', *Federal Reserve Bank of Minneapolis Quarterly Review* 10 (2) (Spring).

Carosso, V.P. (1970) *Investment Banking in America*, Cambridge, MA: Harvard University Press.

Chant, J. (1987) 'Regulation of financial institutions – a functional analysis', *Bank of Canada Technical Reports* no. 45.

Cohen, K.J., Maler, S.F., Schwartz, R.A. and Whitcomb, D.K. (1986) *The Microstructure of Securities Markets*, Englewood Cliffs, NJ: Prentice-Hall.

Davis, E.P. (1986) 'Rising sectoral debt–income ratios: a cause for concern?', *BIS Economic Papers* no. 20.

Greenwich Associates (1986) *United Kingdom Brokerage Services*, Greenwich, CT: Greenwich Associates.

Langohr, H. and Santomero, A.M. (1985) 'The extent of equity investment by European banks', *Journal of Money, Credit and Banking* 17 (1).

Marquardt, J.C. (1987) 'Financial market supervision: some conceptual issues', *BIS Economic Papers* no. 19.

Organisation for Economic Co-operation and Development (1987) *International Trade in Services: Securities*, Paris: OECD.

Peck, A.E. (1985) *Futures Markets: Regulatory Issues*, Washington, DC: American Enterprise Institute.

Robinson, J.M. (ed.) (1980) *Comparative Survey of Securities Laws*, Deventer: Kluwer.

Samatz, A.W. (ed.) (1981) *Securities Activities of Commercial Banks*, Lexington, MA: Lexington Books.

Sherman, M.E. *et al.* (1983) *Banking and Securities: U.S. Lessons of Foreign Experiences*, Cronton on Hudson, New York: Hudson Strategy Group.

Tobin, J. (1984) 'On the efficiency of the financial system', *Lloyds Bank Review*, July.

US House of Representatives (1986) *Restructuring Financial Markets*, Committee on Energy and Commerce, Committee Print 99-DD, Washington, DC: US Government Printing Office.

Wormell, J. (1985) *The Gilt-Edged Market*, London: Allen & Unwin.

5 Features of the New Financial System in the United States

Thomas D. Simpson

INTRODUCTION

It is widely recognized that the period since the mid-1970s has seen some of the most profound financial change in US history. The variety of investments and credit arrangements has expanded at a bewildering pace, aided to a degree by derivative instruments such as financial futures, options and swaps. Such derivative instruments have provided financial market participants with vehicles for adjusting risk exposure. Underlying many of these developments has been an economy that has been buffeted by inflation and disinflation and large fiscal and external deficits. At the same time, the US financial system has become more integrated with those abroad and has faced deregulation in certain areas, factors contributing to more intense competition in the financial market place.

A glimpse of the US financial system at the end of 1988 – as well as a dozen years earlier – is presented in Table 5.1 which shows the indebtedness of domestic non-financial sectors. Over this period, aggregate debt (line 5) increased by more than 250 per cent while gross national product (GNP), a very rough index of the capacity to service this debt, rose by much less; as a consequence, the ratio of debt to GNP, which had been relatively stable for most of the post-war period prior to the early 1980s, has been climbing markedly for some years. Pacing the expansion in debt has been indebtedness of the US government (line 1) which grew by more than US$1.5 trillion over the twelve years ending in late 1988, with by far the bulk of the expansion occurring over the second half of this period. Commercial banks (line 1(a)) acquired only a small portion of the federal debt expansion – their share of outstanding federal debt fell from about a fifth to less than a tenth – implying a massive absorption by the non-bank public, including foreign purchasers. The rise in state and local debt over this period (line 2) was less dramatic, with most again being accumulated by non-bank holders.

Table 5.1 Debt of domestic non-financial sectors (outstanding levels in billions of dollars)

	1976 : Q4	1988 : Q4
1 *US government*	514.8	2,117.8
(a) Held by commercial banks	105.7	192.2
(b) Others	410.1	1,925.6
2 *State and local governments*	233.5	585.6
(a) Held by commercial banks	106.0	151.2
(b) Others	127.5	434.4
3 *Non-financial corporations*		
(a) Debt	570.2	1,874.5
Owed to commercial banks	150.7	552.8
Commercial paper	11.0	85.4
Bonds	276.6	861.3
Other	131.8	375.0
(b) Equity (market value)	787.8	2,565.1
4 *Households*	838.4	3,137.4
(a) Consumer credit	230.4	743.7
Owed to commercial banks	118.0	370.9
Others	112.4	372.8
(b) Home mortgages	529.4	2,131.1
(c) Other	78.6	262.6
5 *Total domestic non-financial debt*	2,496.5	9,049.7
(a) GNP	1,782.8	4,864.4
(b) Debt as percentage of GNP	140.0	186.0

The private sectors – households and non-financial corporations – have also been heavy borrowers, especially in the second half of the period. Businesses (line 3) have tapped commercial banks and the bond market in volume; also of note is the sharp rise in commercial paper, a non-bank source of short-term funds utilized by a growing number of firms. Household debt growth (line 4), too, has been substantial, in both the mortgage and consumer credit categories. The more than US$1.5 trillion advance in home mortgages (line 4(b)) has provided the raw material for a growing array of mortgage securities; in addition, a portion of the mortgage debt build-up has reflected borrowing against accumulated home equity, a type of credit that has proved to be very popular of late while other forms of household debt are losing their tax deductibility. Consumer credit (line 4(a)) has slowed in recent years to a pace broadly in line with income as the interest deductibility of such debt has been disappearing and the economic expansion has matured; earlier in the expansion, consumer credit – especially its revolving component – surged.

This period of rapid debt expansion has also been one of unrealized expectations and severe hardship for many which has placed great strain on certain parts of the financial system, especially in the commercial bank and thrift (or savings) sectors. This has been evident in the earnings performance of the bank and thrift industries; in the case of the latter, massive losses by a large segment of the industry and accompanying insolvencies wiped out the industry's insurance fund, prompting a federal programme of unprecedented proportions for dealing with insolvent institutions and a major industry restructuring. The financial system has been responding to the experience of the late 1970s and 1980s by developing and utilizing new forms of risk shifting. A better understanding of trends in the US financial system can be gained by reviewing the economic background, to be covered in the next section. This is followed by a more detailed discussion of the response of the financial system.

ECONOMIC BACKGROUND

Important economic and financial developments

A major feature of the economic setting over the past decade or so has been the inflation–disinflation process. As Figure 5.1(a) shows, inflation – as measured by the consumer price index – picked up in the late 1970s from already advanced levels, reached a peak of about 13 per cent in the years 1979 and 1980 and then fell off sharply. This inflationary experience profoundly affected the public's expectations of inflation, which was a primary factor boosting interest rates in this period as well as a factor influencing wage negotiations in the labour markets. Many people borrowed large sums, expecting to repay in greatly inflated dollars; real estate investments, which had been performing well in the inflationary setting, were especially favoured. In the event, earnings and prices, including real estate prices, grew much less rapidly in the period following 1981 than had been contemplated, placing debt-servicing strains on many of these borrowers.

Another prominent development bearing on the US financial system has been very large fiscal deficits. These deficits widened sharply in the early 1980s, hovering in the vicinity of US$200 billion or more – in excess of 5 per cent of GNP – in the years 1983–6; the fiscal deficit has been contracting more recently, as shown in Figure 5.1(b), but remains fairly high by historical standards. Pressures on financial markets from large

Figure 5.1 (a) Consumer price index; (b) federal and current accounts

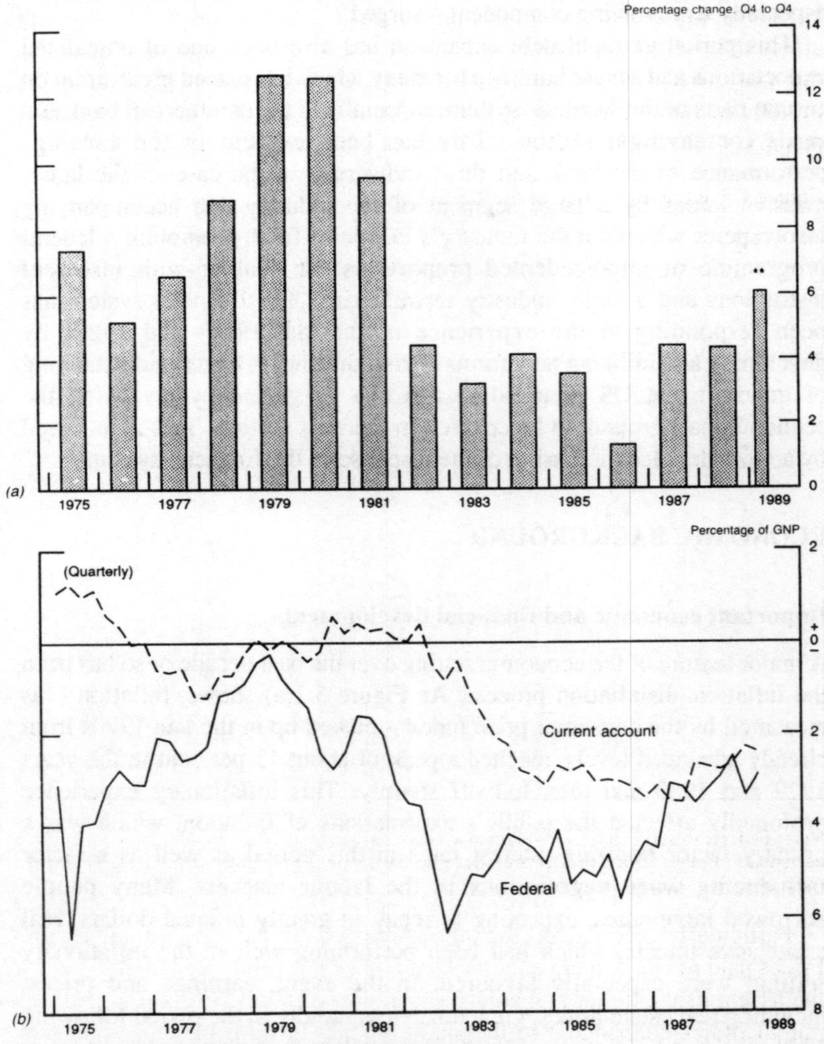

Note: **Growth from 1988: Q4 to 1989: Q2, annual rate.

deficits are widely thought to have been a factor contributing to the dollar's strength over much of the first half of the 1980s (Figure 5.2) and to a worsening current account position (Figure 5.1(b)). This expansion in the availability of savings from abroad probably acted to limit upward movements in domestic interest rates and the extent to which interest-sensitive sectors of the economy, such as housing and investment, needed to be restrained to achieve resource transfers associated with large fiscal deficits. However, the associated worsening of our net export position adversely affected the export industries and those competing with imports. The dollar did move sharply lower after early 1985 – trading in recent years at levels broadly in line with those of the mid- and late 1970s – and the external position of the United States has tended to improve.

Figure 5.2 Exchange value of the US dollar

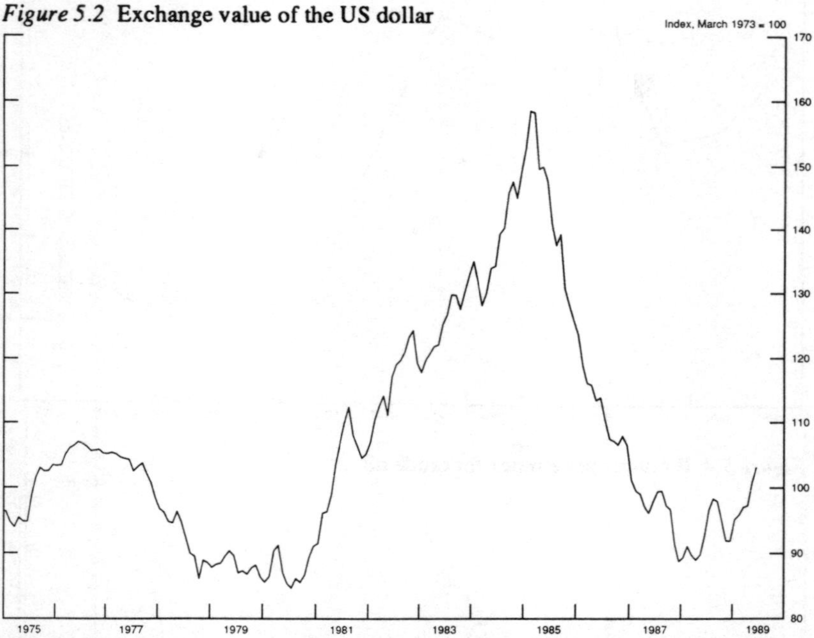

Note: Federal Reserve index of weighted average exchange value of the US dollar against currencies of other Group of Ten countries plus Switzerland. Weights are the 1972–6 global trade of each of the ten countries.

Particularly affected by the strong dollar was the agricultural sector. Prices paid to US farmers over the first half of the 1980s were depressed by the ascent of the dollar and enlarged supplies of non-US producers. Weak output prices contributed to the sharp decline in farm income, shown in Figure 5.3 adjusted for the general level of prices. Weaker income together with historically high interest rates over much of this period placed heavy debt-servicing strains on farm borrowers and stress on many of their creditors; exacerbating the situation was a plunge in the value of farm land used as collateral. More recently, farm income and land prices have begun to recover, relieving stress in this sector.

Energy producers, especially around the mid-1980s, were also adversely affected by external developments, in particular the plunge in oil prices

Figure 5.3 Gross farm income (annual)

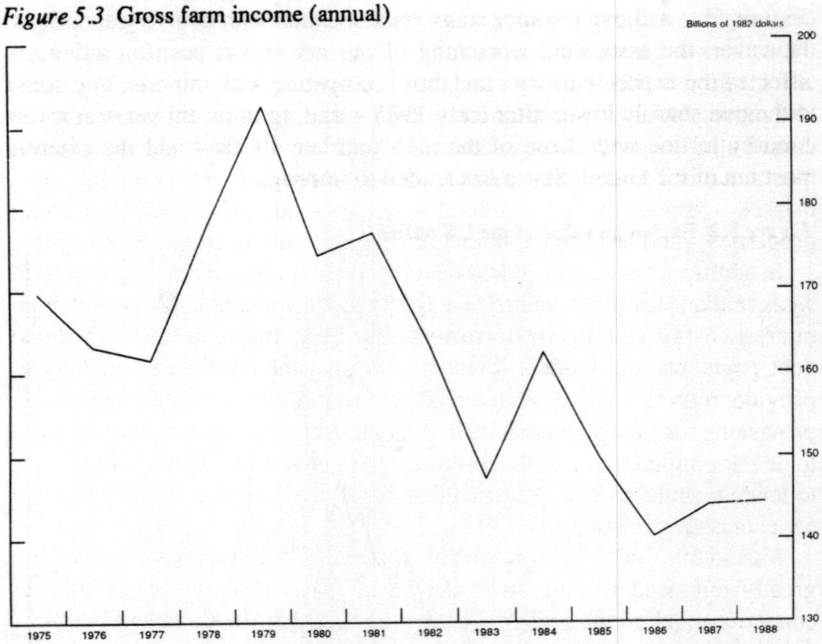

Figure 5.4 Producer price index for crude oil

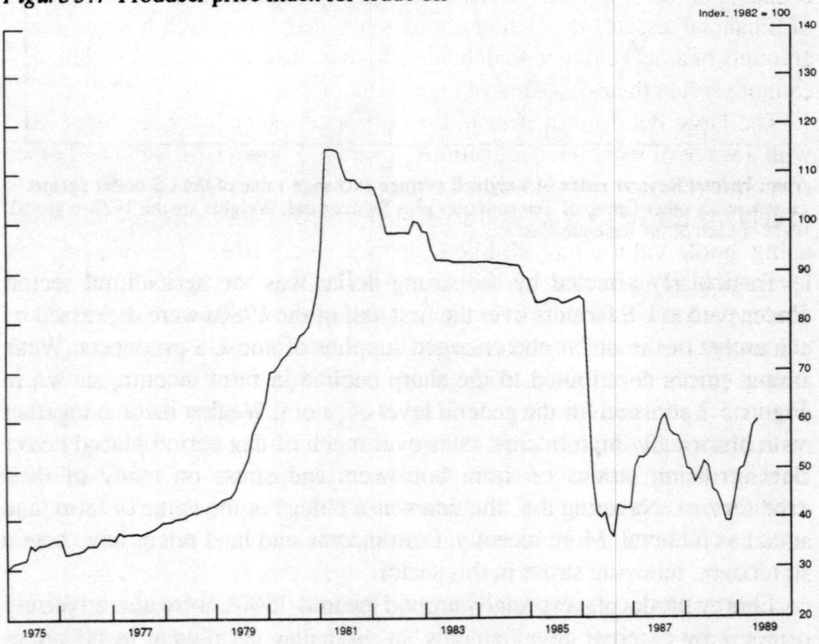

(Figure 5.4). Although lower energy prices enabled the incomes of many of the economy's borrowers to stretch further, energy producers experienced a sharp drop in their earnings and their ability to service their debts. Owing to the geographical concentration of the energy industry, this development contributed to generalized weakness in the southwestern United States, most notably Texas. This weakness showed through to the local real estate market – especially the market for commercial, office and residential properties – and has been a major contributor to the thrift crisis.

In addition, bank loans to less developed countries have soured owing to weak markets for these countries' exports and, for much of this period, high interest costs on the loans. Borrowers have been unable to meet scheduled debt payments and lenders – recognizing that the credits are unlikely to provide returns in line with original expectations – have made large provisions for losses on such debt. A great deal of effort has been devoted to developing internationally co-ordinated approaches that will limit losses to lenders while providing financial resources to borrowers that are needed for economic growth.

Meanwhile, debt growth in the household and business sectors has greatly outpaced income since the early 1980s (Figure 5.5), adding to concerns about credit quality. The degree to which the surge in household debt has been placing strain on the household sector is somewhat uncertain because, in the aggregate, it has been accompanied by a massive build-up of financial assets; those household units that have accumulated large amounts of assets along with debt have built a cushion in the event that they cannot service their debts out of current income.

The large build-up of debt in the corporate sector has been associated with a wave of mergers, acquisitions, leveraged buyouts (LBOs) and other corporate restructurings, in which equity has been retired with the proceeds of debt. As can be seen in Figure 5.6(a), the ratio of debt to equity measured using book values has climbed steeply since 1983. In contrast, the leveraging ratio measured using market values has not shown much tendency to rise over this period owing to very strong gains in share prices; evidently, the stock market viewed this development as consistent with strong corporate earnings despite the additional interest outlays. Many analysts have seen higher debt levels accompanying such corporate restructuring as imposing more discipline on managers to maximize the earnings from corporate assets, thereby enlarging cash flow available for debt service. Nevertheless, the segment of the corporate sector that has added to its leverage is more vulnerable to an earnings disruption or to a significant increase in borrowing costs, and this has been a source of concern to policymakers. A common financing device used in corporate restructuring – especially LBOs – has been low-rated or so-called junk

Figure 5.5 (a) Ratio of household debt to disposable personal income; (b) ratio of corporate debt to gross domestic business product

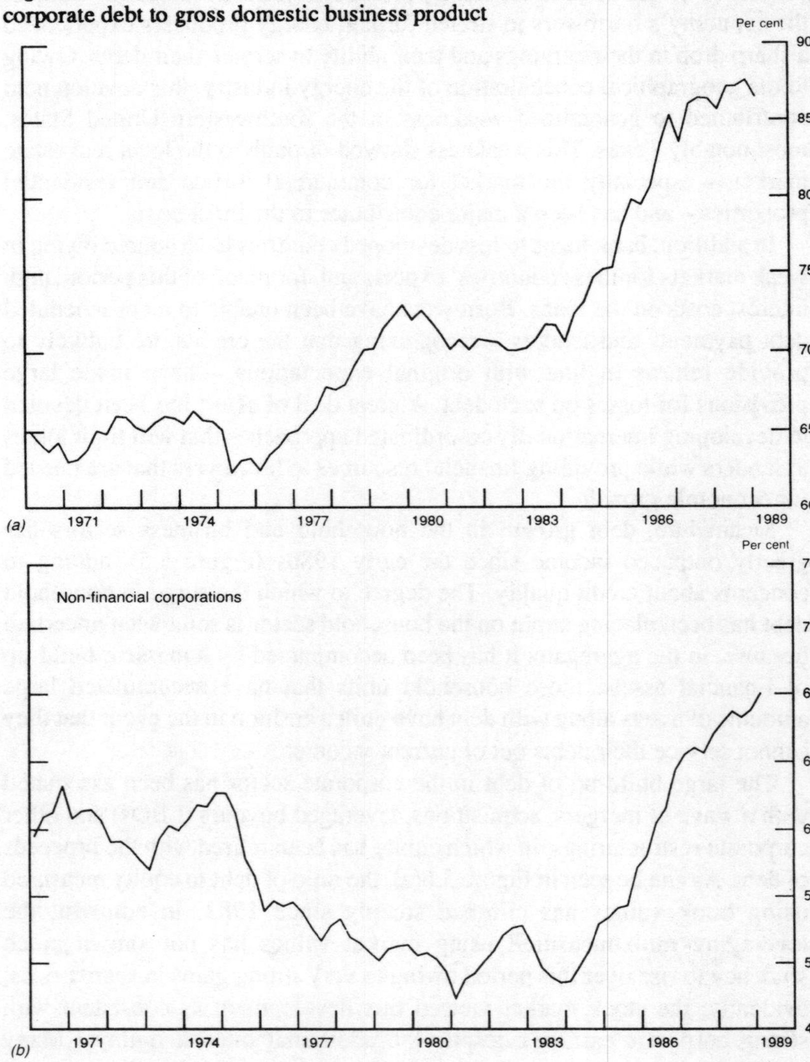

bonds. Figure 5.7 shows that issuance of publicly offered junk bonds rose sharply after 1986 and that the bulk of such offerings has financed corporate restructurings.

A review of major developments affecting financial markets would be incomplete without some discussion of the October 1987 stock market crash. The plunge in share prices on 19 October was the largest single-day

Figure 5.6 Debt-to-equity ratios for non-financial corporations: (a) book value (annual); (b) market value (quarterly)

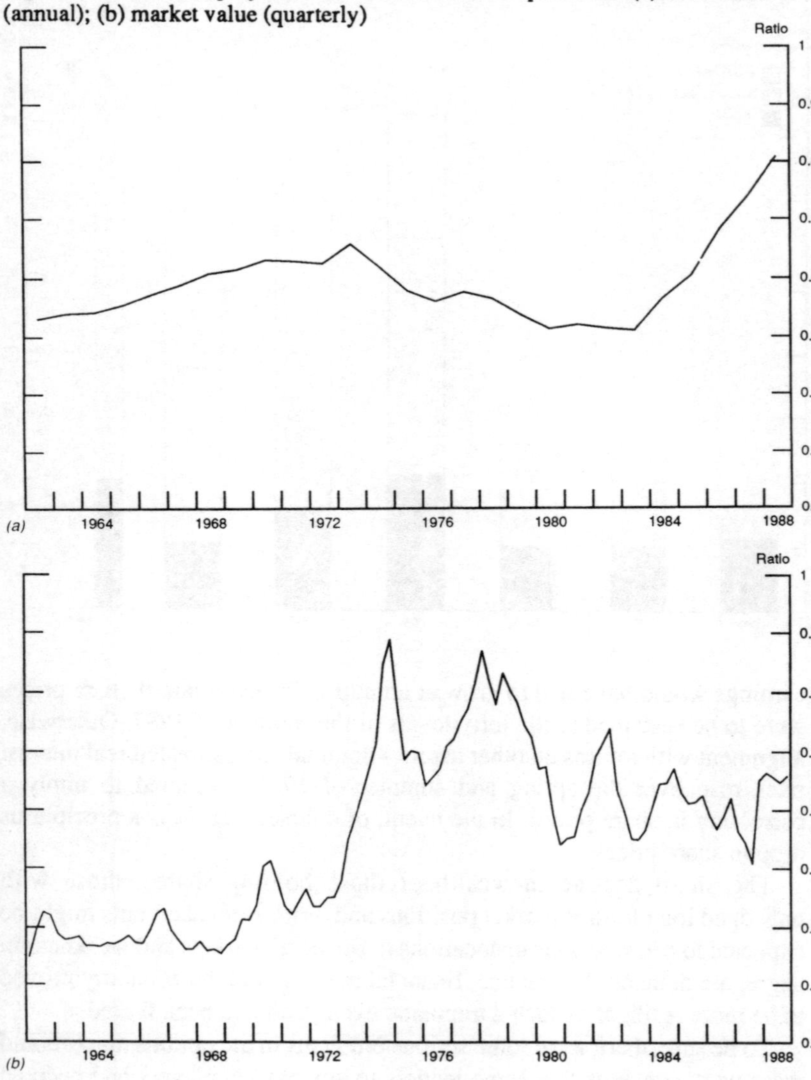

decline on record and, as shown in Figure 5.8, followed some large declines on previous days. At this point there is no consensus of opinion on what caused the sudden drop. What is clearer, however, is that prices climbed to historically very high levels, even when allowing for the rise in corporate earnings shown in Figure 5.8(c). Re-establishing a more typical relationship of price to earnings – and to other asset returns – implied that

Figure 5.7 New public issues of low-rated bonds

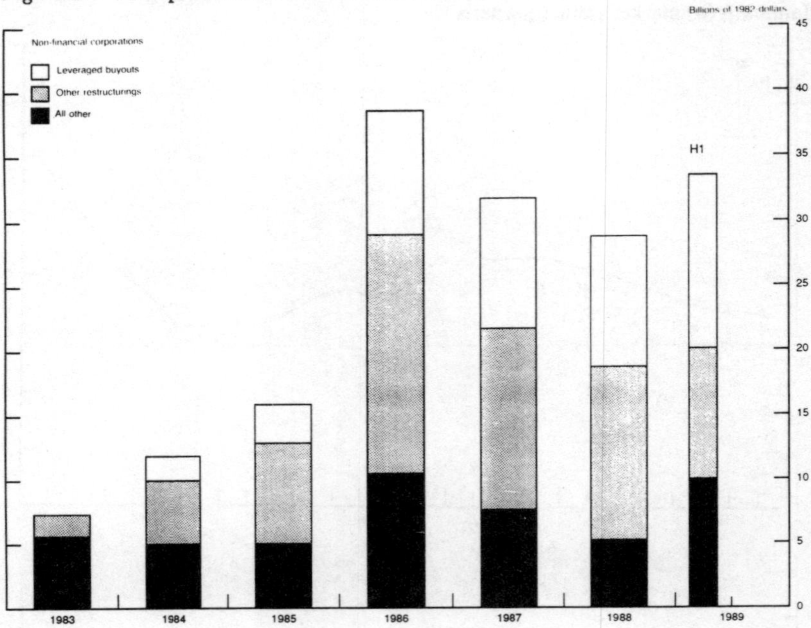

earnings would have had to grow at an unusually rapid rate if share prices were to be sustained at the lofty levels of the summer of 1987. Otherwise, alignment with returns on other assets – nominal and estimated real interest rates rose over the spring and summer of 1987 – seemed to imply a correction in share prices. In the event, of course, there was a precipitous drop in share prices.

The sharp decline in wealth of those holding shares, those with unhedged long futures market positions and writers of naked puts might be expected to cause serious dislocations in financial markets and weakness in aggregate demand. In practice, financial markets and the economy proved to be more resilient to such a traumatic event than had been feared.

To be sure, there were some serious problems in the options markets and there were concerns that some lenders to key market players had become too cautious. In addition, most studies of the crash have concluded that the systems that clear and settle transactions in securities and their derivatives displayed vulnerability. Since the time of the crash, the exchanges and clearing organizations have moved to augment their capacity and strengthen their systems while many market participants have modified their behaviour in ways that should reduce pressures on the system in the event of another market break.

Figure 5.8 Stock market indicators: (a) Dow Jones industrial average; (b) Dow Jones industrial average and S&P 500 stock price index; (c) price-to-earnings ratio

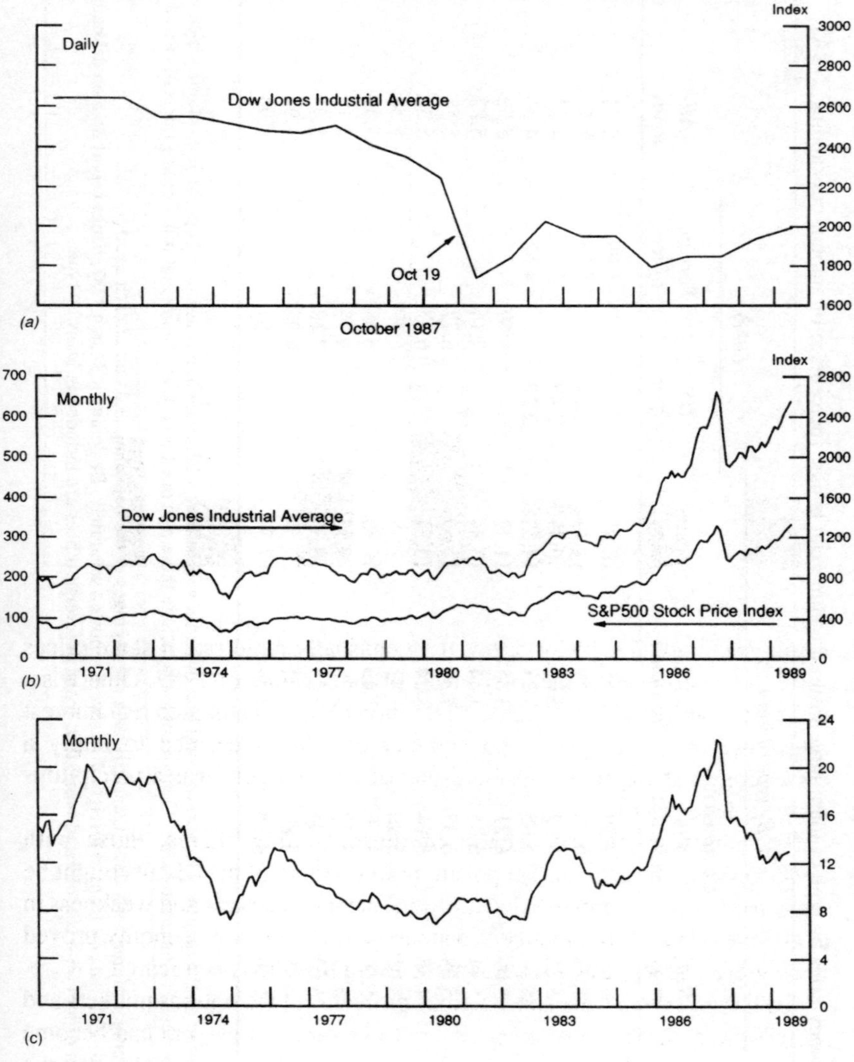

Source: Standard & Poor's

Implications for financial institutions and markets

In reflection of the various strains on the economy and financial system, delinquency rates on bank loans were very high around the mid-1980s, as shown in Table 5.2, but since then have on balance declined. In particular,

Table 5.2 Delinquency rates by type of loan: large insured commercial banks[a] (percentage of amount outstanding, NSA)

<table>
<tr><th rowspan="3">Period[b]</th><th colspan="6">By type of loan</th><th rowspan="3">All loans</th><th rowspan="3">All banks</th></tr>
<tr><th rowspan="2">Real estate</th><th rowspan="2">Commercial and industrial</th><th rowspan="2">Consumer</th><th rowspan="2">Farm</th><th colspan="2">Others</th></tr>
<tr><th>US office</th><th>Foreign office</th></tr>
<tr><td>1983</td><td>6.61</td><td>7.39</td><td>2.65</td><td>10.85</td><td>3.78</td><td>4.95</td><td>5.74</td><td>5.54</td></tr>
<tr><td>1984</td><td>5.79</td><td>6.18</td><td>2.59</td><td>11.14</td><td>2.64</td><td>5.76</td><td>5.11</td><td>5.01</td></tr>
<tr><td>1985</td><td>5.25</td><td>5.59</td><td>3.01</td><td>9.39</td><td>2.47</td><td>5.50</td><td>4.73</td><td>4.78</td></tr>
<tr><td>1986</td><td>5.24</td><td>5.65</td><td>3.27</td><td>11.52</td><td>2.10</td><td>4.52</td><td>4.51</td><td>4.72</td></tr>
<tr><td>1987</td><td>5.09</td><td>6.21</td><td>3.35</td><td>11.77</td><td colspan="2">6.69</td><td>5.52</td><td>5.38</td></tr>
<tr><td>1987 : Q1[c]</td><td>5.44</td><td>6.45</td><td>3.44</td><td>13.84</td><td colspan="2">7.14</td><td>5.82</td><td>5.72</td></tr>
<tr><td>Q2</td><td>5.08</td><td>6.35</td><td>3.30</td><td>12.69</td><td colspan="2">6.77</td><td>5.58</td><td>5.46</td></tr>
<tr><td>Q3</td><td>4.80</td><td>6.14</td><td>3.24</td><td>10.54</td><td colspan="2">6.37</td><td>5.32</td><td>5.17</td></tr>
<tr><td>Q4</td><td>5.05</td><td>5.90</td><td>3.41</td><td>9.99</td><td colspan="2">6.49</td><td>5.34</td><td>5.16</td></tr>
<tr><td>1988 : Q1</td><td>5.36</td><td>5.69</td><td>3.43</td><td>10.89</td><td colspan="2">6.68</td><td>5.39</td><td>5.21</td></tr>
<tr><td>Q2</td><td>5.23</td><td>5.32</td><td>3.28</td><td>9.95</td><td colspan="2">6.75</td><td>5.19</td><td>5.03</td></tr>
<tr><td>Q3</td><td>5.03</td><td>5.04</td><td>3.25</td><td>8.35</td><td colspan="2">7.10</td><td>5.07</td><td>4.87</td></tr>
<tr><td>Q4</td><td>4.91</td><td>4.80</td><td>3.41</td><td>7.59</td><td colspan="2">6.96</td><td>4.94</td><td>4.75</td></tr>
<tr><td>1989 : Q1</td><td>5.10</td><td>4.78</td><td>3.51</td><td>7.59</td><td colspan="2">6.81</td><td>4.98</td><td>4.81</td></tr>
</table>

Notes:
[a]These data are reported on the quarterly Report of Condition by banks with at least US$300 million in assets, except the last column which is calculated for all insured US-chartered commercial banks. Delinquent loans include those past due thirty days or more and still accruing interest, as well as those on non-accrual status.
[b]Annual data are averages of quarterly data. Quarterly data are averages of the beginning and end of each quarter.
[c]Series break: prior to 1987 data on loans in foreign offices were reported separately. Beginning in March 1987, banks report data on delinquent loans in domestic and foreign offices on a consolidated basis; thus loans in foreign offices are included in loans by type.

farm loan delinquencies were running at around 10 per cent or higher but more recently have declined appreciably. Delinquencies on business loans (those on commercial and industrial loans) and real estate loans similarly were running high but more recently have drifted lower. Consumer loan delinquencies, while smaller in level, have tended to climb in recent years while delinquencies on other loans – which include less developed country loans – have remained relatively high. Loan charge-offs, which generally follow delinquencies, rose distinctly around 1985, as shown in Table 5.3, but more recently have tended to level off or decline.

Another indicator of credit quality in the business sector is downgradings of corporate debt in relation to upgradings (Figure 5.9(a)). Over the 1980s the number of downgradings has been very high, particularly in relation to upgrading. Indeed, the period of economic expansion since the 1981–2 recession has been one of unusually heavy downgradings, especially in view of the fact that such downgrading activity typically diminishes as an expansion matures. In part, downgradings in recent years have reflected the sharp rise in corporate leveraging arising from the unprecedented wave of corporate mergers and restructurings. Reflecting downgradings as well as heavy issuance of junk bonds in recent years, the distribution of bonds by rating has moved lower, as shown in Figure 5.9(b); indeed, the median rating of industrial bonds dropped from A in 1983 to BB in 1988.

The period since the mid-1970s has been one of great interest rate risk as well as credit risk. Interest rates are shown in Figure 5.10. Interest rate risk and volatility increased markedly at the end of the 1970s, an event widely associated with the Federal Reserve's shift to a reserves-based change in operating procedure in October 1979. The objective of the operating procedure was to obtain tighter control over the money stock in order to curb inflationary pressures more effectively. A by-product of this change was more scope for movements in short-term interest rates. As can be seen in Table 5.4, both short-term and long-term rates became highly volatile in late 1979 and the early 1980s. Volatility has diminished subsequently but remains above that of the 1970s.

These events heightened the sensitivity of financial market participants to interest rate risk, leading to many behavioural adaptations and new financial products, including financial futures and options. In particular, those depository institutions that traditionally had raised short-term funds to hold long-term assets, most importantly thrift institutions, sought various ways to control and limit exposure to interest rate risk; some did so through changes in portfolio management, including the use of interest rate futures and other hedging instruments.

Other important developments have occurred since the mid-1970s. The

Table 5.3 Charge-offs net of recoveries by type of loan: large insured commercial banks[a] (percentage at annual rate of average amount outstanding, NSA)

	Real estate loans	Loans to financial institutions	Commercial and industrial loans			Consumer loans	Total
			All	US addressees[b]	Non-US addressees[b]		
1981 : Q1	0.01	−0.01	0.38	0.42	0.08	1.06	0.33
Q2	0.00	0.03	0.29	0.39	0.14	0.91	0.27
Q3	0.06	−0.09	0.35	0.43	0.25	0.88	0.29
Q4	0.15	−0.03	0.55	0.61	0.44	1.04	0.43
1982 : Q1	0.03	−0.01	0.36	0.31	0.18	0.86	0.29
Q2	0.10	0.03	0.57	0.72	0.26	0.90	0.42
Q3	0.12	0.12	0.85	1.35	0.29	0.79	0.58
Q4	0.24	0.05	0.92	1.71	0.48	0.97	0.65
1983 : Q1	0.08	0.16	0.75	0.65	0.43	0.87	0.52
Q2	0.17	0.03	0.94	0.81	0.65	0.80	0.60
Q3	0.16	0.18	1.20	1.04	0.89	0.68	0.72
Q4	0.20	0.11	1.22	1.26	1.42	0.85	0.81
1984 : Q1	0.11	0.06	0.78	0.97	0.57	0.69	0.51
Q2	0.28	0.09	1.38	1.62	0.82	0.80	0.84
Q3	0.30	−0.02	1.31	1.40	1.10	0.80	0.83
Q4	0.31	0.06	1.22	1.32	0.96	1.01	0.83
1985 : Q1	0.17	0.00	0.77	0.80	0.68	0.98	0.57
Q2	0.19	0.32	0.86	0.81	1.01	1.14	0.68
Q3	0.21	0.05	1.10	0.90	1.67	1.29	0.77
Q4	0.32	0.23	1.34	1.26	1.60	1.58	0.99

	Real estate loans	*Loans to financial institutions*	*Commercial and industrial loans*			*Consumer loans*	*Total*
			All	*US addressees*[b]	*Non-US addressees*[b]		
1986 : Q1	0.20	0.30	0.85	0.77	1.11	1.58	0.72
Q2	0.36	0.50	1.11	1.02	1.39	1.63	0.91
Q3	0.41	0.48	1.17	1.20	1.08	1.61	0.93
Q4	0.54	0.23	1.45	1.41	1.55	1.72	1.06
1987 : Q1	0.38	0.14	0.75	0.73	0.81	1.64	0.75
Q2	0.40	0.32	0.99	0.94	1.16	1.63	0.82
Q3	0.48	0.34	0.85	0.79	1.09	1.52	0.82
Q4	0.67	1.49	1.30	1.05	2.34	1.81	1.31
1988 : Q1	0.39	1.08	0.78	0.55	1.74	1.62	0.96
Q2	0.73	0.98	1.24	1.24	1.25	1.62	1.22
Q3	0.42	1.03	0.83	0.84	0.77	1.59	1.04
Q4	0.54	0.83	1.07	0.80	2.41	1.73	1.20
1989 : Q1	0.40	0.66	0.59	0.54	0.81	1.74	0.78

Notes:
[a]These data are reported on the quarterly Report of Condition by banks with at least US$300 million in assets. Data are consolidated (foreign and domestic offices).
[b]Available only for banks with foreign offices or Edge or agreement corporations.

Figure 5.9 Debt ratings for non-financial corporations: (a) changes in Moody's corporate bond ratings; (b) distribution of bonds by rating for 1983 and 1988

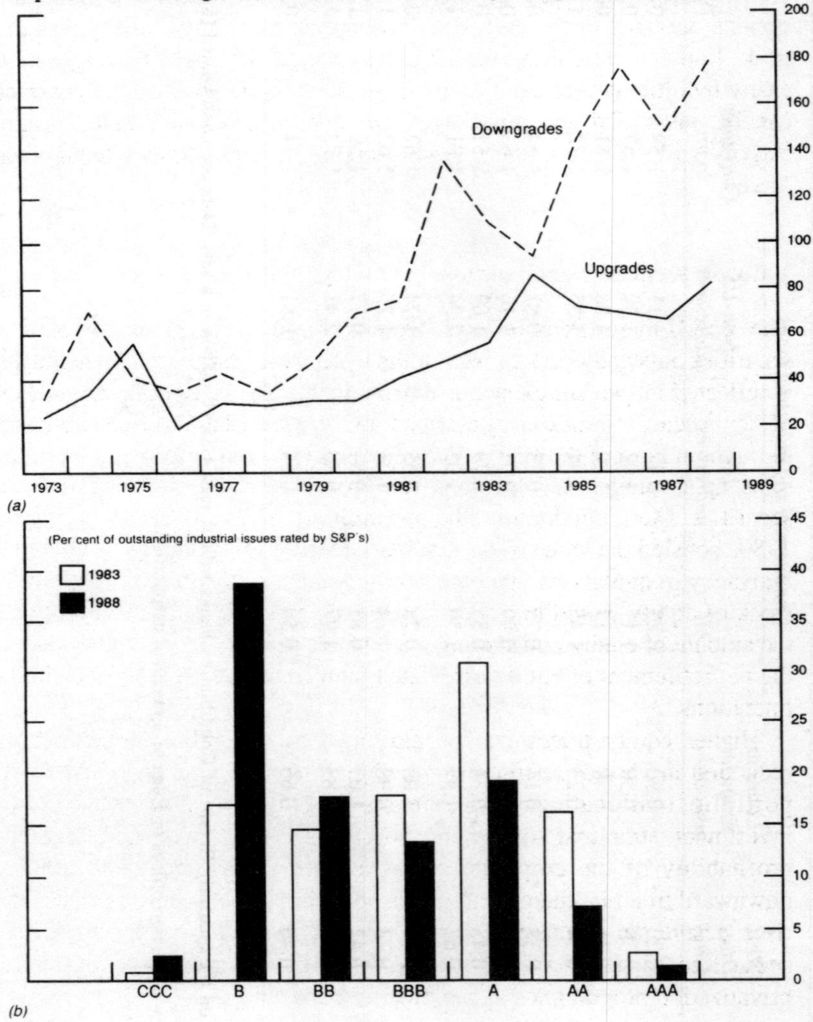

deregulation of deposit rates began in mid-1978 when a new retail deposit instrument, the six-month money-market certificate, was introduced with a regulatory rate ceiling that adjusted with rates in the open market. In early 1980, landmark legislation was enacted, the Depository Institutions Deregulation and Monetary Control Act, that mandated the removal of all interest rate ceilings in an orderly fashion by April 1986. In practice, rate ceilings were taken off in a piecemeal manner, with the final measures

Figure 5.10 Treasury rates (monthly)

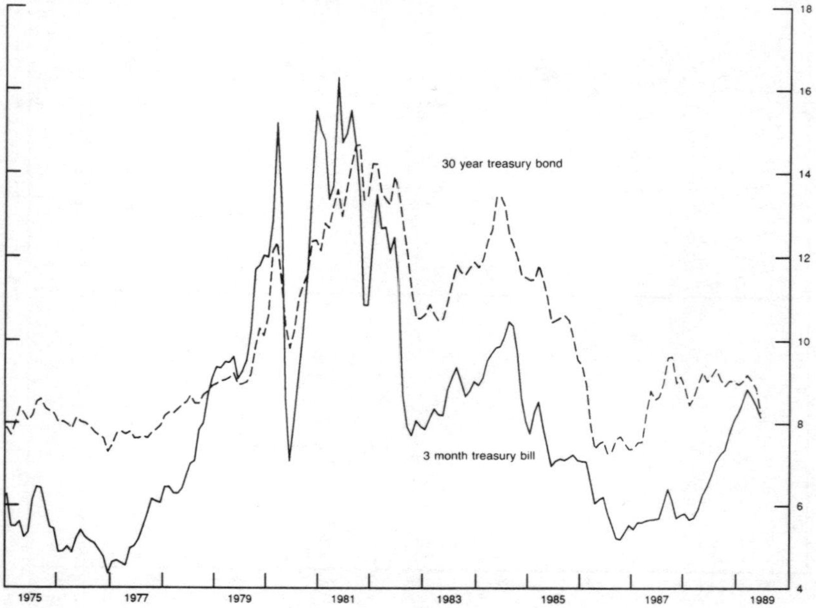

occurring in early 1986; at present, only demand deposits are subject to a constraint, that being the statutory prohibition on the payment of interest on such accounts.

Asset quality problems of US banks along with narrower interest rate spreads took their toll on bank earnings, especially for some institutions. As can be seen in Figure 5.11, earnings as a percentage of assets weakened over the first half of the 1980s, with the erosion being highly pronounced at the poorer performing institutions (the lowest 5 per cent in earnings). The weakest performers have shown some recovery in recent years. In the

Table 5.4 Interest rate volatility (standard deviation of daily changes, in basis points)

	Treasury bill, three-month	*Certificate of deposit, three-month*	*Treasury bond, thirty-year*
1975–9	5.6	5.3	2.7
1979–82	28.7	32.0	14.3
1982–9[a]	8.0	8.3	7.5

Note: [a] Through June 1989

Figure 5.11 Dispersion of bank earnings

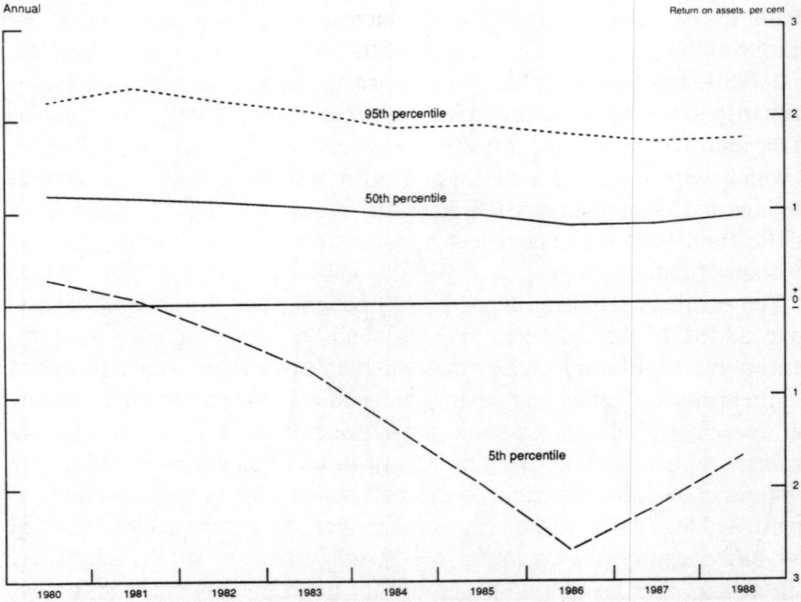

Figure 5.12 Dispersion of thrift earnings

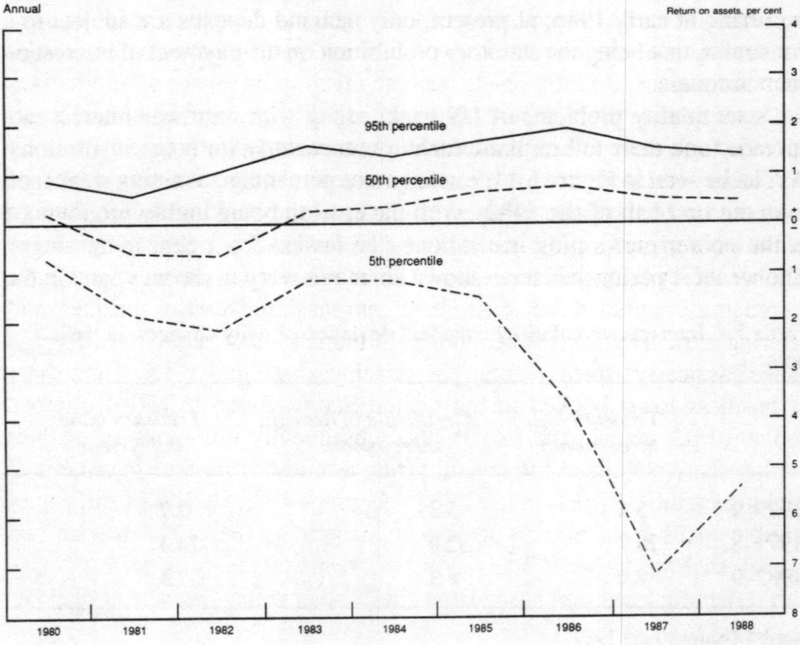

thrift industry (Figure 5.12) earnings were very depressed in the early 1980s by the adverse movement in interest margins accompanying the sharp rise in rate levels. The top half of the industry recovered around the mid-1980s at a time when the poorer earners slipped dramatically, owing primarily to severe credit problems. In recent years, a significant segment of the industry has become insolvent – in many cases by very large amounts – which wiped out the industry's deposit insurance fund (the Federal Savings and Loan Insurance Corporation), requiring a massive infusion of public funds and major legislative restructuring of the industry and its insurance fund.

The earnings problems faced by US banking and thrift organizations have added to their costs of raising funds in the wholesale markets. Moreover, regulatory policy has shifted towards increased capital requirements for banks and savings institutions. As capital requirements became more binding, banks and thrifts sought new ways of conducting business without adding to assets subject to such requirements. This took the form of so-called off-balance-sheet activities, such as standby letters of credit, and loan sales; in the case of the former, the international accord on risk-based capital requirements has sought to cover off-balance-sheet transactions that involve a substitution of off-balance-sheet risk for on-balance-sheet risk.

To the above developments must be added that borrowers and lenders in the financial market place have become much more sophisticated. Against the backdrop of the computer revolution and vast improvements in telecommunications, investors have become much more aware of alternatives and sensitized to yield differentials and risk differentials while borrowers have become more aware of alternative borrowing opportunities.

Closely related to this development has been a rising level of competition in the financial market place. In the banking sector, foreign banks have gained a presence in the credit markets by establishing a large number of banking offices, mainly in major money centres, and have increasingly pursued US customers, emphasizing credit services and offering attractive terms. The number of branches and agencies of foreign banks has nearly tripled over the past dozen years (Figure 5.13). Their share of business loans booked in the United States (Figure 5.13(b)) climbed above 10 per cent in the late 1970s; subsequently this measure of their market share stabilized for several years, as authorization of international banking facilities (IBFs) in late 1981 encouraged a great deal of shifting of eligible loans from branch and agency books to IBFs. The branch and agency share of business loans, however, resumed climbing after 1985, in part reflecting loans purchased from other banks as the loan sale market has burgeoned.

Figure 5.13 Agencies and branches of foreign banks: (a) number of agencies and branches; (b) agency and branch loans as a percentage of loans booked in the United States

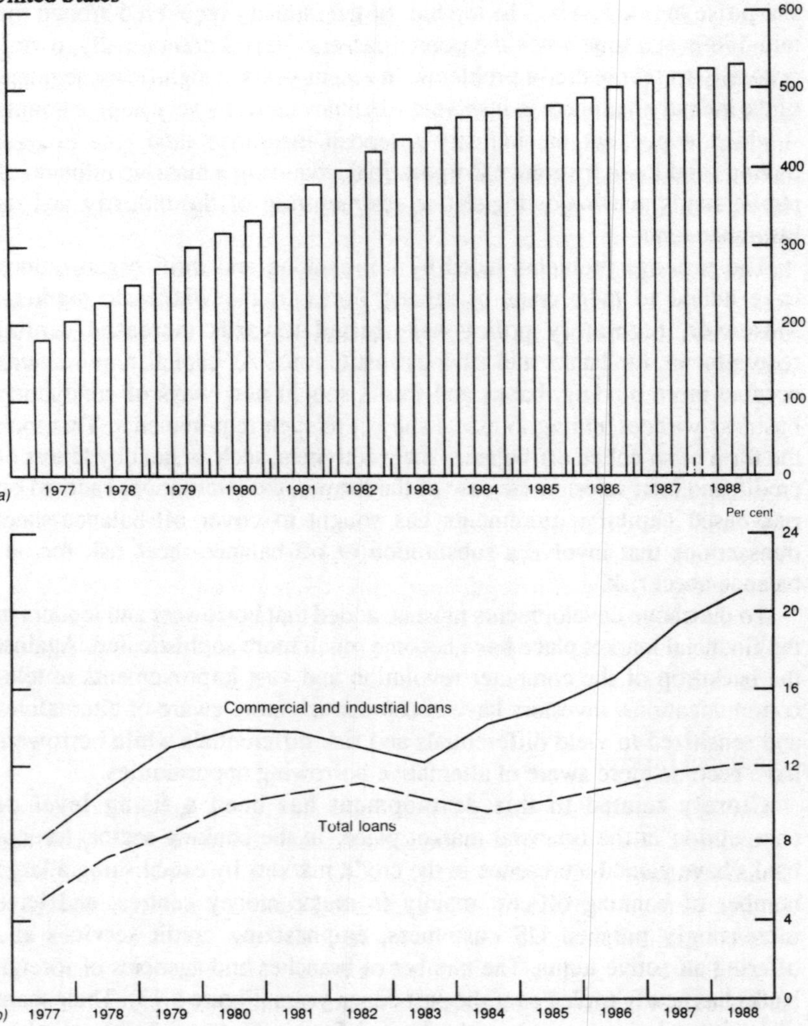

In addition, business access to the open markets has improved over this period, most visibly in the commercial paper market which has expanded several-fold from only about US$10 billion outstanding in the mid-1970s. Many borrowers have gained access to this market through bank credit lines supporting their paper issuance or bank standby letters of credit. Also, a growing number of firms have been able to tap the bond market, for long-term credit, as the so-called high-yield or junk bond market has mushroomed.

In sum, the inflation–disinflation process and shifts in the competitiveness of US producers in global markets – along with large swings in oil prices – has led to some major economic dislocations that have affected the quality of credit rather broadly. This, in turn, has had a major impact on the earnings and solvency of thrift institutions, and to a lesser extent commercial banks. In many cases, the situation has stabilized or improved. Superimposed on this setting has been a tendency for financial markets to become more competitive. In the case of the thrift industry, however, a significant segment has been weakened by extraordinary credit losses – not to mention the segment of the industry that failed – and it will take some time before financial soundness is restored to this sector of the industry.

RESPONSES OF THE US FINANCIAL SYSTEM

Against the background of heightened interest rate and credit risk and growing competition, financial institutions and markets have responded in a multitude of ways, many more than can be addressed in this chapter. Among those covered here are increasing reliance on futures markets as a means of shifting risk, generally more prompt adjustment of deposit and loan rates to changes in open-market rates, off-balance-sheet activities and asset sales by depositories and securitization of credit.

Financial futures

From their introduction in the 1970s, financial futures and options activity has soared. The types of contracts traded and the number of exchanges trading futures and options contracts have risen sharply. Interest rate futures were introduced in 1976 and have come to figure prominently in efforts to shift interest rate risk. The more volatile interest rate environment of the late 1970s and early 1980s was a major contributor to expansion in this market. Interest rate futures are a means available to commercial banks and savings institutions to limit their exposure to the interest rate risk associated with maturity mismatches, traditionally a more serious problem for thrift institutions that have depended on short-term deposits to fund long-term mortgages. Interest rate futures have also been used by underwriters of credit market instruments to limit their exposure to interest rate risk while they are originating and distributing new issues. Another major user of interest rate futures has been securities dealers with large trading account positions.

While a large number of interest rate futures instruments are available, those on treasury bills, Eurodollar time deposits and treasury bonds have come to be dominant in the market. Because the correlation between prices in these markets and prices on other securities is less than perfect, participants using such futures contracts to cover positions in other securities are left with some risk, so-called basis risk. On occasion, hedgers using contracts in these instruments, especially treasury bonds, to cover positions in other securities have incurred appreciable losses owing to differential movements in prices.

Of more recent significance have been futures and options on stock indexes, a development accompanying the appreciation in equities prices following mid-1982. These instruments enable market participants to shift risk associated with generalized market price developments. To some investors, the availability of futures and options was seen as a means of preserving returns on a portfolio of securities; to do this, the investor would sell a futures contract or acquire a put option on a stock price index matching the securities actually held. A related strategy – so-called dynamic hedging or portfolio insurance – calls for the selling of futures contracts (or shares themselves) as equity prices decline or buying them as share prices rise. Such a strategy depends on the ready availability of a liquid market for adjusting futures or cash market positions; the experience of October 1987 demonstrated that such conditions cannot be counted on, especially during those times when they are needed most, and use of dynamic hedging is reportedly down significantly.

Some large investors have come to use index futures as a means of promptly adjusting positions in a portfolio of securities while avoiding the price impacts on individual shares that would accompany large cash market transactions. Use of the market for futures and options is also seen as a low-cost means of participating in generalized advances or declines in market prices; transactions costs associated with positions in options and futures are typically much lower than for cash positions. As a consequence, price movements frequently occur in futures and options contracts before they appear in the cash market; indeed, many sophisticated arbitrage strategies have been developed to profit from disparities between cash and futures market prices. Many of these are computer-driven strategies and, together with dynamic hedging, come under the heading of 'programme trading'.

Some believe that programme trading, such as index arbitrage, has contributed to stock market volatility in recent years, although the evidence on this matter does not lend much support to the view. Others argue that, because of major technological developments, more investors receive relevant information bearing on asset values simultaneously and are able to trade promptly on such information; as a consequence, potentially large short-term price movements are inevitable, with or without the market for derivatives.

In general, the growing availability of financial futures and options has enabled interest rate and market risk to be shifted towards those economic units better positioned and more willing to absorb it. As noted above, the availability of financial futures and options has probably also encouraged more underwriting and trading, enhancing liquidity and affording borrowers greater access to the markets. On the other hand, these markets permit those who are ill equipped to take on large speculative positions; this has consequences for others in the markets as well as the strength of those markets.

Pricing of loans and deposits

At commercial banks, the process of deregulation of retail deposit rates together with competitive forces have led to more prompt adjustment of deposit rates to movements in open-market rates. The resulting pressures on costs have also contributed to more prompt adjustment of loan rates to open-market rates. This has been especially true of small- and medium-sized banks. Larger banks traditionally have relied more on wholesale funds and have long been under greater pressure to keep loan rates in alignment with those in the open market, as their wholesale borrowing costs, largely the certificate of deposit and federal funds rates, tend to move closely with other open-market rates. At the time that the deregulation process began in the late 1970s, deposit and loan rates moved very little at smaller banks, even when open-market rates moved quite sharply. Subsequently, at small- and medium-sized banks both deposit and loan rates have become more responsive to market developments.

The pricing of business loans became more directly tied to open-market rates over this period, especially at larger banks. Contributing to the move from pricing loans off the prime rate, an administered rate, to an open-market reference rate were foreign banks that were aggressively seeking a market share through their branches and agencies. Today, it is very common for business loan customers to have loan commitments containing both prime and open-market base rate options. In practice, customers of the larger banks elect money-market reference rate loans more frequently than prime rate loans, as shown in Table 5.5. In May 1989, less than a third of business loans at the very large money centre banks were linked to the prime rate while about a sixth were linked to the federal funds rate and another fifth were tied to other domestic money-market rates, such as the certificate of deposit or treasury bill rate. Loans linked to foreign interest rates (including the London interbank offering rate) also accounted for a fifth. At other large banks, the prime-based share is about the same as for the money centre banks and the share priced off the federal funds rate and other domestic money-market rates is higher. The bulk of business loans made by the smaller banks – two-thirds of the total – continues to be tied to the prime, although market-based lending by these institutions has been increasing over time.

Table 5.5 Pricing of business loan extensions at US banks (May 1989)

	Percentage of loan extensions		
Reference rate	*Money centre banks*	*Other large banks*[a]	*Other banks*
Prime rate	30	32	64
Federal funds rate	15	26	10
Other domestic money-market rate	19	20	8
Foreign rate	22	4	3
Other	14	18	15

Note: [a]Banks with assets of about US$5 billion or more.

Meanwhile, some larger banks have sought to use deregulated retail deposits as a means of reducing their dependence on wholesale funds. Retail deposits generally have been viewed as a more stable source of funds than wholesale or managed liabilities, especially at times when the availability of funds in the wholesale market may be quite sensitive to shifts in sentiment about the strength of banking organizations. Moreover, some institutions evidently have viewed the substitution of core deposits for wholesale funds as lowering interest costs over the long run; at times, they have used their freedom to set retail deposit rates to bid aggressively for such balances, apparently with the expectation of reducing rates on these accounts after an introductory period or rolling them over at lower rates. As can be seen in Figure 5.14, the share of assets funded by retail core deposits rose appreciably at both large money centre banks and other large banks in late 1982 – associated with a major deregulatory measure permitting banks and thrifts to offer an account competitive with money-market mutual funds – and has subsequently drifted higher. Since the mid-1980s, money centre banks have funded half or more of their assets with core deposits. Viewed somewhat differently, the concern about the quality of large bank loan portfolios, heightened by events involving less developed country debt since 1982, has added to the premium that banks in general, and some especially vulnerable banks in particular, have had to pay for wholesale funds. This, in turn, has added to the attractiveness of federally insured retail deposits to the degree that holders of such deposits by having this insurance protection are not as likely to be sensitive to such developments.[1]

Figure 5.14 Core deposits of large banks (as a percentage of assets)

Note: Banks with assets in excess of US$1 billion.

Capital requirements, standby letters of credit and loan sales

Meanwhile, regulatory capital requirements have stiffened, in recognition of the riskiness of various bank activities and from a desire to limit exposure of the federal deposit insurance fund to risk. For the large banks, capital requirements were tightened both formally, by specifying a minimum primary capital ratio above those that many large banking organizations had in practice, and informally, through the examination and applications process. Because off-balance-sheet activities were initially excluded from formal capital requirements, an incentive existed to expand such activities in lieu of placing loans on the books of the bank.

In particular, standby letters of credit (Figure 5.15) soared from around US$40 billion in 1980 to about US$170 billion in 1985. Through a standby letter of credit, a bank could support the commercial paper or notes or bonds of a customer but avoid maintaining the level of capital that would be required if the customer's obligation had been booked as a loan. The market regards the customer's obligation backed by the standby letter of credit much as it regards the bank's obligation, enabling the customer

Figure 5.15 Standby letters of credit at all insured commercial banks

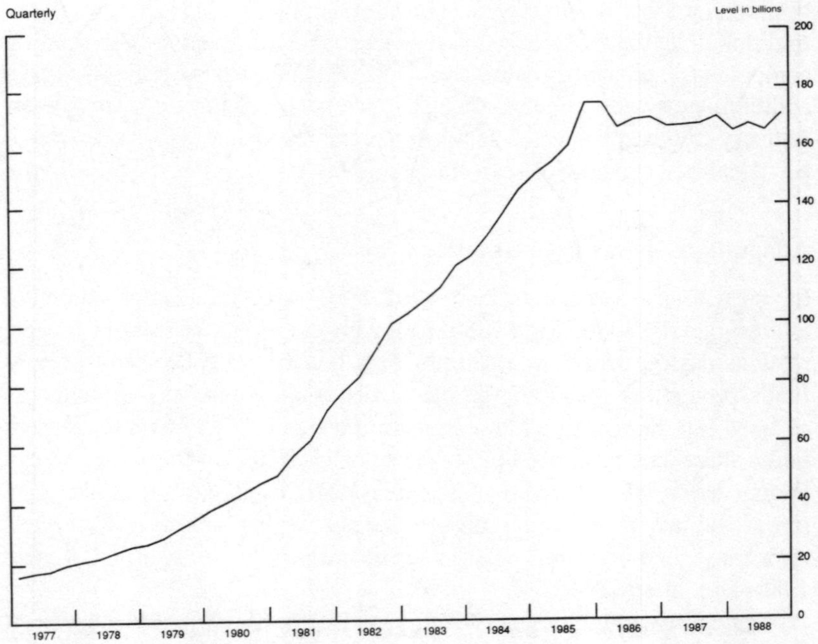

access to markets on terms comparable with those of the bank. This development had been a factor encouraging the separation of the commercial bank credit support function from the funding function. Since 1985, however, the volume of standby letters of credit has declined as regulators came to consider them informally in the examination and applications review processes and as support grew for a more comprehensive risk-based capital standard that would include these and other off-balance-sheet activities posing risk to the bank in the formal computation of capital requirements. The latter effort took on an international dimension when the United States and other Group of Ten authorities agreed to harmonize capital requirements and to base these requirements on the riskiness of the activity, be it on or off the bank's balance sheet.

In addition, larger banks have increasingly originated loans with a view to selling them or participating them out. In this way, the bank can collect origination and servicing fees by advancing credit to an established customer; however, once the loan has been sold the bank need not hold capital against it, provided that the buyer does not have recourse to the bank in the event of default (through standby letter of credit or other guarantee). To date, a good portion of such loans sold by large banks have been sold to other banks – including foreign banks – presumably those facing less binding capital requirements. This development also breaks up the traditional lending function, in this case into origination and funding components, and further unbundles the traditional banking relationship. In addition, a growing number of banks have been structuring sales of their ordinary automobile loans and credit card receivables as pass-through participations in a pool of such claims.

Adaptations by savings institutions

Savings institutions came to realize the extent of their vulnerability to interest rate risk in the early 1980s following the rise in the level of interest rates across the maturity spectrum. This quickly added to their cost of funds, predominantly shorter-term deposits, while returns on their holdings of fixed rate mortgages did not register a compensating increase; indeed, under these circumstances mortgage borrowers became less inclined to prepay their relatively low fixed rate mortgages, leading to a more sluggish upward adjustment of asset returns to the new higher level of market rates. As a consequence, savings institutions incurred massive losses in the early 1980s and failures soared.

Among those that have survived, a number have devoted greater effort to managing interest rate risk. These institutions and their supervisors now follow more closely their interest rate risk exposure by monitoring gaps between maturities of assets and liabilities. Several methods have been used to shorten the repricing interval on assets and to lengthen the repricing interval on liabilities. One widely used method is the adjustable rate mortgage. Such mortgages typically have the same maturity as the standard fixed rate mortgage but carry interest rates that adjust at regular intervals to

Figure 5.16 Conventional home mortgages closed: (a) effective interest rates; (b) proportion with adjustable rate features

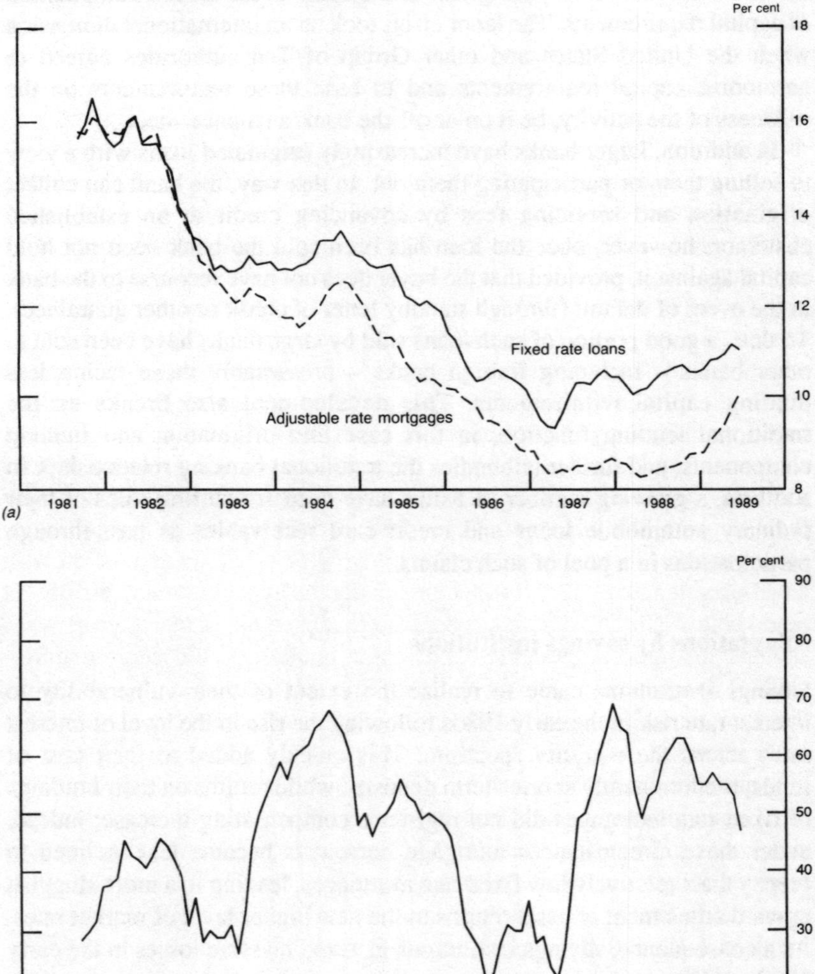

a benchmark rate. Benchmark rates commonly are the yield on one-year treasury securities or a published measure of the cost of funds to savings institutions. As shown in Figure 5.16(b), the share of conventional mortgages made, i.e. new mortgage originations, with adjustable rate features has frequently been one-half or more since 1984; that share tends to be high when initial rates on these mortgages are low in relation to those on fixed rate mortgages (Figure 5.16(a)). Borrowers none the less continue to show a preference for fixed rate mortgages and it has taken rather large rate differentials, at times enlarged by the lender granting concessionary terms in the first year of the mortgage, to attract such borrower interest in adjustable rate mortgages. Moreover, the experience of recent years indicates that many with adjustable rate mortgages are quick to re-finance with fixed rate mortgage credit when rates on fixed rate mortgages fall markedly.

Another more recent method used by savings institutions to shorten the effective maturity of the assets is the collateralized mortgage obligation (CMO). The CMO is a multiclass pay-through bond that is secured by mortgages or mortgage pass-through securities. Repayments (including prepayments) are applied to different classes of bondholders at different scheduled rates. The CMO enables the cash flow from a pool of mortgages, which is inherently uncertain owing to the prepayment or call option attached to the underlying mortgage loans, to be structured into various broad maturity classes. A number of savings institutions have found the short maturity classes of CMOs to be an attractive form in which to hold mortgage assets because they have effective maturities more in line with their deposit liabilities and yields that exceed those on highly liquid money-market instruments. More recently, CMOs have been offered with an adjustable rate feature, further enhancing the appeal to many thrifts. As noted below, CMO issuance has been quite substantial in recent years, with savings institutions thought to be major holders of the short maturity classes. In some cases, thrifts retain the shorter maturity classes of CMOs that they themselves issue while in others they acquire these classes from other issuers.

Another means of lengthening effective liability maturities by a number of savings institutions has been the interest rate swap. In an interest rate swap, the thrift in effect trades an adjustable rate obligation, i.e. a regularly repriced obligation, for a fixed rate obligation. The overall swap market has risen dramatically from virtually nothing in the early 1980s to several hundred billion dollars more recently, with savings institutions representing a significant share of those acquiring the fixed rate component.

As noted above, some savings institutions have used futures and options to reduce interest rate risk. Another more recent device that has come to be used is the stripping of interest from principal in pools of mortgages creating so-called interest-only and principal-only portions. Regarding the interest-only securities, the average length of the interest flow from a pool of mortgages will depend on the level of interest rates. As interest rates fall and principal prepayments pick up, cash flow on the interest-only securities declines. Conversely, if interest rates rise and prepayment activity slows, cash flow on the interest-only portion increases. As a consequence, the interest-only portion is thought to be a hedge against a rise in market rates for an institution having a maturity mismatch in the form of more long-term assets than liabilities. Some thrifts reportedly have acquired interest-only portions of mortgage pools as a hedge.

Meanwhile, the savings industry has responded to maturity imbalances, higher capital requirements and borrower preferences for fixed rate mortgages by originating fixed rate mortgages for sale. In this way, firms in the industry can continue to meet customer demands for mortgages and earn an origination and servicing fee while not aggravating maturity mismatches and avoiding the corresponding capital requirements. Fixed rate mortgages can be sold to other depository institutions but most often are sold to the Federal National Mortgage Association (FNMA) or the Federal Home Loan Mortgage Corporation (FHLMC), two federally related agencies that play a central role in the secondary mortgage market. These institutions pool such mortgages and issue pass-throughs.[2] Another federal institution, the Government National Mortgage Association (GNMA), guarantees payments on pass-through securities issued against pools of federally insured mortgage loans (those insured by the Federal Housing Administration or guaranteed by the Veterans Administration).

These various measures by savings institutions to reduce interest rate risk have been somewhat successful and the industry as a whole is now less vulnerable than earlier in the 1980s to a large unexpected rise in interest rates. Nevertheless, as noted above, a substantial segment of the industry has moved into or close to insolvency. The plight of this segment of the industry, though, is principally due to credit problems arising from depressed local economies or poor credit judgement, especially in areas where new lending or investment powers had been granted. To guard against a repetition of this experience, new legislation enacted in August 1989 imposes stiffer capital requirements on these institutions – they are to be no less stringent than those applicable to banks – and places certain restrictions on investment and lending powers.

Securitization

The securitization of loans, a major recent development, has been most evident in the mortgage market. The principal form of security in this market is the mortgage pass-through, in which holders receive an undivided interest in a pool of mortgages. As Figure 5.17 illustrates, mortgage pass-throughs – represented by the area between the solid and broken lines – have grown from negligible proportions in the early 1970s to nearly US$800 billion in mid-1989 or to a little more than a third of all residential mortgage debt. The strong growth in mortgages around the mid-1980s and borrower preference for fixed rate mortgages helped to boost pass-through volume substantially.

Figure 5.17 Home mortgage debt outstanding

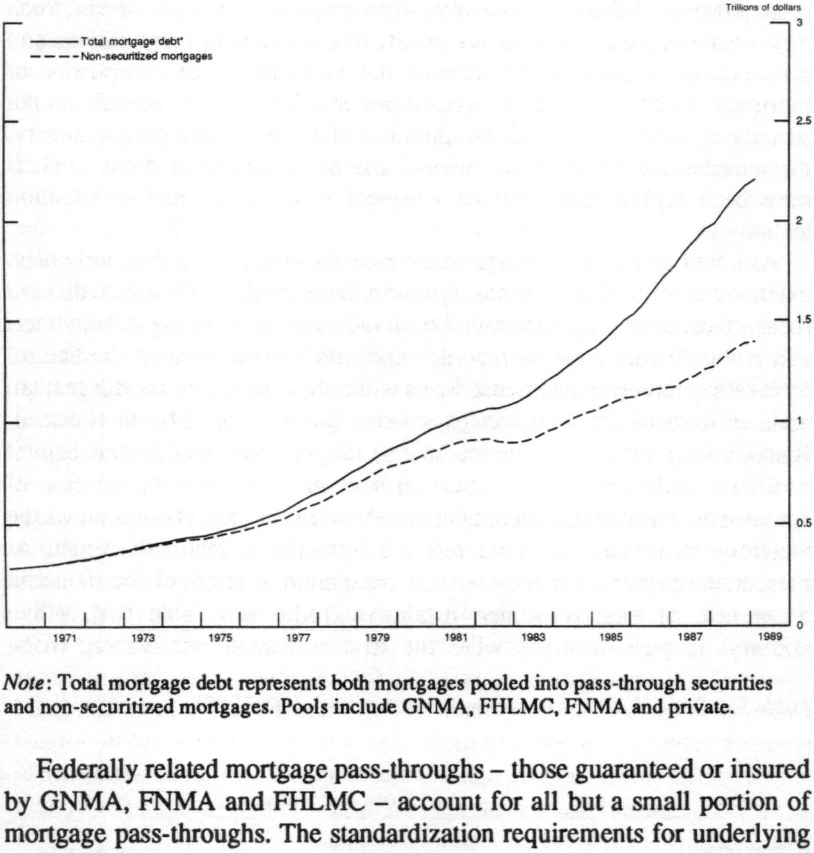

Note: Total mortgage debt represents both mortgages pooled into pass-through securities and non-securitized mortgages. Pools include GNMA, FHLMC, FNMA and private.

Federally related mortgage pass-throughs – those guaranteed or insured by GNMA, FNMA and FHLMC – account for all but a small portion of mortgage pass-throughs. The standardization requirements for underlying mortgages, the liquidity generated by the size of the market and, probably most importantly, the federal support of the pools no doubt has led to the dominance of federally related pass-throughs. Nevertheless, even though such securities are not viewed as entailing much credit risk to investors, they do embody a significant amount of prepayment risk. As already noted, mortgage prepayments tend to rise as mortgage rates fall – reflecting refinancing of existing mortgages and more turnover of homes – and decline as mortgage rates increase; this relationship is a relatively loose one and thus associated slippages add to prepayment uncertainty and risk. Consequently, mortgage pass-through yields contain a premium over federal government securities of comparable expected maturity that largely reflects such prepayment uncertainty. This premium tends to vary with interest rate volatility.

Mortgage pass-through securities have become the raw material for various derivative products. These include CMOs and interest-only and principal-only obligations, discussed above, issued by private entities. Such instruments represent alternative means of dealing with prepayments and prepayment uncertainty. In view of the high degree of complexity of mortgage securities – such as assembling and maintaining records on the underlying mortgages, principal and interest payments and prepayments – the introduction of these instruments and development of these markets have been highly dependent on advances in computer and information technology.

As noted above, the concept of the pass-through has subsequently been extended to other kinds of loans, primarily automobile loans and credit card receivables. In addition, consumer receivables in the form of pleasure boats and mobile homes have been pooled and sold into the market. Credit card receivables represent unsecured loans while the others, like mortgages, are collateralized by the automobiles or other durable goods being financed. Banks selling off such loans are able to relieve some pressure on capital positions while collecting origination and servicing fees. In the case of automobile loans, prepayment uncertainty to the investor is minimal, as the incentive to prepay when interest rates change is relatively small. At present, the amount of securitized consumer credit is relatively small, about 5 per cent of total consumer instalment credit (see Table 5.6). While automobile pass-throughs were the first consumer receivables to be

Table 5.6 Securitized consumer credit outstanding (June 1989)

	Amount (billions of dollars)	*Percentage of total*
Automobile	12.7	4.4
Revolving	17.1	9.0
Other	4.9	2.2
Total	34.7	4.9

securitized in volume, securitized credit card receivables (included in the revolving credit category) have overtaken them recently in size and now comprise nearly a tenth of all revolving consumer credit.

The term securitization has been applied to much more than pools of mortgages and consumer loans and their derivative instruments. Some have viewed as securitization the growing reliance on the commercial paper market by firms that had been heavily dependent on commercial banks – in some cases their paper has bank credit enhancement through standby letters of credit or loan commitments – and also sales of business loans. In addition, the growing ability of many lower-rated firms to tap the public bond market as an alternative to long-term bank financing has been regarded as securitization. As shown in Figure 5.7, issuance of high-yield (or below-investment-grade) bonds has roughly doubled since 1985 and accounts for a significant share of total bond volume. This increase, however, is largely accounted for by offerings associated with corporate restructurings, typically by established firms (in many cases, firms that previously had debt rated as investment grade). Still, the volume of below-investment-grade bonds brought to market by other issuers is quite substantial.

As securitized assets work their way into investor portfolios and compete with traditional securities, the linkage between interest rates on loans that can be securitized and those on open-market instruments becomes tighter. Investor behaviour directed towards maximizing yield – adjusted for credit, interest rate and prepayment risk – tends to bring rates on loans that can be securitized into closer alignment with each other and with competing market instruments. Also, the originators of loans and the underwriters of securitized assets must keep a close eye on yields on assets that they compete with in investor portfolios when they make loans and acquire them for securitization.

A good illustration of tightening linkages can be seen in Figure 5.18, dealing with the commitment rate on fixed rate home loans and the ten-year treasury bond yield, a maturity that is roughly comparable with the expected life of a thirty-year mortgage. The figure illustrates the average change in the mortgage rate, measured in basis points, in the week in which the treasury yield changed, standardized to be a 10 basis point change. In the late 1970s, the short-run responsiveness of mortgage rates was minimal, less than a basis point change per 10 basis point change in treasury yields in the same week; it took a fairly long time to adjust. Responsiveness picked up a little over the first half of the 1980s. The most dramatic change, though, has come in the past few years, accompanying the previously mentioned surge in mortgage pass-throughs; on average in the 1988 to mid-1989 period, the change in the mortgage rate has reached nearly 9 basis points per 10 basis point change in the treasury rate in the same week. Today, active mortgage lenders each day follow closely developments having a bearing on domestic credit markets, such as the foreign-exchange market and indicators of the pace of the economy and inflationary pressures, and adjust their lending rates promptly to such developments.

Figure 5.18 Concurrent-week change in mortgage rate per 10 basis point change in ten-year treasury yield

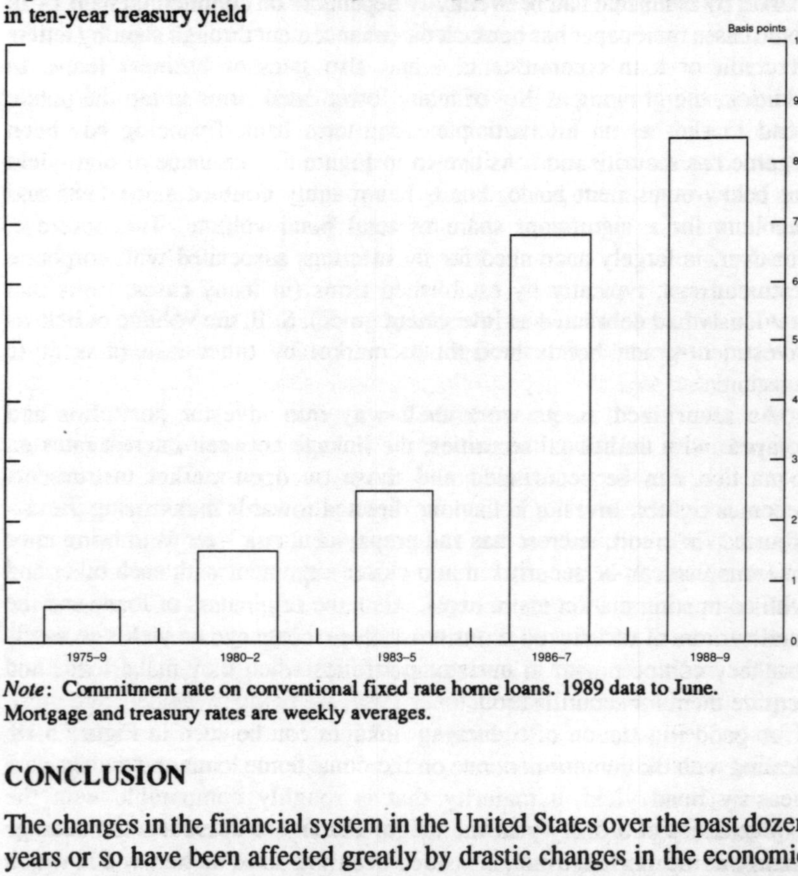

Note: Commitment rate on conventional fixed rate home loans. 1989 data to June. Mortgage and treasury rates are weekly averages.

CONCLUSION

The changes in the financial system in the United States over the past dozen years or so have been affected greatly by drastic changes in the economic setting. Interest rates have swung widely over this period, in large part reflecting changing inflation experience and expectations; in addition, interest rates have come to be viewed as inherently more volatile than was thought in the mid-1970s. While the US economy has been expanding steadily since late 1982 and overall slack in resource utilization has diminished, debt-servicing strains on the part of many borrowers have at times been substantial. This has reflected not only a much diminished inflation rate, including on real estate acquired as an inflation hedge, but in addition a depressed agricultural sector together with weakness in the energy sector and other imbalances associated with a large erosion in the US net export position; in many cases, underlying economic conditions have stabilized or improved and accompanying financial strains have abated. Also impairing the capital position of some lenders have been debt problems of less developed countries.

The confluence of these events – resulting to an important degree from disinflation, global economic slack earlier in the decade and a strong dollar over much of this period – clearly was not envisioned by financial institutions and markets. Nevertheless, it has had a pronounced effect on attitudes and behaviour. Participants in financial markets generally have become more aware and sensitive to interest rate and credit risk. Against this background, there has been a growing array of financial products that enable financial institutions and others to adjust and shift risk exposure to suit their preferences and absorption capacities, some of which have been discussed in this chapter.

Also not envisioned was the plunge in share prices that occurred in October 1987 and the turmoil that accompanied the fall. A number of investors had developed portfolio insurance strategies that they thought would allow them to preserve the large price advances that they had enjoyed and at the same time participate in any further gains in share prices. In practice, these strategies did not work very well as the markets proved to be less accessible and liquid than had been presumed. In response, the use of such portfolio insurance has fallen off – a factor that would probably relieve pressures in the stock market in the event of another large price decline. In addition, the major exchanges have augmented their capacity to handle orders, which could further reduce congestion in the event of another market break. Clearing and settlement systems, an area of considerable vulnerability in October 1987, are being revamped, and more effort is being devoted to domestic and international co-ordination of clearing and settlement in view of the considerable interdependence of these systems.

Capital positions of financial intermediaries – especially commercial banks and savings institutions – have been impaired by heavy economic losses, owing to debt-servicing strains on many of their customers. Measures taken by these institutions in recent years to limit risk exposure and new regulatory restrictions are expected to reduce their vulnerability to economic shocks in the future. The growing use of hedging instruments is one such development that can limit risk exposure. However, many of these instruments – especially those involving mortgages and their uncertain prepayments – contain elements of risk that are not fully known and may not be fully understood by users.

The securitization process is another development bearing on depository risk. Banks and savings institutions have been able to continue to originate and service credit while avoiding the losses associated with defaults or unfavourable interest rate movements, provided that these credits are not sold with recourse to the originator.

Federal exposure continues to be important in the case of the mortgage pass-through securities market, the largest area of securitization thus far. Indeed, it seems in this period of heightened concern about credit quality and financial stability that investors have sought the protection of a direct or indirect federal credit enhancement. Nevertheless, investors are adding securities to their portfolios without such protection, e.g. below-investment-grade bonds and securitized consumer receivables, and as they do they are absorbing the accompanying interest rate and credit risk and thereby lessening the exposure of bank and thrift capital positions.

This development, by affecting the incidence of economic losses and the exposure of the financial system, may affect spending behaviour and the way that the economy functions. Spending behaviour may be affected differently if economic losses are absorbed directly into the public's portfolios than if they are absorbed by bank and thrift capital positions. Probably more importantly, the securitization process has led to a prompt impact of interest rate and credit market developments on loan markets. Indeed, owing to the tighter integration of US financial markets with those abroad, international influences on local credit markets are growing.

NOTES

The views expressed in this paper are those of the author and do not necessarily reflect the views of the Board of Governors of the Federal Reserve System or other members of its staff.

1 The added premium that many banks now pay has encouraged more high-grade corporate borrowers to go directly to the open market for credit because bank costs have been under upward pressure owing to the larger premium they have paid for funds. In essence, the credit quality of banking organizations has fallen in relation to many of their premium customers, making open-market credit relatively less costly to such bank customers.

2 Savings institutions also swap mortgages for mortgage pass-through securities containing the mortgages sold. Pass-through securities are more liquid than the underlying mortgages themselves and can be used as collateral for certain kinds of borrowing.

6 The reform of the French financial system

Didier Bruneel

CAUSES OF THE FINANCIAL INNOVATION PROCESS

Until recently, financing of the French economy depended mainly on the intermediation of banks, and the negotiable securities markets played only a secondary role. From 1980 onwards, these markets have developed gradually and decisively in a context of intense deregulation and financial innovation. An uncertain environment marked by wide variations in inflation, interest and exchange rates has led lenders and borrowers to reduce their risk exposure, with the following results:

— a reduction in exposure period as a result of shortening maturities or by recourse to techniques such as redeemable 'window' bonds, 'exchange clause' bonds and revolving bonds etc.;
— a dampening of the impact of interest rate fluctuations on security values by the use of variable or adjustable rates;
— a development of techniques for hedging interest and exchange rate risks by means of the financial futures and negotiable options markets and the expansion of repurchase or swap agreements (of interest rates or maturities).

These changes have been accentuated by changes in the patterns of the financing needs and capacities of economic agents.

The financing needs of the non-financial corporate sector stood at almost 5 per cent of gross domestic product (GDP) in the early 1980s and have decreased consistently. In 1987 they totalled only 1.3 per cent of GDP. However, the funding requirements of general government (central and local government, social security), which were previously insignificant, are now running at nearly 3 per cent of GDP.

The funding capacity of the household sector has only dropped slightly but has squeezed housing investment. The relative stability of the household financial savings ratio (5.1 per cent in 1980 and 4.1 per cent in

1986) masks an increased preference for financial market securities over traditional bank deposits (a preference which was maintained in 1988, after the October 1987 stock market crash).

The active role played by the authorities in the process of financial innovation and modernization of the financial system is undeniably one of the most salient features of the experience in France. This role is partly due to the need felt by the state to improve its debt management (creation of markets in short-term negotiable securities) or to cut budget expenditure (reduction in the amount of credit granted at preferential rates). But the authorities have also sought to increase competition so as to bring about a better allocation of resources and trim intermediation costs. Finally, the setting up of a unified capital market was a prerequisite for the implementation of a more active interest rate policy and the abandonment of a fossilizing system of credit ceilings.

As a result of these reforms, the French financial system is now more geared to operate along the lines of a 'market economy' than an 'overdraft economy'. This process does of course entail major changes for the banking system and the management of monetary policy.

THE SHIFT FROM AN OVERDRAFT ECONOMY TO A MARKET ECONOMY

What was known in France as an overdraft economy was characterized by

— the overriding importance of bank credit in the financing of the economy,
— a substantial creation of money and a significant 'transformation' (investment financing by liquid resources) and
— interest rates that were kept artificially low (under government pressure) and thus were not fulfilling their theoretical role as automatic regulators.

In this context, economic growth was strong and investments grew as a result of companies' heavy indebtedness (the low interest rates contributing to a 'leverage effect'). However, the price paid for this apparently positive result was as follows:

— a high rate of inflation fed by money creation (the average retail price rise was 6 per cent in France between 1949 and 1976 compared with 2.7 per cent and 3.3 per cent for West Germany and the United States respectively);
— a rapid deterioration in the value of the franc (1 Deutschmark was worth 2.30 francs in 1979 compared with 0.83 francs in 1949);

— a maladjustment in France's industrial potential; artificially low interest rates failed to provide an optimal allocation of resources and encouraged unprofitable investments at the expense of more promising operations.

The growth of financing and investment sources other than banks has moved in four directions: equity and bond markets have flourished; short-term negotiable securities have been created and the money market has been reformed; financial futures and options markets have been set up; exchange controls have been dismantled.

Growth of equity and bond markets

The equity market

Equity issues by companies listed on the Bourse rose from 3 billion francs in 1979 to 67.5 billion in 1986 (45.7 billion in 1987), whereas over the same period capitalization increased from 234.8 billion to 1,150.3 billion (967 billion in 1987) and the volume of transactions moved from 48.1 billion to 427.3 billion (522 billion in 1987).

Measures to encourage new issues

The new reforms were intended to facilitate access to the market for companies which had been excluded either on account of their size or because of their shareholding structure.

— To promote the issue of equity-equivalent securities by family-run businesses or nationalized companies, non-voting shares were introduced, i.e. preference shares and investment certificates.
— To facilitate access to the stock market by medium-sized companies, a 'second market' was put in place as an intermediate between the official and over-the-counter markets. This reform was based on foreign practice (particularly the British unlisted securities market). Conditions for introduction onto this market are less stringent than for the official market.

Measures have also been taken to encourage companies to bolster their capital: registration fees are no longer required on cash increases in capital; from 1983 onwards companies can offer their shareholders dividend payment in the form of shares, etc.

Rising demand for equities

The 'Monory' law of 13 July 1978, which made it possible to deduct as much as 5,000 francs per married couple from taxable income for net investment in French shares, was intended to stimulate personal shareholding. This objective was indeed attained, for in 1981 1.5 million taxpaying households took advantage of the tax deductions and the percentage of shareholders among households rose to 10 per cent, compared with 5 per cent in 1975. However, the decisive factor in the renewed demand for securities has undoubtedly been the marked appreciation in prices since 1983.

This trend reversal is mainly due to the recovery in corporate margin rate. The latter (the share of gross operating surplus in added value), which ran at about 25.3 per cent from 1976 to 1979, had fallen to less than 24 per cent in 1981 and 1982. It moved forward from 1983 and settled in 1986 at 27.2 per cent, thus recovering its early 1970 level.

Privatization operations in 1987 contributed markedly to a further increase in the number of shareholders. The Paris Bourse reacted particularly well to the October 1987 stock market crash since, in 1988, the increase in prices reached 58 per cent. Then, in 1988, stock exchange reform was promoted, the main features of which are the suppression of the stockbrokers' monopoly in operations and the elaboration of a code of conduct for operators.

Table 6.1 Main stock exchanges (in terms of capitalization of French shares and volume of transactions)

	Capitalization	*Volume of transactions*
United States	24	52
Japan	12	18
United Kingdom	4	4
West Germany	2.2	4
Canada	2	2
Switzerland	1.1	3
France	1	1

With the development of the market, operating procedures have been modernized: securities have been dematerialized; there is now a continuous trading market; commissions have been cut. Despite its growth, the Paris Bourse is still only the seventh in the world (Table 6.1).

The bond market

Volume of issues

Having long been a marginal source of financing, the bond market has now expanded considerably. As Table 6.2 shows, the volume of gross issues increased sharply from 1980 onwards, reaching 7.1 per cent of GDP in 1986 and 5.3 per cent in 1987.

Table 6.2 Gross issues

	1972	*1979*	*1980*	*1986*	*1987*
In billions	28.9	65.6	111.7	346.2	282.9
As percentage of GDP	2.9	2.7	4.0	7.1	5.3

On the secondary market, transactions moved up from 63.2 billion francs in 1980 to 1,716.5 billion in 1986 (2,426 billion in 1987). Stock market capitalization of bonds increased threefold over the same period (567.4 billion at the end of 1980, 1,974.0 billion at the end of 1986 and 2,051 billion at the end of 1987).

Measured by the ratio of net issues to GDP, the French bond market is the largest in Europe (Table 6.3).

Table 6.3 Ratio of net issues to gross domestic product

	1985	*1986*
	(%)	(%)
West Germany	4.3	4.5
United Kingdom	3	1.9
France	5.2	5.4
United States	13.8	12.2
Japan	7.7	8.6

Categories of issuer

The notable increase in the budget deficit from 1980 onwards and the desire of the Treasury to place strict limits on money creation led the government to issue bonds on the market. A prudential concern to consolidate bank liabilities and a very restrictive control of bank credit financed by monetary resources encouraged financial institutions to increase their own issues.

Government and bank issues accounted for the greater part of the growth in the primary bond market. Non-financial companies, despite increased issuing activity by the 'large state-owned companies', saw their share in total issues shrink to less than 10 per cent in 1987 as against more than 30 per cent in 1975. Foreign issuers still remain few even though the volume of issues rose to 4.2 billion in 1987 compared with 1.1–1.5 billion in previous years.

Investors

When the changing share of investors is examined, it appears that undertakings for collective investment in transferable securities (UCITS) are increasing (Table 6.4). Although the demand for securities has risen as a result of the improved yields on bond savings, it has also been helped by newly created short-term UCITS.

Table 6.4 Shares of the different categories of investor

	1982	*1986*
Private individuals	47.6	21.0
Undertakings for collective investment in transferable securities (UCITS)	10.2	33.3
Of which, short term	–	16.3
Insurance companies	15.4	15.4
Pension funds	6.5	5.8
Companies, associations, miscellaneous	19.1	22.7
non-residents	1.2	1.8
	100	100

Source: Credit Lyonnais

Three factors have combined to make bond investment particularly attractive: high real interest rates, a steady decline in nominal interest rates since mid-1981 and favourable tax treatment.

Whereas from 1975 to 1980 interest rates on the bond market were only slightly higher than inflation rates, and even sometimes lower as in 1975 and 1979, they rose considerably after this. Since 1982, they have consistently exceeded the rise in retail prices by 4 points.

The tax regime has acted as a stimulus for private individuals. Income from non-indexed French bonds is subject to a withholding tax in settlement of income tax at a rate of 25 per cent (1 per cent higher since 1984). Capital gains realized through the sale of securities are taxed at a rate of only 15 per cent (1 per cent higher since 1984) beyond a certain ceiling of exemption (265,000 francs in 1986). This tax incentive has been even more beneficial since the fall in interest rates from 1982 made it possible to make considerable capital gains.

The demand for bonds has been all the stronger as competing investment instruments have become less attractive. Two measures have had a decisive influence in this respect: the introduction of ceilings on the rate of interest payable on deposit accounts and cash certificates in September 1981 and the progressive increase in tax on these instruments (Table 6.5).

Table 6.5 Rate of withholding tax (percentage)

	Time deposits and registered notes	*Bearer notes*	*Bonds*	*Short-term negotiable securities*
29 Nov 1965–1 Jan 1975	25	25	25	–
1 Jan 1975–15 Jul 1978	33⅓	33⅓	25	–
16 Jul 1978–31 Dec 1979	40	40	25	–
1 Jan 1980–31 Dec 1982	38	42	25	–
1 Jan 1983–31 Dec 1983	45	50	25	–
1 Jan 1984–31 Dec 1985	46	51	26	46
1 Jan 1986–31 Jul 1987	46	51	26	33
1 Aug 1987–	47	52	27	34

Finally the short-term UCITS, i.e. short-term mutual funds (fonds communs de placement, FCPs) and short-term open-ended unit trusts (sociétés d'investissement à capital variable, SICAVs), created in 1982 in reaction to the stiffer regulations on deposit rates, have played an important role in reorienting savings towards the bond market. These UCITS are in a better position than individuals or companies to manage interest rate risks (floating rate securities, repurchase agreements, operations on the financial futures market) and offer their investors a very high degree of liquidity along with a return at market rates; they have accordingly met with much success.

The creation of short-term negotiable securities and the reform of the money market

The expansion of the securities markets was achieved by refining techniques and diversifying instruments. These changes have challenged traditional distinctions made between financial assets:

— the frontier between shares and bonds has been blurred with the appearance of non-voting shares and subordinated loans;
— the frontier between bonds and monetary assets has become less clear as a result of the very high degree of liquidity of SICAV units and the instruments that cut the risks due to rate fluctuations (bond purchases with option of resale, securities with variable or adjustable rates). Short-term UCITS have contributed to making these instruments very popular with investors.

Accordingly it appeared necessary to complete the existing range of products with short-term negotiable securities (for their characteristics, see Table 6.6) in order to offer borrowers the choice of financing their operations either through bank credit in all its forms or by issuing securities with an almost complete range of maturities, and to offer lenders the option between depositing their funds in a bank and acquiring securities at all maturities (and no longer just shares or bonds either directly or through SICAVs and FCPs). As of 1 March 1987 and 1 July 1988, certificates of deposit, commercial paper (issued by businesses) and negotiable treasury bills all have the same characteristics with regard to their minimum amount (1 million francs) and their duration (from ten days to seven years).

On 30 April 1988, the short-term securities outstanding totalled 741 billion francs, of which 371 billion were held by UCITS or non-financial agents.

The growth in these new markets was accelerated by the money-market reform. Although theoretically reserved to credit institutions, the market had been open to certain 'non-bank' entities which were thus able to obtain a market rate return on their sight deposits. This was the case for insurance companies, pension funds, the Stockbrokers' Board (Chambre syndicale des agents de change) and SICAVs. The desire to support the spread of negotiable securities among the public and to limit access to the market for 'Central Bank money' led to a better definition of an 'interbank market' accessible only to credit institutions. The possibility of obtaining unregulated rates of interest on their shortest deposits was therefore gradually taken away from 'non-bank entities formerly admitted onto the money market'. In their liquidity management they have had to rely on repurchase agreements and the buying and selling of negotiable securities, which has contributed to the growth in these new markets.

Table 6.6 Short-term securities negotiable on markets open to all economic agents (as at 1 August 1988)

				Bills issued by financial institutions and finance companies		
	Certificates of deposit (CDs)	*Commercial paper*	*(Negotiable) treasury bills*	*Bills issued by specialized financial institutions*	*Bills issued by finance companies*	*Bills issued by 'Article 99' institutions*
Date of introduction	*March 1985*	*December 1985*	*December 1985*	*December 1985*	*May 1986*	*March 1987*
Issuers	Credit institutions which: —can accept deposits from the public at less than 2 years, i.e. members of the Association française des Banques, mutual banks, municipal credit banks, the Caisse des Dépôts et Consignations —must maintain reserves against their current liabilities	Business entities other than credit institutions, which have been in existence for more than 2 years: —companies limited by shares authorized on the basis of their paid-up capital to solicit investment by the public —public sector enterprises, agricultural co-operative societies and their affiliates with own capital in excess of Ffr 1.5 million —groupements d'intérêt économique (consortia) and general partnerships composed entirely of potential issuers	Treasury	—Specialized financial institutions (Crédit d'Equipement des Petites et Moyennes Entreprises, Comptoir des Entrepreneurs, Crédit National, Crédit Foncier de France, Sociétés de Développement Régional) —Bills at less than 2 years: specialized financial institutions subject to compulsory reserves (CFF, CN, SDR, CEPME, CDE)	—Finance companies subject to compulsory reserves —Minimum capital Ffr 15 million —Mutual guarantee insurance companies (sociétés de caution mutuelle) excluded	—Institutions defined by article 99 of the law of 24 January 1984 (maisons de titres) —Minimum capital Ffr 15 million

Table 6.6 continued

				Bills issued by financial institutions and finance companies		
	Certificates of deposit (CDs)	*Commercial paper*	*(Negotiable) treasury bills*	*Bills issued by specialized financial institutions*	*Bills issued by finance companies*	*Bills issued by 'Article 99' institutions*
Date of introduction	*March 1985*	*December 1985*	*December 1985*	*December 1985*	*May 1986*	*March 1987*
Minimum/maximum maturities	6 months (reduced to 3 months on 1 June 1986 and to 10 days as from 1 March 1987) to 2 years (increased to 7 years in February 1986)	10–180 days (increased to 2 years on 1 June 1986 and to 7 years on 1 March 1987)	4 weeks to 5 years (usually 13 weeks)	2 years (reduced to 10 days on 1 March 1987) to 7 years	2 years (reduced to 10 days on 1 March 1987) to 7 years	10 days to 7 years
Minimum denominations	Ffr 10 million reduced to Ffr 5 million in December 1985 and to Ffr 1 million in July 1988	Ffr 5 million reduced to Ffr 1 million in July 1988; no redemption premium or issuing premium for bills with a maturity of less than 2 years	Ffr 5 million reduced to Ffr 1 million in August 1988	Ffr 5 million reduced to Ffr 1 million in July 1988	Ffr 5 million reduced to Ffr 1 million in July 1988	Ffr 5 million reduced to Ffr 1 million in July 1988
Interest rate	Fixed rate (possible reviewable rate for CDs with a maturity of more than 1 year)	Fixed rate for bills with a maturity of less than 2 years	Fixed rate	Fixed rate (possible reviewable rate for bills with a maturity of more than 1 year)	Fixed rate (possible reviewable rate for bills with a maturity of more than 1 year)	Fixed rate (possible reviewable rate for bills with a maturity of more than 1 year)
Monetary aggregates (if held by non-financial agents and UCITS)	M3–M2	L–M3	L–M3	M3–M2	M3–M2	M3–M2
Compulsory reserves	Yes, on the gross outstanding amount of certificates at less than 2 years	No	No	Yes, on the gross outstanding amount of bills at less than 2 years	Yes, on the gross outstanding amount of bills at less than 2 years	Yes, on the gross outstanding amount of bills at less than 2 years

				Bills issued by financial institutions and finance companies		
	Certificates of deposit (CDs)	*Commercial paper*	*(Negotiable) treasury bills*	*Bills issued by specialized financial institutions*	*Bills issued by finance companies*	*Bills issued by 'Article 99' institutions*
Date of introduction	*March 1985*	*December 1985*	*December 1985*	*December 1985*	*May 1986*	*March 1987*
Secondary markets	—Regulated by the Committee for Banking Regulation, the Banque de France takes measures to ensure smooth operation —Issuers not admitted to this market unless express authorization by the Banque de France	—Regulated by the Committee for Banking Regulation, the Banque de France takes measures to ensure smooth operation —Placing and trading by credit institutions, 'Article 99' institutions, interbank market participants, brokerage firms —Issuers admitted to this market	—Financial futures market (MATIF) created for this instrument in June 1986 (13-week treasury bill contract)	—Regulated by the Committee for Banking Regulation, the Banque de France takes measures to ensure smooth operation —Placing and trading by credit institutions, 'Article 99' institutions, interbank market participants, brokerage firms	—Regulated by the Committee for Banking Regulation, the Banque de France takes measures to ensure smooth operation —Placing and trading by credit institutions, 'Article 99' institutions, interbank market participants, brokerage firms	—Regulated by the Committee for Banking Regulation, the Banque de France takes measures to ensure smooth operation —Placing and trading by credit institutions, 'Article 99' institutions, interbank market participants, brokerage firms
Other characteristics	Issuers must lodge with the COB (Securities and Exchange Commission) and forward to the Banque de France a financial statement, updated at least once a year. Information must be provided on the estimated development in the activity for a period at least equal to the maturity of the issue when it ranges from 6 months to 2 years and for a 24-month period for issues at more than 2 years		—Issued by auction at the Banque de France —Managed 'on current account' at the Banque de France	Issuers must lodge with the COB (Securities and Exchange Commission) and forward to the Banque de France a financial statement, updated at least once a year. Information must be provided on the estimated development in the activity for a period at least equal to the maturity of the issue when it ranges from 6 months to 2 years and for a 24-month period for issues at more than 2 years		

Table 6.6 continued

	Certificates of deposit (CDs)	*Commercial paper*	*(Negotiable) treasury bills*	*Bills issued by financial institutions and finance companies*		
				Bills issued by specialized financial institutions	*Bills issued by finance companies*	*Bills issued by 'Article 99' institutions*
Date of introduction	*March 1985*	*December 1985*	*December 1985*	*December 1985*	*May 1986*	*March 1987*
Other characteristics	—Residents must deposit certificates which they hold with either a credit institution or an 'article 99' institution —Compulsory rating by a rating agency for issues at more than 2 years (from 1 July 1989)	—Optional back-up line provided by a credit institution —Issuer must publish a statement of current assets and liabilities on a quarterly basis —Paper must be domiciled with a credit institution authorized to accept sight deposits —Compulsory rating by a rating agency acting under the supervision of the Banque de France for issues at more than 2 years —Guarantees may be given by a parent company or a subsidiary authorized to issue commercial paper, or a credit institution for commercial paper of Ffr 3 million or less		—Managed 'on current account' at the Banque de France —The outstanding bills issued at less than 2 years must not exceed 15% of credit and leasing operations —Residents must domicile paper with a credit institution or an 'article 99' institution —Compulsory rating by a rating agency for issues at more than 2 years (from 1 July 1989)	—The outstanding bills issued at less than 2 years must not exceed either 15% of credits or 50% of credits with a maturity of less than 2 years —Residents must domicile paper with a credit institution or an 'article 99' institution —Compulsory rating by a rating agency for issues at more than 2 years (from 1 July 1989)	—The outstanding bills issued at less than 2 years must not exceed 15% of the securities of portfolio and the balance between loans and borrowings with financial institutions —Residents must domicile paper with a credit institution or an 'article 99' institution —Compulsory rating by a rating agency for issues at more than 2 years (from 1 July 1989)

	Certificates of deposit (CDs)	Commercial paper	(Negotiable) treasury bills	Bills issued by financial institutions and finance companies: Bills issued by specialized financial institutions	Bills issued by finance companies	Bills issued by 'Article 99' institutions
Date of introduction	*March 1985*	*December 1985*	*December 1985*	*December 1985*	*May 1986*	*March 1987*
	Law 85-1321, 14 December 1985			Law 85-1321, 14 December 1985		
	Decree 88.841, 21 July 1988			Decree 88.841, 21 July 1988		
Basic texts	—Regulations 85-06, 85-19, 86-10, 86-11 and 88-05 of the Committee for Banking Regulation —Governor's letters of 1 March 1985 and 22 February 1988	—Decree 85-1388 of 16 December 1985 and 86-210 of 11 February 1986 —Regulations 85-18, 86-07, 86-11, 86-19 and 88-05 of the Committee for Banking Regulation	No text	—Regulations 85-20, 86-07, 86-19, 87-01, 87-02, 87-12 and 88-05 of the Committee for Banking Regulation —Governor's letter of 22 February 1988	—Regulations 86-12, 86-19, 87-03, 87-12 and 88-05 of the Committee for Banking Regulation of 22 February 1988 of 22 February 1988	—Regulations 87-03, 87-12 and 88-05 of the Committee for Banking Regulation —Governor's letter
Tax treatment		*Income:* *Capital gains:*	optional withholding tax for physical persons at 32% (+ 2%) treated in the same way as income			

Financial futures and options market

Opened on 20 February 1986, the financial futures market (MATIF) originally only traded in one long-term contract (unit value 500,000) covering a notional loan equivalent to a ten-year government loan, redeemable at maturity and bearing an interest of 10 per cent. Actual deliveries are made by equivalent government-guaranteed loans. Since June 1986, contracts on three-month treasury bills have been negotiated.

Trading on the MATIF has exceeded even the most optimistic expectations since, after only one year's activity, the number of contracts traded at an ordinary session was higher than that on the London International Financial Futures Exchange.

An options market opened in September 1987.

The dismantling of exchange control

Seven series of measures were implemented (15 April, 21 May, 8 July, 18 December 1986, 21 May 1987, August 1987, June 1988) in order to give individuals and companies a degree of freedom unprecedented since 1968. Despite a few remaining restrictions, individuals enjoy the freedom to create portfolios in foreign securities or in real estate assets abroad. Companies, too, enjoy a high degree of freedom to manage their business risks and carry out financial operations (investments abroad, currency borrowings, forward hedging operations, securities purchases).

The changing flow of funds in the financing of the economy

The measure of intermediation is taken as the ratio of intermediated debt of resident non-financial agents (credit granted by financial institutions) to their total external financing.

Since 1980, the structure of financial flows has tended to reinforce the role of the financial market at the expense of bank intermediation (Table 6.7). Financial intermediaries that accounted for almost 80 per cent of the financing of the economy in 1981 provided only 40 per cent in 1986. This change in the sources of external financing (excluding self-financing) is mainly due to an increase in the resources collected on the domestic financial markets. In this respect, 1986 was a watershed year. To begin with, growth in total financing of the economy was smaller than in 1985, which can be linked to the improvement of companies' profits and the strengthening of their self-financing. Moreover the drop in the intermediation ratio throughout the year was very sharp. The fall of more than 20 points is due to the slower growth of intermediated financing combined with the increase in direct financing.

Table 6.7 Changing pattern of financing (net flows in billions of francs)

	1981	*1982*	*1983*	*1984*	*1985*	*1986*	*1987*
A Financing through financial institutions	321	413.8	395.7	357.8	378.5	254.6	361.1
B Direct financing	92.2	122.6	161.8	200.4	223.6	352.3	387.1
C Total financing (=A+B)	413.2	536.4	557.5	558.2	602.1	606.9	748.3
Financial intermediation ratio (A/C)	0.78	0.77	0.71	0.64	0.63	0.42	0.48

Financial institutions almost halved their lending, which reflects both the government's policy of financing its budget through non-monetary resources and the weakness of corporate demand for credit. Direct financing grew by 100 billion francs more than in 1985. With foreign financing falling significantly, agents turned in force to the resources raised on the domestic market, in the form of both shares and bonds. Direct financing of companies accounted for only 30–35 per cent of external financing in the early 1980s, but rose to almost 50 per cent in 1985 and 80 per cent in 1986 (65 per cent in 1987) (Table 6.8).

Table 6.8 Financing structure of non-financial companies (net flows in billions of francs)

	1981	*1982*	*1983*	*1984*	*1985*	*1986*	*1987*
A Financing through financial institutions	129.2	169.6	162.5	137.1	138.7	48.6	126.5
B Direct financing	73.4	91.3	109.5	106.1	127.6	194.9	228.5
C Total (=A+B)	202.6	260.9	272	243.2	266.3	243.5	355
Intermediation ratio (A/C)	0.64	0.66	0.59	0.56	0.52	0.20	0.35
Memorandum item: self-financing rate	60.3	64.2	71.2	76.0	76.5	93.4	91.0

The disintermediation process is common to most other OECD countries. Table 6.9 shows the changing share abroad of intermediated financing in external financing. The table was obtained by methods similar to those used for France in the previous tables. Taking into account the dominant role played by financial institutions in financing the French economy in the late 1970s, the change was more pronounced in France than in countries such as the United States or the United Kingdom where direct financing was always important.

Table 6.9 Share of intermediated financing in external financing of non-financial agents

	1978	*1979*	*1980*	*1981*	*1982*	*1983*	*1984*
United States	0.71	0.76	0.57	0.62	0.42	0.48	0.63
Japan	0.54	0.62	0.63	0.61	0.66	0.65	0.68
West Germany	0.91	0.95	0.96	0.98	0.79	0.80	0.82
United Kingdom	0.56	0.62	0.68	0.69	0.81	0.62	0.75
Italy	0.42	0.62	0.59	0.48	0.39	0.30	n.a.
France	0.77	0.80	0.69	0.77	0.78	0.71	0.62

Source: Annual Report of the Bank for International Settlements

THE EFFECTS ON THE BEHAVIOUR OF ECONOMIC AGENTS

Changes in the structure of financial wealth

In the 1970s, the liquid assets held by non-financial agents (included in M3) which are the primary source of funds for financial intermediation accounted for almost 80 per cent of the growth in their financial assets. This share dropped to 56 per cent in 1984 and to less than 33 per cent in 1986, but went back to 48 per cent in 1987 (Figure 6.1).

The trade-off between investments in financial assets and tangible investments

Household trade-off between real-estate investments and financial investments

With the slowdown in inflation, savers have less and less felt the need to purchase real assets (hedges against inflation) to offset monetary erosion. What is happening to the property market is symptomatic. From 1945 to 1981 this market grew steadily in France as a result of some scarcity and a privileged tax treatment, and because the French people could expect a double advantage if they became property owners: they could realize

Figure 6.1 Changes in the structure of financial investment

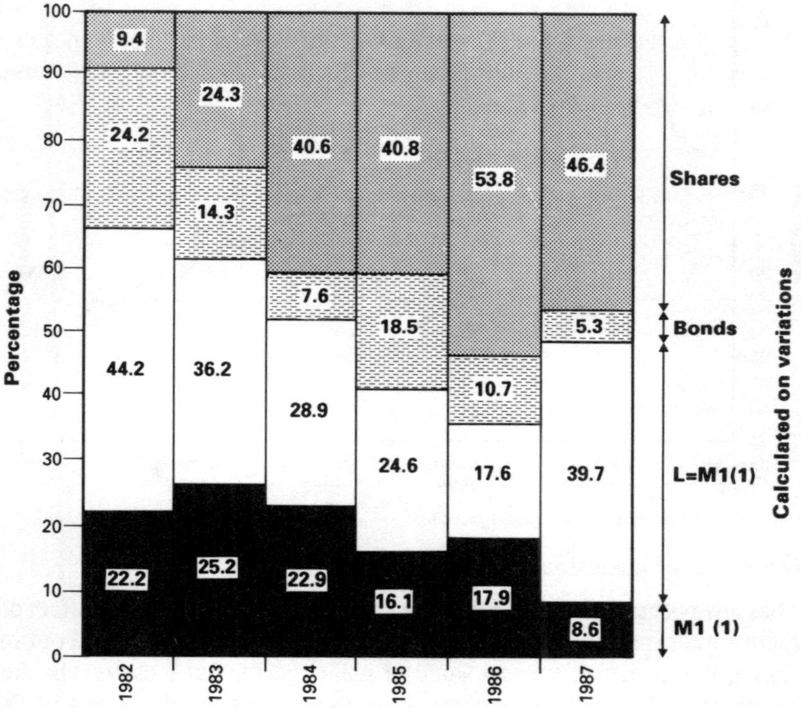

capital gains and, with inflation rising, they could repay their housing loans in a greatly debased currency, more especially as their purchasing power was apparently well guaranteed. Throughout those thirty-five years, the French property market moved ahead undisturbed by any crisis, even that which followed the first oil shock in the majority of the developed countries. This being so, the 1982 shock hit the market all the harder. Prices plummeted and in some cases literally collapsed, with sellers encountering totally unexpected difficulties in finding a buyer. In comparison with financial investments, the property investment profitability seemed weak and the prospects of capital gains much lower (Figure 6.2).

Corporate trade-off between financial investments and tangible investments

The common wisdom is that in a context of high real interest rates companies prefer to withhold capital goods investments and increase their financial assets. This opinion is widely held, but not easy to prove.

Figure 6.2 The 'crowding out' of property to the benefit of the financial market: percentage of households preferring investment in real estate and securities

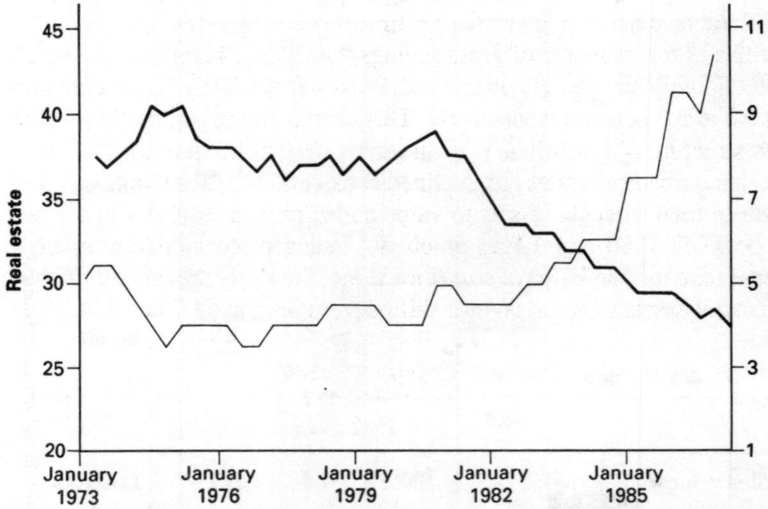

Source: *Economie et Finances Agricoles*

The impact of interest rates on investment

It has always been difficult to provide empirical evidence as to the effect of interest rates on investment. In all the econometric research carried out in France, the incidence appears small or non-existent. But these results are not strictly reliable, as they emerge from studies from the 1960s and 1970s which were characterized by low interest rates and high inflation. The present situation in which real interest rates are high and inflation is low is unprecedented in France.

It is hardly conceivable that physical capital should remain less profitable than yields on financial assets for a long time without the occurrence of switches in investment patterns. Furthermore, short-term substitutions probably affect the realization time for investments. Even if the desired capital volume remains unaffected by the financial conditions, the pace of investment (and hence the capital adjustment profile to its desired level) may well be influenced by interest rates.

More generally, the debt repayment trend that many observers see as accounting for the low rate of investment can also be analysed as a trade-off between real assets and financial assets. In fact, one should talk of financial liabilities. Since the leverage effect has been negative since 1982, companies find it an advantage today to reduce their debt position rather than invest. This conclusion emerges from a comparison of financing costs and profitability.

SOME FIGURES FROM THE NATIONAL ACCOUNTS

From the corporate accounts, drawn up as part of the National Accounts, certain facts emerge (Table 6.10). From 1980 to 1985, purchases of securities as a percentage of gross savings, on the one hand, and the value added of companies, on the other hand, moved from 7.7 to 53 per cent and from 0.8 to 6.5 per cent respectively. This change, however, partly reflects a new structure of portfolios: over the same period the share of monetary assets in companies' assets has declined considerably. Thus the ratio of the growth in total financial assets to value added moved from 4.4 to 6.7 per cent between 1980 and 1985, which is a much more moderate relative increase than for purchases of securities alone. Similarly the ratio of the rise in financial assets to gross savings shifted from 38.5 to 54.7 per cent.

Table 6.10 Some figures from the National Accounts

	1980	*1983*	*1985*
1 Added value (billion francs)	1,463	2,062	2,412
2 Gross savings (billion francs)	169	201	296
3 Changes in claims in money (billion francs)	52	74	5
4 Changes in claims in shares and bonds (billion francs)	13	47	157
5 Gross fixed capital formation (billion francs)	283	354	401
Buying of claims in shares and bonds/gross savings (4/2) (%)	7.7	23.3	53
Buying of claims in shares and bonds/added value (4/1) (%)	0.8	2.2	6.5
Buying of claims in money and in shares and bonds/gross savings ((3+4)/2) (%)	38.5	60.2	54.7
Buying of claims in money and in shares and bonds/added value ((3+4)/1) (%)	4.4	5.8	6.7
Gross fixed capital formation/ added value (5/1) (%)	19.3	17.2	16.6
Gross savings/added value (2/1) (%)	11.6	9.7	12.3

The ratio of gross fixed capital formation to value added slipped from 19.3 in 1980 to 16.6 in 1985. The drop in the investment rate was continuous from 1980 to 1984 with a sharp fall in 1983 when the ratio was down to 17.2 per cent. In 1982 it was at 18.4 per cent. It is difficult to link the slide in investment to the fashion for securities, however. Throughout the period when the ratio of gross fixed capital formation to value added was falling significantly (1980–3) the relative size of securities purchases in companies' assets hardly changed at all. In 1983 when the slide in investment became even more pronounced, liquidity increased sharply, thus reflecting a 'wait and see' attitude on behalf of companies.

This attitude was apparently reinforced in 1984–6 by the exceptionally good conditions on the capital markets. This not only explains the massive transfer of liquid assets towards securities, but also the intrinsic growth of securities portfolios. While the ratio of financial assets to value added edged towards 7 per cent, the investment rate stagnated at 16.5 per cent in 1985 and in 1986 too, according to the first figures available.

If it is beyond doubt that the fashion for financial investments was not responsible for the drop in investment, can it be claimed that it prevented its recovery? There are two extreme answers to that question and it is not easy to decide between them.

1 The reasons justifying the 'wait and see' attitude from 1980 to 1983 (lack of sufficient outlets, for example) have not changed and companies have simply maximized their cash management (trade-off between ordinary bank deposits and financial investments).
2 In a context in which results are markedly improving (the ratio of gross savings to value added shifted from 9.7 to 12.3 per cent from 1983 to 1985) companies prefer financial investment to physical investment.

However, the following remarks can be made:

— In 1987 and in 1988, corporate physical investment went up sharply, against a background of high real interest rates.
— Research conducted by the Office of Central Balance Sheet Data has shown that, in the last few years, firms that have most heavily invested in financial markets have also been front-runners in boosting their production capacity.

Whatever the answer may be, the importance of financial management in companies is increasing significantly.

As the potential losses on operations with poor exchange rate or interest rate risk hedging can be higher than the gains expected from industrial or commercial activity, financial management has acquired more weight in firms in the last few years. The role of the cash manager has undergone a notable reassessment, as he/she now makes a greater contribution to the company's results. He/she is led to deal on markets and to take and manage risks previously left to the banker, as has been happening in some big multinationals since the early 1970s. This is job enhancing, but can also be a source of greater tension for operators. In large firms, financial management (insurance, real estate, financial debt service etc.) tends to be concentrated in a single branch of activity which sometimes includes also financial institutions or, in some cases, a cash management bank. The group's financial institutions can equally be delegated to manage the interest rate or exchange rate risks.

TRANSFORMATIONS IN THE BANKING SYSTEM

Disintermediation

Financial institutions underwent a first wave of disintermediation in 1980 with the rapid growth of the long-term capital market. For almost two years now they have been bearing the brunt of the new negotiable short-term instruments markets (commercial paper and negotiable treasury bills).

The gradual liberalization of exchange control has unleased a third wave of disintermediation.

The first wave, 1980–5: short-term open-ended unit trusts and short-term mutual funds

From 1980, the demand for and the supply of bonds increased considerably. As we saw, the government policy of financing the budget deficit through non-monetary resources boosted the supply. The desire of non-financial agents to take advantage of high interest rates, particularly after the reform of the regulations governing creditor interest rates in September 1981, gave a hefty push to demand.

Banks therefore noted a shrinking in their assets (the financing of the Treasury by purchases of bills) and in their liabilities (deposits at regulated rates). Their reaction to this first wave of disintermediation was to create the short-term SICAVs and FCPs which gathered the funds previously collected directly by banks and invested them on the bond market. They were thus able to recuperate in management fees the whole or a part of the profit they used to make from lending business they had lost. Furthermore short-term SICAVs and FCPs provided them with a captive clientele with whom they could place their own bond issues.

The second wave, 1986: commercial paper and negotiable treasury bills

By bringing together borrowers and lenders of short-term funds, the development of commercial paper resulted in a reduction of bank loans to firms and bank deposits by non-financial agents, other things being equal. Apart from its quantitative impact on banks' assets and liabilities, the creation of commercial paper had repercussions on lending terms in general and the quality of bank risks.

By losing their monopoly as subscribers to treasury bills, but more especially by forgoing a part of the short-term financing of firms that issue commercial paper, banks have noticed a contraction in their better quality assets.

In addition to a worsening in their average risk level, banks have also had to cope with a marketization process. Consistent with trends noted in the United States, the increasing use of commercial paper in the context of a sharp decline in company financing needs has exacerbated competition between financial institutions. An increasing portion of new bank loans are now granted at rates linked to the money-market rate and no longer to the bank base rate, with banks taking only a relatively narrow margin above this reference rate.

To offset the decline in the quality of their risks and the size of their margins, banks have developed new services for companies. For example, they now look after the placing of commercial paper for which is required a back-up line of up to 75 per cent of the amount outstanding. They have also increased their loans to individual clients (consumer loans and mortgages) in a climate of harsh competition and hence of lower interest rates.

The third wave: the lifting of exchange controls

With the gradual lifting of exchange controls, French companies are making increasing use of those international financial techniques that have largely contributed to the development of international financial markets and to the process of bank disintermediation. In particular, French companies are beginning to use the new lending techniques that are taking the place of traditional fixed rate or adjustable rate loans (issues of short-term paper, currency swaps or interest rate swaps) as well as hedging techniques on futures markets or through mutual agreements with other banking or non-banking partners.

As in other countries, this trend is leading to a development of off-balance-sheet operations and accentuates banks' role as provider of services.

Diversification of activities

The capital market function of French banks is growing more important and they are becoming increasingly international.

The importance of the capital market function in bank organization and results

More and more frequently, globalized markets have made it necessary for banks to concentrate their activities on the various domestic and foreign markets under a single authority. In the large French banks, as in banks in

Anglo-Saxon countries and Japan, a central office for capital markets has been set up to centralize operations on national and international markets, relations with companies and financial intermediaries, management of individual and jointly held portfolios (SICAV, FCP) and sometimes the setting up of capital operations in the event of company mergers or acquisitions. Single departments are frequently created for operations in francs and in foreign currencies. Bank groups are increasingly setting up special banks often in consortium form for arbitrage or cash operations. These banks can employ from fifty to a hundred specialists in small flexible groups who deal in specific markets and products, so as to profit from yield differentials on different markets and have a large-scale view of arbitrage possibilities.

These changes are reflected in bank results. In fact it is possible to assess the size of the operations on the new financial instruments in relation to total income. Thus the Banking Commission has carefully examined the size of the item 'miscellaneous products' which includes banks' market operations (management of customers' securities, banks' securities portfolio, foreign-exchange and arbitrage operations). In 1986 these products totalled 25 per cent of the global banking income for those banks belonging to the French Banking Association alone (it was as much as 58 per cent in certain cases), against 17 per cent in 1985 and 13 per cent in 1984.

A further means of gauging the size of these new activities consists in monitoring certain overhead costs. Excluding personnel costs, these increased by 7.6 per cent in 1986, which is faster than the inflation rate. Most frequently these overheads cover the installation of heavy computing systems which are indispensable for most operations using the latest financial instruments.

Internationalization of French banks

The volume of foreign investment made by French banks rose from 6.8 billion in 1978 to 20.8 billion in 1985, tripling in current francs between those dates. The share of foreign branch returns in the combined total of the returns for French banks established abroad (55 out of 299 French-law banks) increased from 18.1 per cent in 1978 to 41.5 per cent in 1985. The off-balance-sheet activities of these branches account at present for more than 60 per cent of total off-balance-sheet operations of all French banks.

The structure of French banks' balance sheets

Table 6.11 shows the increased share of foreign currency operations and transactions carried out with non-residents in the total balance sheet of banking institutions. It also highlights the small share of bank assets in

Table 6.11 Balance sheet of banking institutions (excluding the Banque de France)

Assets	*1977* Amount	*1977* Proportion	*1984* Amount	*1984* Proportion
Claims on residents				
Claims on the Public Treasury	29.6	1.5	117.0	2.1
Credits in postal current accounts	1.7	0.1	2.0	–
Treasury bills in hand	27.9	1.4	115.0	2.1
of which repo's	(12.2)	(0.6)	(5.2)	(0.1)
Claims on the economy	885.6	45.5	2,066.8	36.2
Credits	865.2	44.4	1,967.6	34.5
Francs	(845.9)	(43.4)	(1,892.7)	(33.2)
Foreign currency	(19.3)	(1.0)	(74.9)	(1.3)
Securities	20.4	1.1	99.2	1.7
Francs	20.2	1.1	91.9	1.6
Foreign currency	0.2	–	7.3	0.1
Claims on resident financial institutions	438.2	22.5	1,360.0	23.8
Francs	376.9	19.4	1,039.5	18.2
Foreign currency	61.3	3.1	320.5	5.6
Capital assets	40.8	2.1	107.3	1.9
Other credit items	204.2	10.5	621.9	10.9
of which CODEVI loans	(–)	(–)	(9.4)	(0.2)
Total claims on residents	1,598.4	82.1	4,273.0	74.9

Liabilities	*1977* Amount	*1977* Proportion	*1984* Amount	*1984* Proportion
Liabilities to residents				
Liquid assets held by residents	777.7	39.9	1,639.2	28.7
Francs	771.5	39.6	1,605.3	28.1
Foreign currency	6.2	0.3	33.9	0.6
Commitments with resident financial institutions	526.3	27.0	1,491.4	26.2
Francs	466.1	23.9	1,178.0	20.7
Foreign currency	60.2	3.1	313.4	5.5
Commitments with the Treasury	–	–	5.7	0.1
Loans with residents (including loans issued under CODEVI)	67.1	3.5	306.0	5.4
Own liabilities	71.8	3.7	240.1	4.2
Other liabilities	190.4	9.8	559.4	9.8
Total liabilities to residents	1,633.3	83.9	4,241.8	74.4

Assets	*1977*		*1984*		*Liabilities*	*1977*		*1984*	
	Amount	*Proportion*	*Amount*	*Proportion*		*Amount*	*Proportion*	*Amount*	*Proportion*
Claims on non-residents					*Liabilities to non-residents*				
Credits to non-resident clients	97.8	5.0	466.0	8.2	Liquid assets held by non-residents	28.4	1.4	151.7	2.7
Francs	51.6	2.6	167.5	2.9	Francs	8.5	0.4	21.4	0.4
Foreign currency	46.2	2.4	298.5	5.3	Foreign currency	19.9	1.0	130.3	2.3
Bonds	4.4	0.2	41.5	0.7	Loans from non-residents	9.3	0.5	139.4	2.4
Claims on non-resident financial institutions	244.2	12.5	899.4	15.8	Liabilities to non-resident financial institutions	276.5	14.2	1,165.1	20.4
Francs	3.3	0.2	20.2	0.4	Francs	11.0	0.6	48.5	0.8
Foreign currency	240.9	12.3	879.2	15.4	Foreign currency	265.5	13.6	1,116.6	19.6
Other credit items	2.9	0.1	23.93	0.4	Other liabilities	0.2	–	5.8	0.1
Total non-residents' assets	349.3	17.9	1,430.8	25.1	Total	314.4	16.1	1,462.0	25.6
Total assets	1,947.7	100.0	5,703.8	100.0	Total liabilities	1,947.7	100.0	5,703.8	100.0
Francs	1,577.9	81.0	4,094.0	71.8	Francs	1,595.9	81.9	4,005.9	70.2
Foreign currency	369.8	19.0	1,609.8	28.2	Foreign currency	351.8	18.1	1,697.9	29.8

negotiable securities in francs (3.7 per cent in 1984 of which 2.1 per cent was in treasury bills, against 2.6 per cent and 1.5 per cent respectively in 1977).

However, it should be noted that, in terms of flow, the securities portfolio in banks increased by 21.8 per cent in 1985 and by 27.5 per cent in 1986. These growth rates should be set against those for bank credit: 11.1 per cent in 1983, 9.2 per cent in 1985 and 6.2 per cent in 1986.

If we only consider the assets and liabilities in French francs with residents (by netting-out cash operations between financial institutions and getting rid of the miscellaneous items on the asset and the liability sides) we get the rough picture shown in Table 6.12.

Table 6.12 Banks' assets and liabilities (residents, in francs)

	1977	*1984*
Assets		
Treasury bills (%)	3.3	5.6
Securities (%)	2.2	4.4
Credits (%)	94.5	90
Total (%)	100	100
Liabilities		
Liquidities (%)	77.1	70.1
Bonds (%)	6.7	13.4
Own funds (%)	7.2	10.5
Net liabilities to financial institutions (%)	10	6
Total (%)	100	100

Banks have considerably increased their supply of medium- and long-term loans at variable or adjustable rates. Most medium-term loans and a sizeable portion of the long-term loans to companies are now granted in this form. More recently, variable rates have been extended to housing loans, but this practice has remained marginal. At the same time, a larger amount of banks' liabilities has become sensitive to interest rate fluctuations (Table 6.13).

THE NEW REGULATORY AND SUPERVISORY BODIES

Financial regulation has historically been based on the division of the financial system into the three sectors of securities, banking and insurance.

With the blurring of financial frontiers banking and securities markets have ceased to have separate identities. Nevertheless the regulatory framework is still based on such a division. This 'institutional' approach, whereby each category of institution is place under the control of a different supervisory authority for the entire range of its operations, is relevant since the French banks cover the whole spectrum of financial intermediation.

However, the law encompasses a very broad definition of banking business which gives the French authorities the possibility of submitting many of the financial actors to the same rules. This is why it can be considered that the French authorities have also followed the 'functional' approach, whereby each function or type of financial service or product should be subject to a particular supervisor, independently of the type of financial institution that offers it.

Table 6.13 Banks belonging to the French Banking Association: structure of loans to customers and customer deposits in percentages

	1973	*1984*
Banks' loans to customers (residents, in francs)		
Loans at regulated fixed rate or at non-adjustable market rates	35.1	47
Loans at rates linked to the bank base rate	64.9	53
Total	100.0	100.0
Banks' customer deposits (residents, in francs)		
Non-interest-bearing deposits	47.8	39.1
Deposits bearing interest at regulated rates	33.8	21.7
Deposits bearing interest at rates linked to the money-market rate	15.6	24.5
Bonds (in francs)	3.0	14.7
Total	100.0	100.0

The regulation and supervision of credit institutions

An enlarged definition of banking

The Banking Act of 24 January 1984 introduces more uniformity in the French banking sector by referring to the notion of 'credit institution' ('établissement de crédit') already introduced in the European Directive adopted in December 1977. A credit institution fulfils at least one of the following banking operations:

— collect deposits from the public;
— grant loans;
— make available to customers or manage means of payment.

It must be stressed that on this definition any institution which grants credit, whatever the way this activity is financed (deposits from the public, borrowing on the money or financial markets), is to be considered a credit institution. The definition appears to be far more extensive than is found in most countries where the criterion used for defining a credit institution is their receipt of funds from the public (as for instance in the United Kingdom).

Moreover, the law gives a broad definition of a credit operation which should be understood to mean any act by which a person, against valuable consideration, places or promises to place funds at the disposal of another person or assumes a commitment in favour of the latter in the form of an endorsement, guarantee or the like. Leasing, and in general any rental operation with a purchase option, shall be treated as a credit operation. In addition, any institution which, as a regular activity, enables people to transfer funds, irrespective of the medium or technical procedure used, is considered as a credit institution.

It must also be stressed that credit institutions are allowed to carry out a wide range of activities other than receiving funds from the public, granting credits or managing means of payment. For instance, French banks play a major role in securities activities such as portfolio management or underwriting and trading operations. They also control more than two-thirds of the SICAVs and the FCPs (mutual funds).

Without explicit exceptions, all credit institutions are subject to the same rules (e.g. the same liquidity ratio, solvency ratio). This broad definition of credit institutions implies that there is no incentive for the development of 'non-bank' banks in France. (The law applies to securities portfolio managers acting on behalf of customers, money-market brokers and 'finance companies which control credit institutions'.)

A new organization of banking supervision

Under the new Banking Act about 2,000 credit institutions are supervised by three bodies working closely with the Bank of France:

1 the Committee on Credit Institutions (Comité des établissements de crédit), chaired by the Governor of the Bank of France and responsible

for individual decisions (authorizations to conduct banking activity, individual derogations etc.);

2 the Committee for Banking Regulation (Comité de la Réglementation Bancaire), chaired by the Minister of Finance (the governor of the Central Bank being the vice-chairman) and in charge of regulatory decisions (the creation of new financial instruments, decisions concerning minimum capital, the liquidity ratio, the solvency or risk–asset ratio, the mismatch ratio, the acquisition of equity stakes in non-banking companies, the concentration of risks etc.);

3 the Banking Commission (Commission Bancaire), chaired by the Governor of the Bank of France, with extended powers to control the application of the regulations by credit institutions and to take sanctions in case of irregularity.

The regulation of the stock exchange system

The Stock Exchange Act of 22 January 1988 provides the statutory basis for a modern and efficient Bourse system.

'Brokerage firms' (sociétés de bourse)

The member shareholders of the Bourse are approved incorporated securities companies. These companies enjoy the stockbroking monopoly previously granted to individual official stockbrokers (agents de change) but they may also engage in dealing and investment banking (subject to the provisions of the Banking Act 1984). Many banks have acquired a stake in the capital of brokerage firms.

The Securities Exchange Board (Conseil des Bourses de Valeurs)

The self-regulatory organization covering the seven French Bourses is an incorporated Securities Exchange Board: it authorizes the brokerage firms (sociétés de bourse) and takes action against their failure to meet professional obligations; it sets out the requirements for setting up and managing a fund aimed at guaranteeing all the commitments of brokerage firms towards clients; and it has power with regard to admission to quotation as well as de-listing of securities.

The Board is at present implementing a series of new prudential rules concerning brokerage firms, the first of which will come into force in December 1988:

— a risk distribution ratio aimed at limiting the concentration of risk to one counterparty only;

— a liquidity ratio specifying that short-term debts must be covered by quickly realizable assets;
— a rule demanding that members keep their own and clients' accounts separate so as to guarantee that brokerage firms do not use clients' assets for their own transactions.

The French Bourse Corporation (La Société des Bourses Françaises)

The day-to-day operation of the Bourse (practical organization and supervision) is the responsibility of a specialized financial institution: the French Bourse Corporation.[1]

The Futures and Options Markets' Clearing Company (Société de Compensation des Marchés conditionnels)

The Futures and Options Markets' Clearing Company, also a specialized financial institution, is a fully owned subsidiary of the French Bourse Corporation. It is entrusted with the task of clearing and managing the Paris negotiable options exchange (marché des options négociables de Paris, MONEP) created in September 1987, as well as of supervising and controlling transactions.

The regulation of the futures exchange

The law of 31 December 1987 created a unified futures exchange by the merger of the Bourse de Commerce (commodity futures) and the MATIF (financial futures). This unified futures exchange is governed by identical rules to ensure, in particular, the financial reliability of the market in order to enhance its efficiency and attractiveness.

The Futures Exchange Board (Conseil du Marché à terme) is composed of representatives of all the parties involved in the market (credit institutions, brokerage firms, insurance companies, firms and public authorities). It is responsible for general organization and, to this end, establishes market rules, decides on the introduction of new contracts and sets the terms and conditions of settlement and delivery.

The Paris Futures Clearing House (Chambre de Compensation des Instruments Financiers de Paris) is a specialized financial institution whose capital is held by the main credit institutions and brokerage firms. It looks after the day-to-day operation and supervision of the market. Only members of the Clearing House may intervene in the market (on payment of a fee for membership).

The Securities and Exchange Commission (Commission des Opérations de Bourse)

Created in 1967 the Securities and Exchange Commission (COB) has the responsibility to ensure the protection of savings, the information of investors and the proper operation of markets. Its powers and the matters coming under its jurisdiction have been enlarged by the laws enacted on 14 December 1985 and 22 January 1988.

Regulatory powers

Prior to 1985, the COB had been empowered to issue rulings with respect to the operation of securities exchanges. It has thus issued general rulings concerning such issues as sales of controlling interest, takeover transactions, information to be disclosed upon acquisition of substantial interests in listed companies (1981) and the creation of the second market (second marché) for medium-size enterprises (1982).

The rule-making powers of the COB have now been extended in accordance with the scope of its duties. It is authorized to regulate the operation of the markets which are subject to its supervision, i.e. to issue rules of professional practice for those who invite the public to invest as well as for those who by virtue of their profession are instrumental to the transactions in securities placed by invitation to the public, or who are engaging in individual or collective management of securities portfolios.

The new rule-making power of the COB is not opposing the competence of the other financial authorities but is exercised in close liaison with the latter where the content of the regulations is concerned. In particular, this will enable the COB to specify a number of rules concerning the information of securities holders, professional conduct and certain transactions such as takeover bids and mergers.

Relations with courts of justice

In order to ensure compliance with the statutory and regulatory measures coming within its competence, the COB was already in the past empowered to receive complaints and make investigations. It could also apply to the court for an expert's report on minority interest. Moreover, it was empowered to introduce criminal proceedings for infractions that it had discovered, but this mode of action did not allow rapid sanctioning of stated abuses.

The new provisions are aimed at obtaining rapid cessation of unfair practices, even in the absence of criminal infractions. The Chairman of the

COB is now authorized to apply to the presiding judge of the Paris Court of Appeal 'whenever a practice contrary to the statutory or regulatory provisions is of a nature to injure the rights of the investors'. The presiding judge of the Paris Court of Appeal can grant a temporary prohibitory injunction. He can impose a daily fine for disobedience, payable to the Treasury, and take any adequate protective measure.

Investigation powers

Supervision has been extended from securities markets to all the futures markets, both financial and commodity. Inspections concern professionals, third parties and consolidated subsidiaries, or persons controlling listed companies.

The co-ordination of the French regulatory and supervisory bodies

The French Securities and Exchange Commission and the Banking Commission are allowed to exchange information that they require to perform their respective tasks. A financial markets liaison committee has been created; it includes the Governor of the Bank of France, the Director of the Treasury and the chairmen of the Securities Exchange Board, the Futures Exchange Board, the Paris Futures Clearing House and the COB.

The internationalization of the regulation and supervision of the financial system

The setting up of a single European market for financial services is based on several principles: free movement of all kinds of services; application of the law of the country from which the demand or the effective offer of transactions is originating; mutual recognition of the rules laid down by the country of origin of the intermediaries; control ensured as a general rule by the authorities of the country of origin; minimum of harmonization of the rules applicable in all countries of the European Community.

It should be mentioned that the scope and quality of the prevailing national regulations concerning investor protection vary from one country to another (professional qualifications and reputation, solvency, prior information of the public, authorized marketing methods, code of professional conduct, prevention of fraud). Mutual recognition of local rules and application of the law of the initiator of the contract without prior harmonization of the rules for the protection of the investor would expose the latter to very serious risks.

Banking supervision and the single European market

The French authorities adhere to the basic principles that have been established by the Cooke Committee and will apply common rules which will be defined at the European Community level.

Since the future European Economic Community solvency ratio will be very close to that adopted by the Cooke Committee, it can be assumed that, at least in 1992, all French credit institutions will be subject to a new solvency ratio. With regard to limits on loans of a large amount, French regulations were already strengthened in 1987 in accordance with European Community recommendations. Also the new rules established in 1988 for the liquidity ratio are somewhat in advance of what can be found in most countries.

With the removal of foreign-exchange controls, a mechanism for supervision of exchange rate risk will be set up as in the United Kingdom or Germany. New rules have been adopted with regard to interest rate risk.

Co-operation between national market regulators

The internationalization of securities transactions implies the development of co-operation between national market regulators.

The COB is actively participating in the work of the International Organization of Securities Commissions (IOSCO). The activities of the IOSCO are mainly carried out by two committees, the Committee on Market Development and the Technical Committee on International Transactions created in July 1987. The Technical Committee groups the market regulators of thirteen countries, accounting for over 90 per cent of international securities transactions. Six priority items are on its agenda: international placings and multiple listings; accounting rules for international issues; capital adequacy standards for international firms; clearing and settlement of international transactions; development of the exchange of information and evidence of infractions; off-exchange transactions.

The COB pursues its consultations with the supervisory authorities of other countries with a view to extending the possibilities of exchange of information and mutual assistance in the repression of securities infractions. It should be mentioned that the resolution carried by the Executive Committee of the IOSCO in November 1986 has led to an accord signed by twenty-three countries. Under this agreement the signatories undertake to provide each other, as far as is permitted by local law and on the basis of reciprocity, with the information necessary for the enforcement of securities laws.

Amongst other initiatives in the area of international co-operation, the Council of Europe is working on a draft convention of multilateral assistance in the repression of insider trading. Moreover, there are projects of bilateral accords between France and counterparts in the United States, the United Kingdom, Italy and Quebec.

MARKET TRANSPARENCY AND THE STABILITY OF THE FINANCIAL SYSTEM

Market transparency

Market transparency depends on equal access to information, professional rules for financial intermediaries and the sanction of infractions.

Investors' information

Investors' information exists at three levels:

— information preceding the issue of securities which is checked by the COB;
— periodic information on listed companies which is provided by their obligation to publish annual balance sheets and half-year business returns;
— permanent information on market conditions that is made available by the publication of the official listing and the real-time dissemination of prices and volumes, on screens, through two systems (Chronoval for the general public and Topval for professionals).

Professional rules applying to financial intermediaries

Since intermediaries are allowed to operate on the market for their own account, it is important to guarantee their neutrality towards their clients. On the initiative of the profession, a three-pronged system of measures was chosen:

— 'Chinese walls' between the different services of an intermediary with incompatible purposes or activities (banking, dealing, trust management, broking);
— transparency of relations with clients (time-stamping of orders, order matching, price-supporting transactions);
— special rules for own-account trading of the intermediaries' staff (up to full prohibition) on the basis of their functions.

The sanction of securities infractions

The law provides sanctions for

— insider trading (the relatively new legislation (1970) was complemented on several occasions (1983 and 1988) at the request of the COB),
— supply of false or misleading information and
— price manipulation (a recent rule (1988) creates a special securities infraction of putting obstacles to the smooth and orderly operation of the market, e.g. bearing the market by heavily selling short so as to be able to buy back larger quantities of securities when the price is at its lowest).

The stability of the financial system

The stability of the financial system depends on the liquidity of markets and on the security of the financial centre.

The liquidity of markets (the function of principal or market making)

The liquidity of a market can be defined by the possibility for an operator to undertake a transaction on a large volume of securities without inducing significant price fluctuations. In a centralized market, such as Paris, it is the matching, in a single place, of demand for and supply of securities which should normally provide liquidity. Nevertheless, the liquidity of the market is notably enhanced when there are market makers continuously showing bid and offer prices and holding stocks of securities.

Market making or acting as principal already exists in the bond market and in the treasury bill market thanks to the MATIF which allows market makers to carry out the necessary hedging transactions. Thus the treasury securities specialists (Spécialistes en Valeurs du Trésor) provide the required liquidity on the secondary market by market making in the main government bond or treasury bill issues.

On the MONEP, a fair and orderly market is promoted by the creation of a counterparty of market regularization (contrepartie en régularisation de marché), a function exclusive of any other and performed by a special category of dealers.

On the Stock Exchange under the current system, brokers match up buyer and seller but seldom act on their own account. For small and medium-sized deals, this method works perfectly well. However, a fair amount of skill is required to put through larger trades without disturbing the market. For while buyer and seller may agree a deal through a broker, they cannot do it at a price of their choosing; the fundamental principle of equal treatment for wholesale and retail investors means that the wider market must be offered a piece of the action first. By controlling the flow of stock, deals can still be done at attractive prices, but they can take forty-eight hours or even more to complete.

The setting up, on 9 November 1988, of negotiable options (MONEP) and financial futures (MATIF) markets relating to a stock index (CAC 40 index)[2] has furthered the development of the function of principal on the securities markets. From the beginning of 1989, brokerage firms were allowed to act as principals in dealing with their big clients, at net and freely set prices, without being obliged to refer to the market conditions prevailing at the time of the deal. A 'wholesale market' will then operate at the same time as a 'retail market', thanks to this counterparty in large blocks of shares. It will be necessary to abide by ethical rules. The client will occasionally select between the two markets. It will be forbidden to resort to the block trading market in the case of management mandate.

This reform is aimed first at curbing transactions on French securities made in London where market makers deal with institutional investors at net and single prices for large blocks of shares. It is also designed to organize the liquidity of securities composing the stock indices (CAC 40). Together with this reform, the Paris Futures Clearing House and the Futures and Options Markets' Clearing Company, clearing entities for the MATIF and the MONEP, decided to take account of global positions in futures and options markets to calculate the margin requirements.

Lastly, in line with the conclusions of the Brady Report (in the United States) and the Deguen Report (in France), according to which spot, futures and options markets only form compartments of a single market, a system of 'circuit-breakers' will be set up (each market will maintain its own price limits but a trading halt in one of them will induce a simultaneous halt in derivative markets).

The financial centre solidarity

In France, investors are protected by a contractual scheme of deposit insurance and by statutory schemes of guarantee.

The French system of deposit insurance

Every category of French credit institution has its own scheme which guarantees to reimburse small depositors in case of default. For banks, there is a contractual agreement which concerns all French-franc-denominated deposits from non-bank customers up to 400,000 French francs.

The statutory scheme of guarantee

For credit institutions (établissements de crédit) Section 52 of the Banking Act provides that:

> Where such action appears justified by a credit institution's situation the Governor of the Bank of France shall call upon the shareholders or members of the institution to provide the latter with the support it needs.
>
> The Governor of the Bank of France may also arrange for the assistance of credit institutions as a group with a view to taking the measures needed to protect the interests of depositors and third parties, ensure the smooth functioning of the banking system and safeguard the reputation of the financial centre.

The necessity for this decision and the form it would eventually take are totally in the hands of the Governor. The rescue of Al Saoudi Bank illustrates its implementation.

Brokerage firms are responsible to their clients for the delivery and payment of the securities they have traded. A reserve fund intended to meet 'all the commitments of brokerage firms towards their clients' was provided for in article 6 of the Stock Exchange Act of January 1988.

For markets with a leverage effect (MATIF, MONEP), the clearing centre ensures the successful conclusion of transactions by systematically intervening between parties. These entities are sure to have the necessary resources at their disposal to perform their task.

CONSEQUENCES FOR MONETARY POLICY

These changes in the financial system and in the behaviour of economic agents have modified the mechanisms of transmission and the ways in which monetary policy is applied.

Changes in transmission mechanisms

The regulating function of capital markets should mean that government will not have to intervene so systematically in order to check disequilibria, the free portfolio switches having a spontaneous stabilizing effect.

The role of bank credit as a driving mechanism for monetary policy is now changed. On the one hand, the volume of credit in the financing of the economy is falling. On the other, the stiffer competition from foreign financial intermediaries and capital markets is changing the way banks now fix debtor conditions. The cost of credit is tending to become more variable, particularly in relation to variations in money-market rates, which are increasingly used as a reference instead of the bank base rate. On the whole, banks can now be expected, more so than in the past, to pass their short-rate variations on to their borrowers who will thus assume a greater share of the interest rate risk.

The greater importance of capital markets in financing the economy has meant that the supply of and demand for securities is now one of the main policy vectors for monetary authorities. The decompartmentalizing and deregulating of capital markets makes it possible to draw a yield curve reflecting expectations by agents. This curve informs monetary authorities as to the spontaneous variations that are likely to occur and what economic agents are anticipating with regard to monetary policy. From the point of view of the efficiency of monetary policy, this helps to reinforce the significance of announcement effects and to render the action of the Central Bank more credible.

The abandonment of quantitative credit control, the sharpened sensitivity of the banking system to impulses from the Central Bank and the greater role of capital markets mean that an effective monetary policy depends now on the behaviour of economic agents, savers and final borrowers.

The increased role of free-market mechanisms should make economic agents more sensitive *ex ante* to variations in interest rates which will be spread more widely over the whole of the economy. The impact of rate variations on agents' income (the 'income effect') will be more pronounced as a result of the wider scope of market mechanisms and the growth in consumer loans. The impact on the stock exchange value of financial assets (the 'wealth effect') will be greater as a result of the larger share of securities in agents' portfolios. Anticipated reactions to changes in monetary variables ('announcement effect') will increase because of the privileged role of interest rates in managing monetary policy. The growth of indebtedness and investments in foreign currencies made possible by lighter exchange controls should make wealth values more sensitive to changes in exchange rates.

Conversely, agents should react by seeking to protect themselves against interest rate risks, in particular by improving the structure of their balance sheets (self-financing and recourse to external own funds). According to the state of prepayments, one might see a growth or a decrease in variable rate loans and investments and, for large corporations, hedging on the new markets (MATIF and options market etc.). These new possibilities for protection should on average lengthen the time-lags for monetary policy to have an impact, whereas variability in the extent of their use might make the time-lags more unstable.

New ways of implementing monetary policy

The shift from an overdraft economy to a financial market economy did not involve a change in monetary policy direction. However, it led to the replacement of credit ceilings by indirect control instruments.

The maintaining of money stock objectives

The Central Bank was led to introduce a monetary aggregate reform on 1 January 1986 and the authorities are therefore not faced with a situation of such uncertainty that it requires them to modify the intermediate target nature of monetary policy, as happened in Canada and to some extent in the United States and the United Kingdom. Yet in a financial system where the capital market is tending to become unified, product substitutions may be both numerous and frequent. For example, an unexpected turnround in interest rate expectations may give rise to switch movements between short-term securities included in a given monetary aggregate and long-term securities not included in that aggregate. These switches do not necessarily imply that non-financial agents have changed their behaviour as regards their demand for goods and services. Interpreting changes in an aggregate is therefore more difficult, as a slowdown (or speed-up) in its rate of change may have a different meaning as circumstances change.

To take these uncertainties into account, monetary authorities are monitoring several aggregates. In 1987 targets were fixed for M2 (+4 to +6 per cent) and for M3 (+3 to +5 per cent). In 1988 a target was only fixed for M2 (+4 to +6 per cent).

The increasing role of interest rates as an instrument of monetary policy

The decline in direct quantitative credit control procedures is the logical result of changing financial patterns. The growth of alternative financing sources for companies (commercial paper, equity and bond market, external borrowing where necessary) and for the Treasury (negotiable treasury bills) makes accurate control of bank credit or of money creation by the Treasury an illusion. Interest rates will therefore become more and more important.

One of the difficulties facing the government stems from the fact that, as France belongs to the European Monetary System, conflicts may arise between exchange rates and monetary aggregates. In theory two points seem obvious.

1 It is not possible to fix an objective for the exchange rate and an objective for money supply growth at the same time.

2 It is not possible to hit two targets with a single instrument (in this case, interest rates).

In practice, however, as France belongs to the European Monetary System, it does try to achieve both an exchange rate objective and a money supply objective. In the event of a conflict between these two, a priority should be defined, at least in the short term (in 1979 excessive money creation was tolerated to prevent the franc from appreciating; in 1981–2, a destruction of money was allowed to combat a decline in the franc's value).

In the medium term, there is no lasting conflict between domestic and international objectives if the domestic targets are accurately fixed and expectations are not biased. Respect of the exchange rate objective reflects both a desire to improve European integration and a concern to harmonize economic policies so as to improve credibility and achieve better results in curbing inflation. The money growth objective must therefore be consistent with an inflation rate which is compatible with foreign-exchange-rate stability.

The possibility of conflict cannot be excluded in the short term, however, even though improvements in communications between the domestic and international markets are tending to make inflation expectations at home and abroad more homogeneous. In some cases, the domestic situation and changes on the foreign-exchange market may separately make it necessary to act in opposite directions on interest rates (e.g. a depreciation of the exchange rate and a decline in domestic activity not accompanied by inflation). In most cases, intervention on the foreign-exchange market and adjustment of compulsory reserves should make it possible to deal with these situations.

CONCLUSION

The changing patterns in borrowing and lending now seem irreversible. The progress in technology which has made financial innovation possible has also made economic agents more interdependent and capital markets more international. This is likely to continue.

In 1992 such trends are planned for the members of the European Community. It is obvious, however, that free movements of capital and freedom of transactions within the Community will *de facto* imply a globalization of the trends, if only because of the presence in Europe of American and Japanese banks with their impressive bridgeheads, especially in the City of London.

Two facts should be remembered, however. First, whatever may be in store for the French financial system, banks will continue to play a major role. Even if large corporations have become the partners of banks rather than their customers, small and medium-sized firms and households will go on needing banks for financing purposes. In comparison with non-financial agents, banks can always boast a specific difference. They remain the institutions that create money and, even if they have lost the monopoly of the functions they assume (financing of the economy, assets 'transformation', management of means of payments, transfers and common risk pooling, brokerage), they are still the only ones able to perform them all. Second, cycles do exist and the growth of capital markets in France is merely a return to a situation which prevailed throughout the second half of the nineteenth century.

NOTES

1 The French Bourse Corporation has been approved by the Committee of Credit Institutions and is supervised by the Banking Commission.

2 A competing stock index options and futures market (Options Market of France), set up on the initiative of several credit institutions, was approved by the authorities and has been open to the general public since 8 November 1988 (OMF 50 stock index).

BIBLIOGRAPHY

De Boissieu, C. (1983) 'Overdraft economy, financial market economy, interest rates', Paper presented at the Symposium, Keynes Today: Theories and Policies, University of Paris, September.

Bruneel, D. (1985) 'Government objectives and action on the level and structure of interest rates', *Cahiers économiques et monétaires de la Banque de France*, nos 24, 25, December.

——(1986) 'Development in the French capital markets in recent years', Paper presented at the SUERF Symposium on Shifting Frontiers in Capital Markets, Cambridge, 27–30 March 1985, in D.E. Fair (ed.) *Financial and Monetary Policy Studies*, vol. 12, Dordrecht: Martinus Nijhoff.

——(1986) 'Recent evolution of financial structures and monetary policy in France', Paper presented at the Conference on Domestic and International Aspects of Macroeconomic Policy, University of Illinois at Urbana-Champaign, 12–14 September.

Bruneel, D. and Patat, J.P. (1983) '10 years of monetary control in France (the impact of credit ceilings)', *Cahiers économiques et monétaires de la Banque de France* nos 17, 18, December.

Bruneel, D. and Facq, J.M. (1984) *Financial Innovation and Monetary Policy in France*, Basle: BIS.

Metais, J. and Szymczak, P. (1986) 'Changes in the French financial system – innovations and deregulation', *Notes et Etudes Documentaires* no. 4820, La Documentation Française.

Patat, J.P. (1987) 'The financing of the economy and monetary policy in France: from regulation to market mechanisms', Paper presented at the Symposium on Money and Financing, Oran Institute for Economic Science and Centre of Applied Economic Research for Development, June.

Report of the Conseil National du Crédit.
Reports of the working groups at the Commissariat Général du plan on the medium-term prospects for the financing of the French economy and monetary policy.

7 Towards a European financial system

Paolo Clarotti

By the adoption on 25 March 1957 of the Treaty of Rome, which came into effect on 1 January 1958, the six founding states allotted the Community the task of 'promoting, in the whole of the Community, an harmonious development of economic activities, an unceasing and balanced expansion, an enhanced stability, an accelerated raising of the standard of living and closer links between the states which it brings together'. The means for putting this aim into effect are framed 'by the establishment of a common market and by the progressive reconciliation of the economic policies of the states' (article 2). The aim therefore urges the creation of a common market involving a freedom of trade within a market economy, framed about by common rules and policies.

With a view to the realization of this aim, the Treaty of Rome envisages the putting into effect of what are generally called the four freedoms:

— the free movement of goods, which involves the suppression of all restrictions relating to quantity and of all similar regulations;
— the free movement of workers, which involves the suppression of all employment-related discrimination and of all nationality-related conditions of work;
— the freedom to establish a business and the freedom to provide cross-border services, both for companies and for self-employed people;
— the freedom of movement of capital, inasmuch as it is necessary for the functioning of the common market.

Mr Delors, President of the Commission of the European Community, the executive voice of the Community, declared that the common market as conceived by the 'founding fathers' of the Community is a 'true economic entity, aware, interdependent and, by this very fact, capable of triggering the synergy necessary between our countries to combine even better our economic and monetary policies'. In other words, the putting into effect of the four freedoms referred to above must result in the formation of a bigger market, similar to those which exist at present on a smaller scale inside each member state, where there would be no further obstacle either to the movement of goods or to services transactions.

Since the subject of this chapter is financial systems, we shall be considering the problem of setting up the extended market in relation to financial services: what is the present situation and when will it be possible to attain the objective of a single financial system or entity in the European Community? I shall examine these two points in succession.

THE PRESENT SITUATION WITH REGARD TO THE DEREGULATION OF FINANCIAL ACTIVITY IN THE COMMUNITY

In this chapter, I shall consider financial activities in the strict sense of the words, i.e. organized financial markets (exchanges etc). I shall not deal with insurance companies which are also classified as financial institutions but which bring with them their particular set of problems, because of space limitations.

The banking sector and other financial establishments

The Community's first act in this domain was the directive of 28 June 1973 which set up the right to establish a business and the right to offer services. This directive set out the principle of non-discrimination between national and Community companies. With regard to the right to offer services, however, it limited that right to services linked with the movement of capital freed in pursuance of the two directives which the Council adopted in 1960 and 1962, and which were essentially concerned with the payment of short-term commercial operations and with transactions related to securities quoted on the Stock Exchange. Taking into consideration that some member states were committed to broader measures of freedom, the Council considered it necessary to add to the directive a list of the services which were freed. This decision was based on article 61, paragraph 2, of the Treaty which stipulates that the liberalization of banking services should be carried out in accordance with the free movement of capital.

It is appropriate to point out that the directive was followed by two judgements in the European Court of Justice; in June 1974 the Reyners judgement, in the matter of the establishment of business, and in December the Van Binsbergen judgement, in the matter of provision of services, which declared that the articles of the Treaty on these matters (articles 52 and 59) were directly applicable from the end of the transitional period arranged by the Treaty (1 January 1970), without it being necessary to have a specific directive. The directive of 1973 had been proposed in July 1965 and came into force after eight years of discussion!

The putting into effect of the principle of non-discrimination was certainly a move forward compared with the previous situation, but in practice it did not give rise to important advantages in the mutual penetration of markets. Indeed, each member state's legislation was very different, and for a bank to have to conform each time it wanted to work in another country to rules very dissimilar to those that existed in its own country constituted a serious obstacle to the broadening, in geographical terms, of its activities. In addition, in certain Community countries (Denmark, France, Ireland, Italy) a clause existed according to which the national authorities could refuse to admit new banks and even new branches, national or foreign, by reason of the lack 'of economic need in the market'. This criterion was to be applied in a discretionary way, which could make all Community-wide banking activity practically impossible. For these reasons the Commission in December 1974 proposed a first co-ordination directive; it was adopted on 12 December 1977.

This directive defines certain minimal conditions for access to the business of credit institution (minimum capital reserves, competent and reputable directors, at least two in number, a business plan etc.) and most importantly it suppresses the clause concerning economic need (there is a temporary measure, however, allowing its application until the end of 1989); furthermore it sets up a system of ratios of solvency and liquidity which must be monitored by the Commission and by an advisory committee composed of senior representatives of banking supervisory authorities. The first co-ordination directive made it mandatory that there be collaboration between such authorities when a bank has branches in a country other than that in which it has its head office; it is a first step towards 'home country control' of which more will be said below.

Following a number of banking crises which had international repercussions (e.g. the Banco Ambrosiano case), the directive of 23 June 1983 set out the principle of a banking supervision on a consolidated basis. In other words, the national authorities must supervise the subsidiaries, both national and foreign, of banks which have their head office in their territory. While the first directive was not directed at all financial institutions (but only at credit institutions, i.e. those whose business consists of receiving deposits from the public and of granting credit), the directive concerning supervision on a consolidated basis is also applicable to the former when they are part of a group having a credit institution as a parent (a bank in the ordinary sense of the word).

At the same time work was started to establish rules concerning the presentation of both the annual and consolidated accounts of banks and financial institutions. This work resulted in a directive adopted on 8 December 1986 which not only standardized the format of balance sheets and profit and loss accounts but also co-ordinated rules governing valuation. This directive filled a gap because it complemented the work of the fourth and seventh directives on company law (on annual accounts and on consolidated accounts respectively) which did not automatically apply to banks.

Again in 1986, on 22 December, the Commission published two recommendations on banking. Recommendations, unlike directives, are not mandatory, but the Commission felt obliged to use them in the two areas of activity in question because there was a consensus in the advisory committee and they were dealing with an evolving situation where premature directives might create what would be an inadequate long-term solution. The recommendations concerned limits to large credit risks and the setting up of a system of deposit guarantees in all the Community countries.

Limits to large exposures (i.e. exposures of more than 15 per cent of the bank's own funds) were fixed, for each risk, at 40 per cent of such funds and, for all such risks, at 800 per cent of the latter.

Concerning the deposit guarantee schemes, which existed at the time of publication of the recommendation in only six member states (Belgium, Great Britain, France, Spain, the Netherlands and Germany), the recommendation invited the six other member states to install such a system of guarantees. Subsequently Italy and Luxembourg have instituted an interbank guarantee fund and Denmark and Ireland have introduced deposit insurance; work is going ahead in the two remaining countries with a view to achieving similar arrangements. It will only be when a system is in place everywhere that the Commission will be able to take the initiative and issue a directive standardizing the existing systems. In the same way, in the light of experience gained in the application of the recommendation concerning large exposures, a directive will establish a definitive framework for monitoring this regulation.

We can see that from the inception of the Community until 1985 very few initiatives resulted in a Community instrument. Since then, however, the Commission has taken other initiatives which have almost all come to fruition. We shall examine these in the second part of this chapter. There is good reason nevertheless first to remind ourselves of the context in which they are situated. In 1983, the Commission had published a programme document on the necessity of achieving financial integration within the Community; however, the document did not anticipate any really new initiatives aimed at facilitating this, but only the traditional instruments which permitted a very slow advance towards the desired goal.

The change in the composition of the Commission at the beginning of 1985 and the arrival of the new President, Mr Delors, caused it to change its approach and to become much more ambitious, not only in financial matters, but in all matters relating to the Community's internal market. A new programme document was prepared and presented to the European Council at the Milan summit in June 1985. This was the famous White Paper on the completion of the internal market, which defined a precise objective – full achievement of the single planned internal market by the end of 1992 – and a new approach: mutual recognition of national regulations as a complement to the former approach based exclusively on the standardization of these regulations. It is interesting to note in this respect that the Milan summit approved this programme (with the exception of the fiscal section, which need not concern us in the present context) and especially that the Single European Act, which came into force on 1 July 1987, repeated the deadline of 31 December 1992 for the completion of the internal market.

On the question of freedom of capital movements, the new document was much more incisive than the previous one and provided for complete deregulation within a relatively short time. It must be said that, in the meantime, the economic climate had improved and that as a result of the fall in the price of crude oil and a simultaneous decline in the value of the dollar the negative balance of payments of certain Community member countries had become positive, facilitating the liberalization measures that had been announced.

The new approach of mutual recognition had moreover been encouraged by certain judgements of the European Court of Justice, notably in the case of the 'Dijon Cassis', which stated the principle that a product, validly made and put on sale in a Community country, could be exported to another country of the Community without hindrance, even if the regulations relative to the product in the latter country were different from those in force in the former. Of course, the Court subjected the principle to four safeguards (the protection of public health, fairness of conditions of competition, respect for fiscal law and the protection of the general interest) but what was important in the judgement was the declaration of the principle of the mutual recognition of regulations.

In the White Paper the Commission took this on board and, notably in the sphere of financial services, argued that it was no longer necessary to harmonize the whole body of supervisory legislation in order to deregulate financial services completely. It was sufficient to harmonize the essential elements of the relevant regulations; the complete list of necessary harmonizations was given in an appendix. All the non-harmonized regulations were made the subject of mutual recognition along with its corollary, the principle of 'home country control', already mentioned at the outset; this means that, within the framework of the common market, the monitoring of a bank's activity from its entry into the market place, i.e. from its authorization, to the measures to be taken in case of crisis, including eventually the decision to enter into obligatory liquidation or winding-up, must be the responsibility of the competent authority in the country of the head office of the bank in question.

In the list of initiatives to be taken with a view to achieving the integrated financial market, most have already been put into effect. They are, in addition to the two recommendations on large exposures and the guaranteeing of deposits (1986) already dealt with, the previously mentioned directive dealing with annual accounts and balance sheets of banks (1986), the directive concerning the removal of the obligation on branches of foreign banks to publish separate accounts (1989), the directive which defined banks' own funds, the so-called second banking co-ordination directive and the directive which established a common solvency ratio for all European banks, also approved in 1989. Among those which remain to be brought to fruition, all those figuring in the programme cited above have already been the subject of a proposition on the part of the Commission. Others, not part of this programme, have been proposed and will be examined in the second part of this chapter, but first let us look more deeply at those directives which have already been adopted.

The directive concerning the own funds of credit institutions

The proposal was made in 1988 and resulted in a unanimous agreement of the Council of Ministers on 17 April 1989. It is important since it aims to define the common concept of capital which is often used as a criterion in banking regulations. Banking regulations of all Community countries require that banks maintain adequate capital, that there should be a minimum ratio of capital to risk assets and that large risks should be limited in accordance with the amount of bank capital. These conditions do not prevent other uses of banks' capital funds.

The Commission and the Council accepted most of the amendments of the European Parliament, notably the one by which the member states would have the possibility of including irredeemable securities in own funds. These securities include the 'perpetuals notes' in Great Britain, the 'titre participatifs' in France, the 'Genussenscheine' in Germany etc. The directive also took into account the major part of the recommendations on capital adequacy of the Committee of Banks Supervisors (the Cooke Committee) of the Group of Ten countries. Items which can be considered as own funds and can be included at 100 per cent of their value are capital, published reserves and funds set aside against general banking risks and included on the balance sheet. Revaluation reserves and other items not shown in the published accounts but which are known to the supervisory authorities (the irredeemable securities mentioned above) plus subordinate funds and the financial obligations of members of co-operatives or friendly societies can only be included at less than 100 per cent of their total value.

The agreement on the concept of the own funds of banks is one of the foundations of standardized prudential regulations which, in turn, are an essential prerequisite for the creation of a common financial market.

The second banking co-ordination directive

The second co-ordination directive, sent to the Council in February 1988, together with the introduction of a common Community capital ratio will provide the minimum necessary harmonization to enable mutual recognition of supervisory systems, which in turn will allow the principle of banking control by the country in which the head office is sited (home country) and a single bank authorization, valid for all Community countries. This covers both the establishment of branches and direct cross-border transactions. In order to achieve these aims, the text expressly prohibits the separate capitalization of foreign branches of Community banks previously demanded by nearly all Community countries. It also stipulates that, on the subject of monitoring liquidity, the host country will continue to exercise all its responsibilities until the time of subsequent measures of co-ordination, measures which will not call into question the principle of mutual recognition. Another stipulation concerns the comprehensive supervision to be exercised by the authorities of the home country. This supervision must be global in character and encompass not only financial conditions but also accounting and administrative procedures and especially internal controls.

Furthermore, the necessity to avoid allowing banks to enter into activities which may have too high a risk factor demands that limits on participation in non-banking business be imposed; 15 per cent of own funds for a single participation, 60 per cent of own funds for all participations.

Lastly, the second banking co-ordination directive establishes the conditions of free provision of banking services beyond national frontiers. This means dealings carried out directly by a bank with clients in another country, whether or not the bank has a branch in the country in question. At the present time, such transactions are carried out betweeen countries which have abolished all restrictions on capital movements and even with some countries where such restrictions are still in existence as long as there is special authorization. There is not yet a Community framework of regulations for such transactions; these depend, in effect, on the degree of tolerance shown by the relevant authorities.

The second directive undertakes to define the terms for allowing the unrestricted provision of banking services so as to safeguard the interests of the public in the country which is the recipient of these services, subject to the jurisprudence of the European Court of Justice.

This fundamental directive was approved by the European Council of Ministers on 15 December 1989.

The directive relating to the capital ratio

In April 1988, the Commission sent to the Council a proposal directive concerning a Community ratio relating to the monitoring of the capital adequacy of credit institutions. This was to be a ratio formulated by dividing own funds by risk assets. This has already been tested in the form of the 'observation ratio', which was provided for by the first co-ordination directive and which has been followed up to now by 250 European banks. These banks represent approximately two-thirds of the total assets of all the banks in the Community.

The ratio on risk assets will have as its numerator the own funds as they are defined by the directive adopted by the Council. The total amount thus calculated (from which certain items must be subtracted to avoid double counting, e.g. shares owned by the bank) will represent a minimum percentage – 8 per cent is the rate – of risk assets. The risk assets will be the denominator of the ratio under discussion. The risk assets include on the one hand assets shown on the balance sheet, such as loans, and on the other hand risks which do not appear on the balance sheet, such as guarantees, underwriting and other commitments. As these assets, whether on the balance sheet or not, do not all represent the same degree of risk, each risk category is the subject of an *ad hoc* weighting before the number which will be the denominator of the ratio is reached.

The previously mentioned Cooke Committee in Basle had the same aims as those of the Community. Based on experience gained in the use of capital ratios, it set up a similar exercise and came up with a risk assets ratio which was not very different from the one which resulted from the work carried out within the Community. On this issue there was close collaboration between Brussels and Basle.

Let us now turn to what has been achieved in the sector of stock exchanges and other long-term financial markets.

The stock exchanges and other financial markets

It is important to note that the directive of June 1973 also applied to the activities of intermediaries and jobbers on stock exchanges and to those trading in transferable securities in general. A partial exception was made in the case of stockbrokers for whom work on an *ad hoc* directive had been started. The previously mentioned Reyners and Van Binsbergen judgements made such a directive unnecessary. That does not mean that there are no problems in this sphere: there are a large number, but they are becoming fewer. One of the major problems was that in some countries (France, Italy etc.) brokers were considered to be government officers, part of the government sector, and therefore theoretically excluded from the liberalization process by article 55/1 of the Treaty. Present thinking following reforms carried out in most European exchanges is to consider this type of broking as being a *de facto* business, and it is likely that the official government aspect will soon be abandoned or will become a totally secondary feature of their activity.

In the sphere of dealers trading in transferable securities, the Commission then undertook a number of co-ordination measures intended to achieve the three following objectives:

— to ensure effective investor protection;
— to promote the efficient operation of markets in transferable securities;
— to encourage further interpenetration of national markets in transferable securities.

The realization of these objectives will contribute to the creation of a genuine common capital market, which means that the work undertaken in the sphere of dealing in transferable securities is included in the context of the creation of the single market by 1992. But the Commission had started to take action well before the White Paper of 1985 on the single market.

In order to achieve these three objectives, in July 1976 the Commission published a recommendation including a code of conduct concerning transferable securities transactions. This code, which is not a binding instrument, proved itself to be insufficient and the Commission proposed a number of directives, most of which have already been adopted by the Council. These are the directive on conditions for listing on stock exchanges (February 1979), the directive on share prospectuses (March 1980) and the directive on the six-monthly reports to be published by listed companies (February 1982).

These three co-ordination directives constitute an indispensable base from which to progress towards the realization of the third objective mentioned above, i.e. the interpenetration of the transferable securities markets of the member states. In fact, these three directives, by co-ordinating the conditions relating to access to stock exchanges, are of a type which will facilitate the access of Community securities issuers to the transferable securities markets of all the member states. This access was made even easier by the liberalization of capital movements related to all transactions on transferable securities, both quoted and unquoted, set in place by the directive of 17 November 1986.

The three directives which have just been mentioned form only the first step towards the realization of an internal market, since each member state remains in charge of all formalities and regulations to be carried into effect in order to list a share on its markets. This means that an issuer of securities who wishes to gain simultaneous admission for his securities to the exchanges of several member states has to conform to the particular regulations of each of these member states, even if the regulations already conform more or less to Community requirements.

Moreover, on 20 December 1985, the Council adopted a directive concerning undertakings of collective investments in transferable securities. Based on a common regulation of the operating procedures and investment policy of these organizations, the directive establishes the principle of control in the country of origin (home-country control). It ensures that an approved organization in a member state will be able to sell its units in other member states without being subjected to new approval. Likewise the control of the operation of this organization will be enforced exclusively by the competent authorities of the country in which it has its head office. This directive was complemented by another which was adopted at the same time by the Council of Ministers and which refers to the free circulation of units of such undertakings within the Community (third directive concerning the movement of capital).

Further steps to encourage the interpenetration of transferable securities markets have recently been taken. On 22 June 1987 the Council adopted a directive concerning the mutual recognition of prospectuses of admission to stock exchanges. The effect of this directive will be that when an issuer of securities wants these securities to be listed simultaneously on several exchanges in different member countries, he will have to draw up only one prospectus which will be approved by the competent authorities of one member state and recognized by the other member states without being subject to new controls. It must be made clear, however, that this directive does not yet establish the principle of automatic admission to exchanges.

On 12 December 1988 a further directive was adopted covering the transfer of large blocks of shares, ensuring that such transfers should be sufficiently overtly carried out that the market be duly informed of major movements of shares affecting prices quoted on the exchange. This directive must be considered along with two other important initiatives, the directives concerning insider trading and the share prospectus.

Let us examine first the directive aiming to standardize regulations relating to share prospectuses. The text of this directive was formally adopted by the Council on 17 April 1989. The substance of the text is essentially similar to that of the directive on share prospectuses of 1980 but includes the principle of mutual recognition which, as we have seen, was the subject of a separate directive. As far as the problem of Euro-securities is concerned, they have been completely excluded from this directive as they were from the other because they are not generally offered to the public.

With regard to the second of the above-mentioned directives, in June 1987 the Commission presented a proposal aimed at prohibiting insider trading. The international press had given considerable coverage to security-trading scandals which have taken place mainly in the United States, but also in certain member states. Such scandals were likely to be prejudicial to the creation of an integrated European financial market and it was vital to set up procedures aimed at preventing those with inside knowledge from profiting from their privileged position in order to earn money to the detriment of the investors. Only a system containing severe penalties, such as those recommended in the proposed directive, would have been able to ensure that the extended frontierless finance market will have the obvious honesty and openness to allow its development. The European Communities Council of Ministers endorsed the Commission's views and adopted this directive on 13 November 1989.

All these texts make up the necessary instruments for the protection of investors in the larger frontierless internal market which is in the process of being created.

INITIATIVES UNDER CONSIDERATION

As has already been seen there is good reason to make a distinction between initiatives which have already been the subject of Council decisions and those which are still being discussed. Let us now examine the latter ones starting with those concerning the banking sector.

The banking sector and that of other financial establishments

The Commission's proposals

There are four proposals.

The proposal for a directive on the matter of mortgage credit of February 1985

The Council has already begun to discuss this text, which aims to put into effect the right of establishment and the free provision of services in this particular field, in which up to this time there has been practically no interpenetration of markets. This is not only because of the differences in regulations governing this activity, but rather because of their incompatibility. Until now, institutions specializing in mortgage credit have remained inside their own frontiers. The reason for this is that, if they had wished to become international, they would have had to modify their financial techniques radically (which would pose administrative problems) or infringe their control regulations (which was forbidden).

The Commission's proposal aims to eliminate these problems by putting forward the principle of mutual recognition of financial techniques. This proposal was almost unanimously approved by the European Parliament. It was seen as a first concrete application of the principle of mutual recognition. The European Parliament only suggested some redrafting amendments which the Commission put into its modified proposal of May 1987; the discussion in the Council was suspended, however, because the majority of the delegations were of the opinion that agreement on the second co-ordination directive (mentioned above), bearing in mind that mortgage credit is especially mentioned as being part of the banking activities covered in its appendix, will make it possible that the solutions intended there will be sufficient to achieve the aims of the proposal on mortgage credit. Only the experience of the implementation of the second banking co-ordination directive after 1993 will show if the decision was justified. If not, the Commission will urge the Council to resume the discussions on the above proposal until its adoption.

The proposed directive relating to the reorganization and the liquidation of banks

This proposal, which also received the support of a large majority of the European Parliament, was the subject of an amended proposal in January 1988 and discussion in Council should start before the end of 1990.

This proposal also aims more at mutual recognition than at real harmonization. It puts forward the principle that, in the case of a financial crisis in a bank, the reorganization procedures decided on by the authorities in the country in which the bank has its head office are applicable to its activities throughout the Community. The authorities in countries where the bank has branches cannot stand in the way of these procedures, nor can they seek to apply different measures. In the same way, in the case of failure of the reorganization measures or when the bank's situation has deteriorated in such a way that there is no point in applying such procedures, it is the function of the home-country authorities to decide upon putting it into liquidation. This liquidation will be centralized because it will only be the procedure in operation in the home country which will be applied; it will also be universal because it will affect the totality of assets in existence in the Community.

The proposal of a directive against money laundering

The international press recently carried stories about instances where very important sums of money originating from illegal operations, notably drug trafficking, had been 'laundered' by well-known international banks. In several countries, both within and outside the Community, initiatives have been taken at government and sometimes at bank level to contend with this type of occurrence. The Committee of Central Bank Governors of the Group of Ten published a recommendation in December 1988 at Basle which supported such initiatives. The Commission could not dissociate itself from this problem, especially after having played an important part in the signing, in December 1988 in Vienna, of an International Convention on the fight against drugs. Thus the Commission proposed in March 1990 a directive to ensure that there will be standardization of action throughout the Community to prevent the 'laundering' of illicit money. The major issue contained in the proposal is the 'criminalization' of such practices.

The proposed directive on the capital adequacy of investment firms and banking institutions

By far the most important initiative has been left to the end. The reason for this is that it influences the banking sector, the stock exchange sector and the sector of transferable securities. This initiative deals with the drawing up of a proposed directive intended to finalize a special set of regulations to deal with the group of risks which come under the heading of market risks involving transferable securities. The directive will be applied to the institutions which operate in the field of transferable securities in the broadest sense of the word, including the different instruments created by financial innovation. The document is a follow up to the proposal for a directive on investment services in the securities field which I will mention later.

Over a long period, in different Community states, the activity of banks was subjected to capital and liquidity ratios which had to take account of the essential risk which they ran: credit risk – the risk that the borrower will not pay back the debt, or that he will not pay it back within the agreed term. During the last few years, banks have increased exponentially their transferable securities transactions and, by the development of the phenomenon of 'securitization', they have increasingly replaced the traditional loans with agreements to acquire securities issued by their clients, securities which they subsequently trade with third parties. This development has not brought new risks, since they have always existed, but it has underlined their increasing importance relative to traditional financial risks such as foreign exchange risks, interest rate risks and risks related to banks' holdings of securities, either in the context of transactions on behalf of clients or in the context of transactions carried out on their own behalf, notably as market makers. From this arises the necessity to complement the traditional capital ratio by adding new requirements. The United Kingdom was the first country in the European Community to establish such requirements, very complex in nature; other countries have been studying them. It was necessary for the Community to intervene in order to avoid the introduction of different regulations in the various Community states, rendering useless the work done towards the creation of a single market by the application of home-country control. A proposed directive was put before the Council in May 1990. As has already been said, it will apply equally to banks and to other securities dealers which are not banks, so as to avoid the creation of unfair competition between the two types of financial institutions.

The scope of the proposed directive extends fully to banks because several of the main risks dealt with by the directive, such as the risk of losses from interest rate and exchange rate movements, apply to banks' traditional activities such as deposit-taking and lending, as well as to their investment business.

As regards provisions against market risks on securities positions, the directive has to take account of the capital requirements imposed by the previously mentioned Capital Ratio Directive which implicitly makes some provisions for risks other than credit risks. It would thus be inappropriate to require banks already meeting the requirements of the Capital Ratio Directive to provide additional capital against market risk in general; to do so would put them at a disadvantage in comparison with non-bank investment firms from elsewhere in the Community and in third countries.

The proposed directive therefore offers banks a choice of two main options. Under both these options, *all* banks are required to:

— provide additional capital against foreign-exchange risk unless their foreign currency open positions are subject to a limit calculated as a

percentage of their own funds (this is necessary because the Capital Ratio Directive does not take account of foreign currency risks);
— set up their own systems to monitor and control market risks (other than foreign currency risk) on their overall business.

However, with regard to market risk on open positions in equities and fixed rate securities and counterparty risk, the proposal allows the supervisory authorities in each member state to choose between two alternative approaches: *either* (a) to continue to apply the requirements of the Capital Ratio Directive *or* (b) to set capital requirements on the short-term 'trading books' of each bank, calculated in accordance with the rules for security-trading institutions as set out in the proposed directive in substitution for the requirements of the Capital Ratio Directive. Bank supervisors can choose either to apply one of the options to all banks in their charge or to decide which banks should apply which system on a case-by-case basis.

The provision of the 'trading book' option allows banks to have their capital requirements in this area of business measured in the same way as investment firms. Thus the trading book option is consistent with the goal of ensuring a broadly level playing field between firms undertaking investment business which are banks and those which are not banks. This option is also desirable on prudential grounds, because the requirements in the proposed directive provide a more comprehensive treatment of the various risks in investment services business than the Capital Ratio Directive, which is mainly concerned with credit, as opposed to market, risks.

Other work being undertaken by the Commission

All the initiatives mentioned in the programme annexed to the 1985 White Paper have been the subject of proposed directives or of Commission recommendations. A considerable number of the former have already been approved by the Council. Work undertaken by the Commission is aimed at producing new initiatives, the need for which was not foreseen when the White Paper was drawn up.

Included in this work one can identify five different areas whose importance and urgency are very different.

The most important and most urgent work concerns the revision of the 1983 directive on consolidated supervision. After seven years in operation it is obvious that there are several loopholes. A planned directive should correct the main weaknesses. The first of these is a stronger co-ordination of methods of consolidation, without going as far as complete harmonization. The 1983 text imposed consolidated supervision but allowed member states the freedom to determine their own methods and also the extent of the consolidation. Next is the need to include the supervision of certain groups which do not have a bank controlling them, whereas the 1983 directive was only aimed at groups controlled by banks. Then there is the application of certain regulations to financial holding companies. A proposal is to be presented to the Council before the end of the first half of 1990.

Of necessity, the carrying into effect of the extended financial market will increase cross-border operations. At the present time these operations are almost exclusively the province of companies of above average size. Under the present system, smaller companies or consumers, who rarely attempt cross-border operations, are often unpleasantly surprised by their cost when they do. It is vital that all those interested in such transactions be well informed of the costs involved. Greater openness in these matters would encourage increased competition and, consequently, an eventual lowering of costs. In February 1990 the Commission issued a recommendation which aims to achieve this objective. In fact, the Commission recommendation might well be used as an instrument to put this into effect, in order to avoid cumbersome legislation. However, such a solution could not be excluded in the future if experience shows that the recommendation, which is not a binding instrument, is not sufficient.

Supervisory authorities demand that banks periodically furnish them with a whole series of very detailed statistical data on the different asset and liability transactions carried out, whether or not they figure on the balance sheet. As most of the supervisory measures will be standardized, it is thought appropriate that these statistical data be standardized too. The basis for this initiative is provided in the drafts of the balance sheet and the profit and loss account shown in the 1986 directive. It is likely that these initiatives will result in a proposed directive sometime in the 1990s.

We mentioned above the recommendations concerning large risks and deposit guarantee schemes. At the time of writing, a majority of the member states have applied them. But some member states have partially applied them and others have not applied them at all. It was agreed within the Banking Consultative Committee, created by the first co-ordination directive of 1977, that in the case of only partial application of the recommendations the Commission would change them into proposals for a directive. This would be done with a view to arriving at a Council decision which would make the above texts mandatory. During 1990, the Commission is expected to proceed to the finalization of new proposals concerning large exposures which would contain the text of the recommendation, adapted to cope with certain new circumstances. A similar proposal for the deposit guarantee scheme will follow later.

We now turn to the stock exchange and other securities markets.

The stock exchange and other securities markets

The Commission's proposals

In December 1988 the Commission adopted a proposed directive whose aim was to regulate all investment services, such as security trading, investment advice, portfolio management and dealing in derivative contracts arising from financial innovations such as options, swaps etc. This proposal, which is similar in structure to that of the second banking co-ordination directive and which is unusual in that it is directed at all firms offering investment services, whatever their legal status, be they banks, finance house, securities dealers, stock exchange brokers etc., contains many important regulations. Special mention must be made of the following regulatory requirements.

— There must be minimum capital for investment firms, to be determined according to the type of activity undertaken.
— Management must consist of persons of experience and probity.
— There must be rigorous accounting and internal administrative control.
— There must be a complete separation of funds managed on behalf of clients from funds administered on behalf of the company providing the investment service.
— The supervisory authorities must be regularly provided with all required information.
— A system of investors' guarantees must be established, designed to indemnify investors in cases where a firm goes bankrupt.

By means of such co-ordination this directive should facilitate the provision of cross-border services within the Community.

Also in December 1988, the Commission adopted a proposed directive designed to harmonize regulations relating to takeover bids. In order to ensure that all shareholders are treated fairly, the proposed directive establishes a threshold at which a full offer for all shares must be made. The threshold chosen as a point where the bidder would have at his disposal a minority holding considered to be sufficient to influence voting has been fixed at one-third, although member states will be free to fix a lower threshold.

Moreover, with a view to protecting minority shareholders and to avoid the launching of partial and purely speculatory offers, the directive establishes that a bidder must make a bid for all the company's securities.

The bidder will also have to draw up a bid document containing all the conditions of the planned transaction. This document must be published or made available to the public and, once published, it can only be withdrawn by the bidder in a limited number of cases which are strictly defined by the directive.

An essential element in all bids is the fixing of a time limit for acceptance. This should not exclude revised bids, however, but here again these can only be allowed within certain limits. A characteristic of the system set out in the proposal is the obligation of the management of the company for which a bid is made to decide on the time limit in a report distributed to all affected shareholders.

Lastly, as well as making provision for the establishment of an authority, in each member state, to monitor the above regulations, the directive also provides for other measures aimed at protecting the recipients of a takeover bid. It does this by giving them certain guarantees, in particular by the provision of full and accurate information and by imposing the fundamental principle of the equality of treatment of shareholders. It should be noted that the latter also applies if the shareholder lives in a member state other than that of the company which is the subject of the bid.

The Commission has also put forward in 1989 a proposed directive intended to ensure the mutual recognition of a share prospectus published in one member state, with a view to its being recognized as a prospectus for purposes of a listing on a stock exchange in another member state.

Other initiatives being undertaken by the Commission

The Commission is considering whether it would be appropriate to extend mutual recognition to the half-yearly reports published by companies listed on a stock exchange.

As well as initiatives intended to set up Community statutes, the Commission is playing an active part in promoting a series of measures intended to establish the interconnection of financial markets within the Community. Deserving of mention in this context are the efforts made to establish a system of Community clearing for transactions in transferable securities, and the efforts made towards the dematerialization of securities, i.e. the replacement of share certificates by computerized records in security-holding accounts.

This impressive picture of initiatives designed to make possible the creation of a European financial system is far from complete. It has been aimed exclusively at establishing measures which have a direct application to banks and similar institutions and to those who are professional operators on stock exchanges and more generally in all security transactions. There are further initiatives aimed at a broader stratum of economic operators and even the totality of the population and there is not sufficient space for a description of them in this chapter.

I shall restrict myself to mentioning two issues. First, the programme announced by the Commission in May 1987 concerning the complete freeing of capital movements. This resulted from the previously mentioned directive of November 1986 (the fourth directive of capital movements), and was finalized in June 1988 by a directive aiming to suppress all remaining restrictions on the exchange of foreign currency. Second, the programme document presented by the Commission in January 1987, which dealt with the establishment of a system of Community-wide payment cards. This programme anticipates standardization directives which are now in the process of being prepared. There is a code of conduct for the relations between the card issuers and traders, which was published in December 1987. There are also consumer protection measures regarding automatic teller machines (ATMs) and electronic funds terminals at points of sale (EFTPOS), which were formulated as a Commission recommendation in November 1988.

The ultimate goal is that all European citizens should be able to use their payment card not only in their home country but also in all other Community countries, to enable them to buy goods from shops, to pay for petrol, public telephones, motorway tolls or to obtain money from ATMs. In other words it is intended to establish the Community-wide validity of payment cards. This will be a concrete and spectacular proof that the European financial system is no longer a utopia but a reality.

An obvious synergy exists between the Commission's plans which have just been explained and the tendencies which have appeared in different European financial markets towards their deregulation. The goal to attain is the setting up of a European financial system, distinguished on the one hand by a greater freedom of operation and on the other by a more rigorous monitoring of the solvency and the soundness of financial institutions with better protection for depositors, investors and consumers.

Index